M000314317

LZ SITTING DUCK

LZ SITTING DUCK
The Fight For FSB Argonne

On the 3rd day the battle, someone had Armed Forces Radio playing and the National Anthem came on. This picture was taken of L/Cpl Ken Silka standing for the National Anthem.

JOHN ARSENAULT, LTCOL, USMC (RET)
THOMAS GOURNEAU, USCG

LIBERTY HILL PRESS

Liberty Hill Press
2301 Lucien Way #415
Maitland, FL 32751
407.339.4217
www.libertyhillpublishing.com

© 2021 by John Arsenault, LtCol, USMC (ret)
Thomas Gourneau, USCG

All rights reserved solely by the author. The author guarantees all
contents are original and do not infringe upon the legal rights of any
other person or work. No part of this book may be reproduced in any
form without the permission of the author. The views expressed in
this book are not necessarily those of the publisher.

Printed in the United States of America.
Paperback ISBN-13: 978-1-6628-1313-9
Dust Jacket ISBN-13: 978-1-6628-1314-6
eBook ISBN-13: 978-1-6628-1315-3

TABLE OF CONTENTS:

BOOK DEDICATIONS

John Arsenault

I want to dedicate this book to my wife
Tammy Jo and my daughter Claire.
These two women have saved me from my demons,
inspired me to stand fast and face the nightmares and ghosts.
To them I will be forever be indebted.
And to all of the Marines who gave so much
to our brotherhood and nation.
Their sacrifice will always be remembered and honored.

Thomas Gourneau

I dedicate this book to all the Marines and Navy Corpsmen
who served with the 1st Bn, 4th Marines, 3rd Bn, 12th Marines
and the supporting air support during this assault on FSB Argonne.
I also dedicate this book to my family, friends and supporters
who helped make the book possible.

Authors Note: The use of the term "Marines" in this book includes our Navy Corpsmen. We are all brothers.

1st Bn, 4th Marines, Area of Operations
Operation Purple Martin
March, April 1969

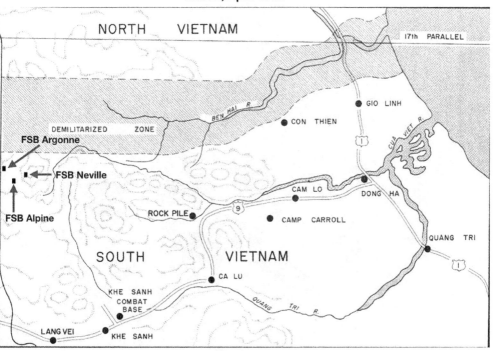

The Tactical Area of Operational Responsibility (TAOR)

1:50 Military Topographical Map of FSB Argonne Battle space

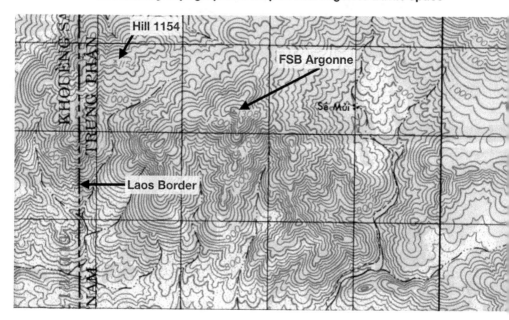

Tactical Map of Hill 1308 (FSB Argonne) and the surrounding area

ACKNOWLEDGEMENTS

SPECIAL THANKS GO OUT TO ALL WHO CONTRIBUTED THEIR accounts and others who also contributed, including: Harold "The most photographed Marine in Vietnam" Wilson, Byron Moore, John Kier, David Bobbitt, Thomas Tucker, Thomas Breeds, Mr. Katz of the website Pop-A-Smoke (https://www.popasmoke. com/), Karl Marlantes, Bing West, Jim Land, Jack Mclean and to those I may have forgotten. A special thanks to Mark Abplanalp, who singlehandedly collected and organized the names, locations and contact information for many of the Marines from 1/4 and also Thomas Gourneau, who initiated this effort with unyielding determination and launched this book. Without their efforts, this story would not have been told.

For further reading on the subject of the 1st Bn, 4th Marines in Vietnam, please see the following books available:

Matterhorn, by Karl Marlantes.
ISBN: 978-0-8021-1928-5

The Body Burning Detail, by Bill Jones.
ISBN: 978-1-4766-7517-6

Loon: A Marine Story, by Jack Mclean.
ISBN: 978-0-3455-1016-7

FOREWORD

HERBERT. E. PIERPAN

Major, 0302, Infantry Officer
Battalion Operations Officer, 1st Bn, 4th Marines

MUCH HAS BEEN WRITTEN ABOUT THE AMERICAN MILITARY involvement in the Republic of South Vietnam during the late 1950s, 1960s, and early 1970s. For those U.S. Armed Service Personnel who volunteered or were ordered there, each has their own personal recollections of what they did there. Unfortunately, many did not have the opportunity to tell their story, and others returning to the States after their in-country time preferred not to talk of their experiences and get on with their lives, while others over time went to their graves never revealing personal feelings and experiences about their participation in the Vietnam War.

Many books have been written about what turned out to be the more popular named battles that took place during the war. These battles were popularized by the press and the military, while many other books and articles of general interest, both real and fictional, have been published concerning the war.

Many military participants in the Vietnam War have returned to Vietnam individually or as part of small tour groups, most oriented to the area of the country where they served and desired to revisit. Although the country infrastructure and government has changed and former United States military bases are no longer present, the tours have brought healing to many who have visited, plus given family members who accompanied their spouse, parent or relative an understanding of the terrain and the climatic conditions they endured.

For many, the war is a long past memory that can be reignited by a friend, past unit buddy or just an innocent individual's inquiring and desire for information from one who had been there during the war, or maybe just a student gaining information for a school research assignment. This book is just that, sharing experiences and recollections with former military friends, unit buddies, or just unleashing memories of one particular Marine Operation, the battle for Fire Support Base Argonne.

Fire Support Base Argonne is wedged in the far northwest corner of the then-Republic of South Vietnam.

Operation Purple Martin was a helicopter-borne operation conducted by the U.S. Marine 1st Infantry Battalion, 4th Marine Regiment and its attached detachments of support personnel, which commenced at 8:00 AM, March 20, 1969. The mission was to seize and secure the hilltop and the immediate surrounding terrain of the hill to permit an artillery battery of the 12th Marine Artillery Regiment to be helicopter lifted onto the hilltop and set up their guns and act as a forward fire support base supporting friendly units that would be operating in the area.

This book is about Fire Support Base Argonne, one of those lesser, but just as intense no name or unpublicized battles that took place during the Vietnam War.

The word Argonne was an unfamiliar word to most young Marines. A few remembered the name from World War I history, but to most an unfamiliar word that became very popular and familiar as the operation unfolded. Ask anyone who took part, and they will tell you how fiercely contested the battle was that lasted over two weeks. The landing zone and immediate area of the landing zone, even after heavy artillery preparation prior to the landing, was populated with heavily entrenched, well camouflaged, well-fortified positions by North Vietnamese Army soldiers.

The chapters in this book are written by individual Marines who took part in or supported the operation and landing of what eventually became known as Landing Zone Sitting Duck. Each participant will tell you they are lucky to be alive, whether in the air or once on the ground. They are only lucky to have survived because of their fellow Marines, working as a team, supported by some of the best supporting arms with particular credit to artillery, mortar and fixed wing support that was brought to bear on the North Vietnamese Army soldiers.

Each chapter will provide a narrative and view from a participant's vantage point. As anyone who has been in combat knows, it can be an intense, terrifying, brutal, and definitely a memorable experience. If it were not for good planning, leadership, small unit teamwork, training, good weapons, equipment, logistics, supporting arms, individual bravery and the will to survive, one does not have a fighting chance. It seems all these were in play during the battle for Argonne, thanks to the brave and persistent Marines who prevailed during a very trying time.

This book is to honor all those who took part in Operation Argonne, especially to those who gave their all.

Herbert. E. Pierpan
Colonel, USMC (RET)
Navy Cross, 20 March, 1969

PREFACE

THE SUMMER OF 1985, I WAS NINE YEARS OLD. MY FAMILY decided to take a summer vacation to the Washington, D.C., area in our new Oldsmobile Delta 88; oh, the days of large cars that when scrapped could produce the steel for ten Honda Accords.

It was a hot summer, and the dense crowds attended the newly created Vietnam War Memorial, though the conflict in Vietnam was not yet a subject most would care to discuss willingly. I recall my mother approaching a park ranger, asking for locations of the names of the fallen from my area, the Upper Peninsula of Michigan.

Panel 28 West, Line 13. My mother raised her camera to photograph the name etched there in the shining black granite:

"David Emanuel Ovist"

I wondered about the name at the time, unaware of how this young man would come to shape my future research.

As the years went on, the conflict in Vietnam began to enter the mainstream. *Full Metal Jacket; Platoon; Apocalypse Now; Hamburger Hill; Good Morning, Vietnam*. Hollywood began to address the issue as time passed and wounds slowly began to heal.

As a kid, the normal pastimes of youth in rural America— hunting, Little League baseball, swimming and summer hockey— failed to hold my attention. I grew older and technology evolved. I found at my fingertips new research tools, and through diligence I found a website listing the names of the 58,220 Americans who gave their lives for their country in Vietnam.

From there I was able to track down David's old unit: G Battery, 3rd Battalion, 12th Marines 3rd Marine Division. Using this information, I was able to locate the names and contact information of David's comrades-in-arms. This information renewed my desire to learn more. Without hesitation, I reached out to the people I had found, hoping that someone would return my message and help me learn more about David, his time in-country, and, ultimately, how he met his end in a place known to history as Fire Support Base Argonne.

Among the early contacts were David's fellow Marines, Larry Deason, John Dunlop, and Carl Deagan. To my surprise, all three returned my e-mails, and, remarkably, all recalled each other from their time in-country nearly a half-century prior, as well as strikingly recalling David. Mr. Deason especially was grateful for my interest in his time and experience during the war, and I noted in his voice a touch of sorrow at his recollections of the subject.

After the conversation with Mr. Deason, I was determined to explore the bond that drew these men together, learn of their struggles and explore the far-flung jungles of Vietnam, the very area in which these youths—most not old enough to buy alcohol, many scarcely a year out of high school—patrolled, defended, assaulted, fought, perished and had at their fingertips the full might of the United States war machine. My five trips (soon to be six) have led me to within five hundred yards of the ruins of LZ Argonne, now partially reclaimed by the indifferent jungle.

With each trip my desire and passion to know more of the conflict and its combatants increased, leading me to this work, an attempt to honestly convey in their own words the struggle that took place there from the perspective of the men who fought.

Few have expressed publicly what they experienced in Quang Tri Province in March 1969. With each account of these brave men, I come to learn more about the fallen; more of Cpl. David Ovist, a friend to family and a friend of many. But most of all, to the individuals who helped this idea become a reality, I am able to show never-before-seen photographs and return-trip pictures fifty years after the battle for LZ Argonne.

LZ Argonne's legacy includes the awarding of three Navy Crosses within the first twenty-four hours of battle and reflects the heroism of Delta Company, the 1st Battalion, 4th Marines and the Headquarters group.

I have collected these individual stories from that battle in March 1969. These accounts include all perspectives, from officers to enlisted men, from air to ground units. For many it has been the first time they have been able to tell their tales. To the reader, I hope you will understand the nightmares these guys see, the diseases and illnesses they may still have from an almost unbearable life as a "Grunt Marine." From my research and discussions with these Marines, I've learned of the physical suffering experienced from the general operational tempo of this war. Hunger, lack of sleep, being in the field long enough to have your clothes rot off your body, open sores of jungle rot and having to carry seventy pounds of gear in a WWII "Field Transport Pack," smaller than a children's book bag, are some of the things these men endured.

I hope this effort will provide you with a better understanding of PTSD, suicide awareness and the tragic outcome of the Vietnam War.

Thomas Gourneau

INTRODUCTION

BULLETS FLEW THROUGH THE CH-46 MARINE CORPS HELI-copter like angry hornets, and pieces of aluminum flew around inside. We were landing at the abandoned Marine Corps, Fire Support Base (FSB) Argonne, on the border with Laos, just south of the DMZ. The NVA had taken over the base, they were ready and waiting for us. We would be completely surrounded when we landed inside the perimeter of the NVA's mountain top base. We landed at "LZ Sitting Duck."

This story is told by the Marines who fought there. None of us are authors or writers, we tell our own stories as they happened. Each with our own perspectives, observations and descriptions of heroism, confusion and grit of battle and war. The Marines in this book want you to know of the heroic actions taken by the young Americans who fought on this nondescript mountain, FSB Argonne, hill 1308, Vietnam March 20th. 1969.

For each of us, these are our stories, nightmares and ghosts from a time when we were young, when we fought as hard as we could, at a place no one cared about, just a mountain top that was a good place for men to fight and kill each other. This is the story of those who survived, died, or became horribly wounded, the story of a small Marine unit in Vietnam, surrounded, cut off and fighting for survival. Just one story of many in this war, one story that each of us has carried for over fifty years.

John Arsenault, AKA L/Cpl "Little John"
3rd Platoon, Delta Company, 1st Bn, 4th Marines

CHAPTER 1

CLEAN AND CLOSE

Robert P. Brougham
Captain, 2502, Comm Officer
H&S Company, 1st Bn, 4th Marines

ARGONNE FIRE SUPPORT BASE WAS THE FIRST STRATEGIC
operation location I heard referenced to shortly after arriving
in-country RVN and joining the 1st Bn/4th Marine Regiment in
October 1968. At this time, the command group and all rifle companies were currently in-the-field at Argonne FSB on the border of
Laos, just below the DMZ. "Wow, nothing like jumping directly
into the pressure cooker!" There was no farther north and west
outpost of US troops in RVN! I was advised that because the command group and many of the staff were in transition with some
being in rotation to CONUS or being transferred to other duty
in-country (i.e. "Short" Duty), I should report to Admin in Quang
Tri or at the new field base of operations at Vandegrift Combat
Base (formally the location of LZ Stud) and to get my working
orders there. There was no need to join the troops in the field
at Argonne FSB. Thank God! I just did not feel ready for total
immersion and exposure, yet. Thanks again! I chose to report
and meet the returning 1/4 Staff at Vandegrift when they returned
from the field.

During this waiting period, I did come to realize what "short" really meant in a free fire combat zone. On an otherwise quiet evening in the Officer's Billet in Vandegrift (playing cards, reading, small talk, writing letters), an incoming 120mm rocket flight (eeeEEEE) and blast detonated close to us on base (Really **big boom**)! All at one time, ten fellow officers and senior enlisted were running, assholes and elbows, to the small bunker at one end of the large, reinforced tent. Another **big boom** and another **bigger boom** closer to our position. The NVA were indiscriminately "walking" the rockets across the base. In the shuffle, I connected with my very, very "Short Timer" Gunny, who forcibly pushed me away from the small, single "beaver slide" entrance to the bunker. We wrestled our way inside. Rats everywhere were falling from the ceiling/sides of the bunker with each blast. **Boom, boom**!

The Gunny finally said, "No offense, **sir**!" S-m-i-l-e." **Boom boom**, farther away.

"No problem, Gunny.... How many days left now? Four? Now, that's short! You're excused!"

Besides learning to always know your next spot to "dive for cover" and to realize it's CYA first and foremost, I was challenged with a totally vertical learning curve to find out who/what/where was required of me. Initially, I did learn that: 1) In the aftermath of Khe Sanh and Tet'68, all I-Corps Marine units had been given the Primary Objective to remove all aggressors and stockpiled enemy equipment from in-country RVN and to plug the gap of incoming supplies from infiltrating through the DMZ (Operation Scotland I/II – Tet '68 Clean-up). Argonne FSB, because of its location, was the perfect place to deploy to help meet this objective by plugging the gap of traffic both North and South on the Ho Chi Minh Trail. There was no doubt some unit would be called to fulfill this mission in the near future and since 1/4 had occupied this FSB in the past and knew the lay-of-the-land, it was inevitable they (and I) would go there in the near future; 2) In order to enforce the Primary Objective, General Davis, the new I Corps Commanding General, made it clear that Vandegrift Combat Base would be I-Corp's westernmost Base of Operation replacing Khe Sanh but would not be the static base as Khe Sanh turned out to be.

2

To implement this more dynamic mode of operation, he ordered all regiments to deploy their battalions with their rifle companies and supporting arms to the field on a constantly rotating basis; i.e., there would be no build-up of assets in one place as was done with Khe Sanh. The rifle companies' place was in the field. This meant that each Bn would be twenty to thirty days out in the field, complete their mission and then return to the Base Camp for resupply and rehabilitation for the next twenty to thirty days. They would then return to the field when, where or however needed mutually supporting other Bn's within the Regiment. Therefore, there was to be a constant field rotation of operating units. In addition, to effectively apply given resources, General Davis adhered to the concept that "All Marines are riflemen first," whatever their MOS. Therefore, each Bn would field an Alpha Command Group (Beta Command Group in reserve) which would consist of the Bn Commanding Officer and direct supporting staff (S1, S2, S3, S4, Artillery Liaison Officer, Air Liaison Officer, Motor Transport Officer, Communications Officer, Chaplain, Bn Surgeon), to provide "on-the-spot" field command decisions. In addition, armed Headquarters Company personnel (cooks and kitchen crew/motor pool/Admin/maintenance/comm) would be deployed with the Alpha Command Group to set up and maintain a static field FSB/LZ protective perimeter in the assigned sector to support the rifle companies' search and clear missions in the surrounding countryside (depending on the circumstances, a rifle company with supporting arms rather than Headquarters Company would provide this perimeter set-up and security mission in any hot zone or where there was an assessed need for enforced defense and/or supporting arms).

When the Bn returned from Argonne in November '68, the required personnel changes were made quickly and efficiently, including a new CO, Lt. Col. G.T. Sargent. I was made Communications Officer on his staff and was assigned a combat and in-country experienced Gunny to replace my short-timer. Already, lessons learned from Argonne were being discussed, including the fact that communications were particularly difficult due to the geographic location as well as the location of

3

the established CP on the FSB. (It was located on the reverse or western slope of the mountain facing Laos. Somehow, we had to communicate over the mountain on which we were located to the support units to the east!) Additionally, Comm repair/replacement parts as well as qualified radio repair technicians were in short supply. In other words, changes must be made to improve communications and make parts readily available when the Bn returns to Argonne. The return to Argonne, in fact, seemed to be of the highest priority and the primary objective of the new CO.

But first, there was re-fit and rehab, organizational evaluation and assignment, and initiation of planning for and implementation of the next field operation, and the next, and the next, and the next.... Over the next several months, there was a whirlwind of activity to successfully achieve our primary field objective of removing the aggressors from Western I-Corps. They were in hiding and we had to go looking for them. For the most part, they consisted of seemingly loosely organized NVA Regulars and their equipment (mostly small arms, 50 cal. machine guns and mortars) and supplies (rice, ammo, 60/82mm mortar rounds and fuses, clothing, utility tools). It was noted that those who resisted were well equipped, dug in (often in bunkers with stockpiles of supplies) and were there to stay. It was thought they were setting up for the next offensive, which would most likely be TET '69 in March. It was therefore imperative that we clear these pockets of aggressors and block them from consolidating forces. With this in mind, the Alpha Command Group and rifle companies were helicoptered to many different LZ's and FSB's in NW I Corps including Gazelle, Catapult, Neville, Marilyn, Mack, Alpine and more. Each time the Alpha Command Group would move, headquarters company or a rifle company would set up a secure perimeter and we would establish a comm/fire support center, dig our fighting holes and/or set up a hooch to sleep and focus on supporting the rifle companies executing search and clear operations in the adjoining hills and terrain. Many times, we were in the direct line of small arms fire from the company's activity around us and almost always were mortared on a daily (and nightly) basis. The same type plan/execution was used in two civic action operations at the Quang Tri

Refugee Village and the local Montagnard Village close to Quang Tri. The air, artillery liaison officers of our unit were seasoned and creative. Over the five months I served with them, we called in fire missions from fixed wing A4's and F-8's, an OV-10 Bronco, UH-1 and AH-1 helicopter gunships, "Spooky," the battleship *New Jersey* and all the assortment of 105mm, 155mm, 175mm guns and 8" howitzers within range. When needed, we brought artillery with us on the LZ for direct fire support.

Besides the seemingly endless Alpha Command duties hopping from LZ to LZ or FSB, there were a couple of communications issues that I needed to resolve to make our "return to Argonne" succeed: lack of replacement parts, qualified radio repair techs and the ability to communicate to our supporting arms from the reverse slope of FSB Argonne. I approached the parts replacement issue by taking a full inventory of parts available and sourced adequate quantities of those we needed. This sounds simple but it was actually quite a chore because most radio men were assigned to field units with some of their own parts and supply. And the inventory and techs were mostly in Quang Tri where non-inventoried parts were stockpiled, not in Vandegrift where they were needed. I had to pull this all together.

In this situation it sure helped to have a seasoned and creative Gunny. We ended up establishing a "forward" comm repair station with the right mix of replaceable parts and a dedicated repair tech at Vandegrift. This allowed the units returning from the field to get immediate equipment repair/replacement instead of waiting for parts and equipment to be repaired and transferred between Quang Tri and Vandegrift. A definite waste of time. The operation worked so well that at times I had to temporarily assign additional tech support to handle the load. In fact, the 7th Radio Battalion CO stationed at Vandegrift took a tour of our operation and asked Col. Sargent if they could utilize our service. As far as improving the communication between Argonne and supporting units to the rear, we planned to set up properly equipped relay stations with strong signals to assist our effort 24/7 if/when comm became marginal. We knew that this would work but also wanted to be assured we had a direct line of communications. Yes, we would use our standard omnidirectional antennas (RS-232), which always sort-of worked. But we needed something better. So, we "acquired" the latest "high-tech," portable, multiple-array antenna with a built-in telescopic base pole from the nearby Seabee unit. The Gunny wouldn't tell what he bargained for it, but if it gave us the "edge" we needed to improve communications, would it really matter what he negotiated? This piece of gear could be priceless.

With these two primary Argonne prep objectives completed, there was another unrelated project to complete. Lt. Col. Sargent assigned me a project to set up a mobile UHF radio trans/receiver (VHF is commonly used between ground and support units) so he could communicate directly with fixed wing aircraft – B52's, A4's, F8's in the field. This was a special project because of the 240V power needed to activate the mostly obsolete UHF equipment (the radio was very large, filling the full back seat of a standard military Jeep and was powered with vacuum tubes.). The only thing to support such a large piece of equipment and to make it mobile was another rather obsolete piece of equipment–the "Mighty-Mite," a smaller version of the standard military Jeep. This combination worked well, even though the Mighty-Mite's muffler had a hole(s) in it and there was no replacement or repair parts available. Frankly, it sounded like a tank. This sound effect, we rationalized, could be interpreted as a psychological tactic against the NVA to make the aggressors think we had tank support. The first time we used this tool was on night convoy between Vandegrift and Quang Tri to set-up a community action program at the refugee camp there. Everything worked satisfactorily but the noise from the Mighty-Mite was so loud, one could not hear the radio transmission clearly. We decided to try it again on a planned mission to FSB Alpine (step off point to FSB Argonne). This time we would separate the power source from the radio so the transmission could be heard more clearly. It worked perfectly and with the Regimental CO witnessing the event. After the transmission, the Lt. Col. pulled me aside to personally meet the Regimental CO, introducing me as the CommO who was responsible for the fixed wing air communication link. Both were pleased and I was complimented. This adulation only lasted a short time because the Lt.

Col. later criticized me for not being clean shaven in meeting the Regiment's Commanding Officer. He made it clear, I was to be clean shaven at all times in the future. Yes, sir! Okay, even though I knew I was just made the object of the Marine Corps "high/low" attitude adjustment to make a point, the bottom line was that I was expected to be clean shaven in the future. So, to avoid another conflict, my mantra became: "clean shave avoids close shave" or to paraphrase it, "clean and close"! At the time, I was quite disgusted with myself for being the object of criticism, which would pass, but I was certainly not aware that this "close shave" incident would become a significant event memorable for the rest of my life. Later in the day, Col. Sargent, in an effort, I think, to rectify a rather abrupt confrontation between us, publicly gave me and my crew a commendation for a job well done with enabling the radio transmission and awarded us a privileged "wash-day" in the streams below the FSB. The "out-of-the-wire" walk down the hill to the stream for sheer enjoyment was actually not very comfortable for myself and others in the group (there were about ten of us) because we were lightly armed without full battle gear and little ammo supply. After all, this was NVA territory and we had no briefing on the current NVA activity outside the wire. We were all quite nervous at first, but everyone loosened up (perhaps, a little too much, under the circumstances) and a guard was posted at all times. In the end, all went well and we all crossed back through the wire unscathed and refreshed. However, refreshed as we felt at the time, no one could forget that in two days it would be March 20 – return to Argonne day.

After almost a full day and night of air and artillery prep, the day finally arrived. Personally, I was relieved because the air assault of LZ Argonne initiating Operation Purple Martin for 1st Bn 4th Marines was the culmination of many planning meetings and tons of preparation. It was now time to make it happen. The fact that I was overdue for a much-needed R&R was put aside for now and the Col. had agreed I could take the leave after the operation was completed. "Let's get on with it!" Operation Purple Martin included the entire 4th Marine Regiment with all 4 Bn's assigned to assault and occupy strategic locations in the northwestern I-Corps. The 1st Bn 4th Marines and the assault on Argonne was the spearhead of the operation. The code name for 1/4's accumulation of supplies to support this operation was "Blue Eyes," in recognition of our CO, Col. Sargent, whose eyes were always an intense, penetrating blue grey.

I may have been in a field support position as Comm Officer for the Bn, but when in the field, I was well prepared and as ready to protect myself as any grunt could have been. I always carried an M-16 with a couple of bandoliers of ammo and a couple of frags. I carried a 45 pistol as well as a personal, ankle holstered 32 cal. pistol. I always carried adequate ammo for all my weapons as well as my collapsible utility tool (always dug a fighting hole as 1st priority after landing in a new location, when possible). I usually didn't carry much food stuff, but this time I loaded up for the "long haul" with some comfort food from home including a small canned ham and a flask of brandy to share. I was always willing to carry an 81mm mortar round, if needed, and handed it over to the mortar crew as soon as we landed. On this mission, I couldn't carry any additional weight because I was taking our newly acquired portable telescopic multiple array antenna, hoping we would not have to use it, but if we did, it would improve our communications.

As we approached the loading pad, I was told I would be the commander of the first helicopter of the second assault wave. What? I supposed this meant there would be the first assault wave with two or three CH-46 loads of Marines landing before ours. Hopefully, the LZ would be reasonably cleared when we got there. I would be positioned in our aircraft as the first in/last out. The good news was that I would be in close contact with the crew chief, who was wired-in to the current status of our flight and landing. I could listen in and be prepared for what may come. As we loaded, the "word" was that, in spite of the intense artillery and air prep for the last day and night, the **zone was hot!** In fact, an Army recon helicopter and crew of five who made first landing in the morning were hit by close range small arms and 50 cal. fire, killing the pilot and co-pilot and badly wounding the others. The crew was evacuated but the abandoned chopper was left on the upper LZ. The first wave was therefore landing on the lower LZ.

As if the "pucker factor" was not intense enough, I had the additional "burden" to look out for my recently assigned new Gunny. He had previously told me this was not his first tour, but he had been stationed in Da Nang for his entire first tour and for the past three months of this tour in a non-combat position. He had no experience with a field grunt Bn or in a free fire combat zone. As expected, he was very apprehensive as we loaded the chopper and it really showed. In spite of this, I felt I should keep him with me to help coordinate the set-up of the command post after we landed, as I had done many times before with other members of the team. He had other plans. As we were completing the loading, he told me he "forgot something." No problem, we'll adapt. Let's get on with it. The next thing I knew, he had off-boarded the chopper and was walking out of the loading area, back toward the LZ perimeter.

"Oh well, that actually took a lot off my back. I'll deal with it later!"

Truthfully, nothing is worse than having someone aboard who doesn't want to be there. There were other Marines begging to come aboard and they were with me. Right now, there was a most critical mission to get started and it would have to be without him.

Finally, we were airborne and on approach. I was told we were off loading on the upper LZ. "What? How about the disabled Army UH1?" As we descended, the outgoing gun fire suddenly became intense. Our mounted 50 cal. was firing into the heavy foliage approaching and surrounding the bleak, exposed opening in the canopy of the jungle on the west side of the hill returning fire to muzzle flashes visible on the ground. I wasn't aware of any incoming hits on the chopper. The Army Huey was still on the LZ! Our approach was from the south. The pilot brought us in at a fast clip, turned the nose to the west/southwest as he lowered the craft toward the ground. He didn't land completely but skill-fully lowered the ramp on the seemingly solid level surface just off the LZ while avoiding the stationary Army Huey. This guy was good! **Out! Out! Go, go, go!** As soon as boots hit the dirt, we all scattered in every direction to go wherever there was cover. Being one of the last ones out, the ramp/chopper was lifting as I was departing. "Watch that last step, Lt.!" I was ready for it. I jumped and ran for the closest cover downhill, which seemed to be an artillery or mortar crater – not deep enough. There was the din of small arms firing all around. I became part of that little hole. Then suddenly, I had the sensation of being totally alone. The gun firing seemed to be all around me with rounds whizzing overhead, but all was pretty calm at my center. The ground I was attached to, was at about a 30 percent incline and I had a panoramic view west down the hill to the lower LZ, the heavy jungle canopy beyond, and to the hills in Laos. My first thought was I had to check in with the Col. and find the command center. There were a couple of bunkers surrounding me which were pretty trashed and mangled, with caved-in roofs and were not habitable. The Army Huey still sat on the LZ above as a reminder of a plan gone wrong and the lethal spontaneity and possible terminal existence as a result. There were bodies of NVA visible through the openings of one of the damaged bunkers in rigid, grotesque positions. And there were no Marines, no anybody alive in sight. Looking west, down the hill were scattered bunkers and trenches with wisps of smoke hanging in the air. Most of them inhabitable, some probably booby-trapped. And there were no people. The constant sound of small arms fire had to be coming from someone. Where was everybody? Then, I spotted a bunker with intact roof about thirty feet down the hill with a Marine-issue RC-232 antenna above. I cautiously headed in that direction. And then I saw… a Marine, a Comm guy! "Hey Lt., about time you got here!" Hmmm. I looked around.

The chosen CP looked small and looked so very exposed – a target. Yes, the CP was sitting on the reverse side of the hill but openly, defiantly facing west to Laos and incoming fire. Definitely a NVA turkey shoot with, I'm sure, pre-registered targets. There was a flap over the entry. I opened it a crack. It was totally jam-packed with everyone busy talking on the PRC-25 radios (looks like comm is a go!) and otherwise, hunkered down. I asked for the Col. who I knew would give me the directive to move the CP. If not, I would recommend it. I was told the Col. was not there but was spotted just outside a minute ago. I started to look around. I didn't take more than a few steps before I saw the Col. crouched down on top of a large rock formation north and east of the CP. I couldn't believe it! He was totally exposed. My first thought was that, just maybe, he knows something I don't know. Have the NVA abandoned the hill? Is the FSB secure? Before I could stop myself, I said, "Get the Hell down from there!" Big S-M-I-L-E, "It's okay, Lt., there's an AK in that bunker. Take a look."

Meanwhile, with the sound of gun fire all around us, I, with command obedience, reflexively crawled over to the bunker, looked inside at the tangled blend of humanity, sandbags, galvanized steel, a trashed 50 cal. on a tripod and body parts. There were also heavy gauge chains linked to the 50 cal. tripod leading to metal bolted cuffs around the ankle of one of the gunners. Perhaps, this was NVA style discipline! One thing was for sure, that guy was not going to abandon his post. And yes, there was an AK47 with a broken stock among the mess. Broken stock? The Col. lost interest. Later, I saw one of our engineers several feet away from the bunker with a long cord "de-boobytrapping" the corpse with the AK the proper, safe way. Someone was interested after all. As the Col. and I were making our way back to the CP, I mentioned that I thought the current CP was very exposed – a target. Yes, he wanted to relocate the CP, ASAP. Yes, sir! I then left him and sought out my comm personnel to advise the men what I committed to do and to open discussion of how to do it. We all agreed we would start moving what we could up the hill to a location a few were familiar with that provided cover, protection and better communication. We would start now.

Also, while discussing the move, I was advised by the men that the communications with some of our support weapons on Alpine were not very strong and the relay was not much better. This was expected. Okay, it was time to try the new antenna. The set-up was a little more involved than I had practiced back in Vandegrift, due to the slope of the hill, the contour of the land and the excessive exposure to enemy fire. The only place to position it was on the southeast side of our current CP position on the hill, which was close to the upper LZ, overlooking a severe drop-off of about 200 feet and totally exposed. All the troops were busy with preparing the CP move, which would not be completed until later tomorrow, so I decided I would set up the antenna myself. My immediate thoughts were that sometimes in life there are times when duty and common sense are in opposition. This was one of those times and I've never shirked duty before. Let's go! I had more than a few rounds zing by (there were snipers reported throughout our position) but they were either very (or not) interested in what I was setting up and left me alone or pretty damned poor shots. Anyway, mission accomplished, complete with guy wires, and the hook-up improved the communications besides. Now it was time to gather my comm guys, dig a fighting hole or find a protected location to hunker down. It was rumored there would be a counterattack. I had spotted an empty bunker just north and east of the CP that had a solid roof and was backed up to the large rock formation where I found the Col. earlier. There was a severe drop off to the north, so it was protected from that side. I checked inside and didn't find any visible booby-traps. I gathered some of the guys ("The Line Chief, what was he doing here? Oh yeah, back at Vandegrift, he practically pleaded with me to give him some field time. Frankly, these are the only guys you want around when things get hot. They want to be there!"). Several of us found refuge for the night. I chose a spot up front in the bunker with a viewing hole toward the CP about twenty-five feet away where I could view and hear any activity from that direction.

Things had quieted down somewhat. I snoozed a bit, kept watch and as dawn broke, I splashed water on my face in preparation for the day. At the same time, I heard the colonel's voice. "Where's the CommO?" At first, I thought I was hearing things but suddenly, I was wide awake, realizing the Col. was asking for **me**! I instinctively looked out the viewing hole and the Col. was standing on top of the CP, talking with someone. My thought was, "He is assembling the morning meeting and he wants to get the status and details of moving the CP." My second thought was, "I better shave this face, now, before going out (clean shave/close shave!) or I'm in deep shit!" As I took my handy battery-operated Norelco out of my pack and started shaving, I looked out the viewing hole at the colonel, twenty feet away, still standing on the

12

roof of the CP. He was preoccupied with someone/something and had not moved from the top of the CP. I had time to get reasonably presentable before joining the meeting! "Who was he talking to? Why is he standing so exposed on the roof?"

And then in an instant, I saw the shadow of a projectile strike the top of his head. His upper body was enshrouded in smoke and debris. What was left of him was lifted off the bunker and deposited on the ground behind the bunker. Several others close by were struck by debris and were knocked off their feet. They had visible gaping wounds. All who were mobile were hustling for cover. I was totally shocked, stunned! In total disbelief. I looked around the dimly lit bunker and said something like: "The Col. has taken a direct hit by a Chi-Com '82mm! He's gone!" Suddenly, I realized I could have been right next to him–"clean shave/close shave" saved my ass! **Oh-My-God**! I got up immediately and rushed over to the command bunker to see what I could do to help. I think there were a couple more incoming rounds. I don't know, I was dazed. The atmosphere was chaotic but very sober, almost religious, at the same time. The colonel was KIA, the new 2nd Lt./S2 was KIA, eight or ten key staff personnel were WIA, some seriously. None of my comm people were hit.

I have very little memory of what happened next other than I let those in charge do what they had to do. Maj. Pierpan was the highest-ranking tactical officer on board, was the staff S4 Officer, and probably was responsible for directing the operation since day one. He aptly took charge. Things were in good hands. Meantime, I sought out my people, especially my ranking corporals, to further discuss the CP move and to assure them that "things happen and we must carry on. Me included." This was a tough one. The Col. was my boss and somehow, I felt we had developed a degree of mutual respect. I did enjoy his sometimes whimsical behavior and personal approach, which complimented his absolute focus on the mission. He was an inspirational, "take it to 'em," tough-ass Marine. R.I.P. Col. Sargent! You'll get the proper recognition you worked so hard to achieve! But now it was time to move on. It was only our second day on Argonne, we had a mission to complete. "Carry on, let's get it done."

13

Later that day, I did helplessly watch chopper air currents totally destroy my recently erected array antenna. Rather suddenly, out of the blue, a chopper carrying a 105mm gun appeared over the Upper LZ and began lowering the gun in place there (the Army Huey was finally shoved to the side sometime earlier). The antenna was located just to the south and west of the LZ. If I would have known the guns were being placed, I would have taken the antenna down. Regardless, the downdraft air currents of the chopper were just too intense for the support structure of the antenna. Down into the abyss it went. No way to salvage that one.... Oh well, let's get the new CP set up quickly higher on the hill, which should give us better comm.

The relocation was starting to come together. The proposed new CP was located on the uphill slope southeast of the upper LZ on the edge of a rather flat cleared area with sparsely set large trees surrounding it to the north, south and to the east and open to the LZ or west. The proposed CP itself was in a natural recessed area with protective berms and thick foliage surrounding it on all sides. Opposite the proposed CP, to the north and west of the clearing, was an extended branch of land projecting northwest. As we were starting to transfer backup equipment to set up the new CP, a reinforced squad or platoon of D Company troops moved into the area. They had apparently aborted their assault landing yesterday due to a malfunction of their chopper and had to transfer to another one that arrived some time after the initial assault. Whether they were located in the area the night before, I don't know, but they seemed to now be responsible for this sector of the perimeter.

I don't know where I was or what I was doing at the time, but one of my responsible corporals alerted me to the fact that presently, a fire fight was progressing in the clearing close to where we had our proposed CP. My Comm guys had been working in that area last night and part of this day without any NVA harassment. "What was happening at our supposed 'protected and secure' area! Let's go!" We used some low, linear trenches in the clearing to approach the firing line and saw there were about ten to fifteen Marines in a semi-circle firing on an improvised or partially damaged bunker or reinforced hooch on the northeast border of the clearing. One could clearly see a single aggressor was firing back from protection of a "spider trap" located in the floor of the hooch. He would periodically pop up to fire several shots and when someone threw a frag in the door facing the clearing, he would throw it back, fire a few shots and duck back down into the "spider trap." I took a few shots at his clear silhouette, all the while thinking, "This is the guy who pulled the trigger on the colonel. I'm going to get him!" From my position, he was very visible and totally exposed. There was no way I could miss him. Who knows? At least, I had an opportunity to release my pent-up anger. Finally, one of the Marines, under protective fire, used a short fuse frag to officially subdue him in his trap. "Great job!" I just couldn't help wondering whether this NVA had a chain around his ankle, too? I didn't have a chance/nor did I care to look.

After the firefight was over, there was talk of snipers in the area. Why didn't they harass us now or when we were working on the new CP? Actually, I think this "spider trap" guy was the suspected elusive sniper all along. He could easily pop-a-shot from cover at close range and no one would know where it came from. The Comm guys and I had been in that area for about a day and were not aware of being shot at, but there was always a din of small arms fire throughout the day and fortunately, we were not the target. All of us still remained cautious of the threat. Some of the D Company Marines mentioned that earlier that day, their CO led a squad down a trail into the dense jungle projecting to the northwest from the clearing and were ambushed. The CO and another Marine were in the kill zone and didn't come back. They were presumed to be KIA. The remaining Marines now wanted to organize a patrol to retrieve them, but it was getting late in the day and it would have to wait. Besides the time factor, a couple of the men close to us were running out of ammo. Not knowing whether they had re-supply, I threw them my two bandoleers and gave them a couple of frags. I hoped I wouldn't have to use them, but these guys needed them more than I did.

It was getting late in the afternoon and we had to get back to our work, so we left the area. As we were leaving, a tall, blond Marine with an Aussie hat flipped to one side ran across the clearing in the direction of the northwest extension by himself, with his weapon in the assault position. We all watched as he disappeared into the dense foliage. A bold move, considering the ambush earlier in the day! I thought I heard him fall (sniper, tripped and fell, took cover?). I've often thought about whether he made it or not. He was definitely on a lone mission.

As we got back to the area of the CP, it was starting to get dark and I decided to take one last look at whether I could salvage anything from my array antenna. It was hardwire connected, so it should be still hanging over the drop-off, if the wire didn't break. The others went on. I noted the 105's (I believe there were two in-place) were now in operation and as I approached, one of the artillery crew advised me to get down and take cover. They were about to fire a mission. He told me they were firing "grape shot" directly into the dense foliage at the bottom of the west perimeter, so the gun's barrel was horizontal or below. I noted they had used the sandbags and other debris from the destroyed bunker west of the LZ to construct a decent parapet, so I decided to hunker down in front of it, facing the direction of fire. I knew there would be backwash but I was fully protected with helmet and flak-jacket. As I sat down, there was a young PFC Marine with a dazed, bewildered look on his face, walking directly up to the face of the gun position. As the breech closed behind me, I grabbed his arm and yanked him to the side of me. In so many words, I told him to shut up and cover up. The next thing I knew, there was a rush of the fired round outward and backwash of debris from the gun blast.

From the corner of my eye, I noticed a mushroom-shaped cloud of debris from a ground impact about ten feet to our left. What? The Marine I pulled down was to my left and I noticed him with raised head looking in that direction. He didn't keep his head down. Yep, it was the debris and shrapnel from a Chi-Com '82mm impact. The NVA were shooting at the 105mm gun and we just happened to be there. As the dust cleared, the Marine with me looked to the right toward me and at first, his face looked very pockmarked, then it was totally drenched in blood. He had faced the '82mm blast and took a frontal hit. I had to get him to a "doc"! I went to get up and I fell against the parapet. My left knee could not support any weight and there was blood dripping from the left side of my face. Fortunately, there was a makeshift triage center just down the hill about twenty feet. When I say makeshift, that is an understatement. It was several half-shells stretched over a twelve-inch-deep indentation in the ground without any rein-forcement protection. Crawling room only. I managed to get up on my right leg and pushed the PFC ahead. He wasn't walking very good and there was a lot of blood from his upper torso. We were fortunate that it was a downhill trek and we dove in the hatch, abruptly arousing a corpsman sitting by the door flap. All I could say was, "This guy needs a lot of help!" The left side of my face was bleeding but not nearly as much as the PFC. The "doc" said, "We can help him but we're too overwhelmed to help you." What? Where was the Col. (actually a Harvard-trained physician – our Bn surgeon)? I knew he was aboard. The corpsman took the, by now "very wilted" and almost unconscious PFC farther into the triage tent and left me at the entrance.

The next thing I knew, our Bn Surgeon crawled over with some gauze and antiseptic pads and told me, "This is all I can give you right now."

"But I can't walk?"

"Sorry, I have to go!"

"How about a Medevac?"

"There's no more coming in today."

"Thanks, bye!"

Okay, I had to locate my Comm guys. Luckily, I just left them about an hour ago and knew where to find them. I hopped (unfor-tunately) uphill for about fifty feet, past the artillery pit (Yep, the artillery crew saw it all. "Hey, you okay?" All I could do was shake my head, No. I found one of my responsible corporals close to our progressing new CP, getting ready to hunker down for the evening. In fact, most of the Comm guys were there. They were concerned with my condition and saw that I was immobile (the bleeding had pretty much stopped but my utilities were coated with blood and now the knee was swelling up and stiff). Was I going to lose my leg? We all knew there would be no more chop-pers to get me out of there tonight. So, they were stuck with me.

But right now, they were most concerned about the rumor that there would be a counterattack this evening.

We all decided that I was pretty much close to a "piece of meat" (true!) and could hardly survive any counterattack (true!), so we decided I would take my weapon with ammo and get into one of the many holes in the middle of the group where I would be protected. A 4'X8' piece of plywood was placed over my "fighting hole." Pending no attack, they would get me out with the first chopper in the AM. I now had time to reflect and found myself very despondent at being disabled by Chi-Com shrapnel at the hands of the NVA Regulars and there was the possibility of losing my leg; then being rejected treatment by a field Navy corpsman and given "picnic lunch" first aid bandaging and antiseptic for my wounds; and now I was a burden to and "buried" by my own men, awaiting a Medevac that may or may not arrive. "God, help me!" Fortunately, it was a quiet night. We didn't get attacked and I did get some rest, knowing that if anything happened, I would be alerted by those around me. "Thanks, guys."

At first light, I was startled awake by the "thwark, thwark, thwark" sound of an incoming chopper. I pushed the plywood aside (I tried but couldn't get up) and yelled as loud as I could, "Corporal G!" I saw a head pop up about twenty feet away. He looked in the direction of the LZ, "Hey, the Lt.! Get a stretcher!" Someone grabbed my arm and lifted me out of the hole. I started hopping in the direction of where a chopper could unload or take passengers (remember, the LZ now had 105's on it). They put me on the stretcher and hustled me to the docking area just as the chopper laid down its ramp on the side of the hill close to where my antenna was once placed. That was certainly the wrong place for my antenna. Marines immediately started to unload ammo boxes for the 105's. We waited with several others for them to finish and to get the signal from the crew chief to board. I was waved in first. The stretcher was placed mid-ship on the floor. "See ya, Lt.!" After my guys left, there was a literal charge of desperate passengers boarding. As about ten to fifteen Marines piled in, on, and over me, I saw a plume of smoke outside the lowered ramp from an '82mm incoming. We had to get out of there! As the new passengers found some space, they started firing rounds into the jungle about 200 feet below. The crew's 50 cal. was already firing full-automatic. Simultaneously, the ramp started to close as the chopper started to leave the docking. As the chopper got airborne and away from the docking, two men desperately jumped and grabbed the ramp as it was closing. The chopper was moving forward quickly. The ramp closed with their hands still visible on the top of the ramp and bleached white with strain before disappearing with their attached bodies, dropping to the jungle below. I hoped they made it, but doubted it. It was their desperate choice and all inside were busy laying protective fire or otherwise helpless to assist. What a pathetic last visual of the combat on the venerable Argonne FSB – two Marines taking their lives in desperation rather than supporting the mission of their fellow Marines.

The chopper rose quickly, then leveled out. There was total silence in the cabin and not a tearless face on board. "Chop, Chop, Chop!" Next stop, Quang Tri Field Hospital. I was off boarded last (first in/last out). None of my fellow passengers seemed to be wounded or disabled like me. They just seemed to scatter in all directions like the landing on Argonne. There was no reception from the hospital, most likely because they didn't expect us. But they were ready. There was a wheelchair and then a gurney, then an operating table. In the operating room, they must have given me a spinal because I heard one of the operating physicians say: "Yep, he got hit pretty bad!" As I heard this, I lifted my head up to see my left leg being pumped like a manual farm water pump with blood squirting out large gaping holes on both sides of my knee. Clinicians were picking shrapnel from my face, arms, back and head.

"Hey, am I going to lose my leg?"

"You'll be okay."

Next day, Da Nang. Next day, USNH Guam Orthopedic Hospital for the next two months. "You have numerous shrapnel wounds and surgical incisions which will heal. We left some shrapnel tags intact. Your leg will be okay, but you have shrapnel imbedded in the patella which will stay with you for life. You will never have full extension of your leg and will require physical therapy for the next few months. And — you're going home!"

CHAPTER 2

KNIFE BOY SIX FOUR

Larry Deason
SGT, 0848, Field Artillery Ops Chief
Golf Battery, 3/12, Assigned to 1st Bn, 4th Marines

I FIRST MET DAVID OVIST IN DECEMBER OF 1967. HERE ARE some of my thoughts on this nice guy who joined the Battery.

He was a big kid, quiet, strong-looking, one of those farm boy-looking guys, just bone and muscle. I met him and first thing I said was, "What happened to your arm?" That was a stupid thing to say the first time you meet somebody but he had this big discoloration on his arm. He said when he was young he got burned. I left it at that. His name was David Ovist. He was from the Upper Peninsula (UP) of Michigan. He had to try to explain where that was because I'd never heard of it. He said he grew up on Lake Superior. I asked him if that wasn't Lake Gitchigumi? (Gitche Gumee is Great Lake in Ojibwa.) I'd remembered it from the poem. He displayed a shit-eating grin. I learned that was about all you'd get from him. Me, being the aggravating SOB that I am, I could normally get a rise out of most anyone. Not David. I kind of liked him. He was one of those people you meet who just seems so easygoing but has a way about him that is calming. After a while, they started letting him sit in with experienced radio operators in FDC so he could see how to perform his job. When it's busy, you definitely do not want a novice.

I was getting to know David a little better as we spent some time together. The guys in communications called him "Ovie." I started calling him "Big O." We were both 6'2", but he had about forty pounds on me, all muscle. He told me about growing up pretty much in the wilderness. He grew up around moose, wolves, wolverines, badgers, Indians, a pet bear, horses and a deer. Well damn, I was hanging out with a modern-day Daniel Boone. The bear lived in the house with him.

While stationed at Quang Tri, somebody came up with a football and we had a game of tackle. FDC, Communications, Motor Pool, Docs and the rest of the Battery played the Cannon Cockers, Gun Grunts. There were some cuts, bumps, and bruises running barefoot in that sand. Big O was pretty good; I found out later he was a high school track star. Luckily, he was on my team. At Quang Tri we were about five miles south of Dong Ha and watched the fuel dump explode there one day when it was hit by a NVA 152 mm artillery round fired from North Vietnam. We were out of their range, fortunately.

In March 1968, the scuttlebutt was we were headed to Khe Sanh. Not good. Not good at all. That place had been getting the shit kicked out of it twenty-four hours a day. We'd heard that there were about 5,000 Marines up there, surrounded by 50,000 NVA, and they were taking incoming artillery from Laos plus rockets and mortars constantly. Planes couldn't land to resupply, so they were parachuting everything but half the time missing, so the Marines were running low on ammo, food and water. The NVA were tunneling under the fire support base and had trenches dug up to the wire. One of my best friends from high school and enlistment buddy was killed in February at Khe Sanh. Incoming mortars killed Sandy Shull; he was a radio operator with the 81 Mortars, one of the FO teams with 1st Battalion 9th Marines, "the Walking Dead."

In April, the Battery was headed to Dong Ha, where we turned west onto Route 9. We drove through the base at Dong Ha on northwest toward Cam Lo when we came under rocket attack.

I'd never heard or experienced a rocket attack before. About 200 yards in front of us was a civilian bus loaded with people. I don't know how many were on that bus, they were in it, on it and hanging off the sides when it took a direct hit from either a 122 or 140 mm rocket. That bus all but evaporated. That was my first time to see body parts plus dead and wounded scattered everywhere. It was sickening but I was glad it wasn't Marines. We got around the mess, didn't stop fearing we would be the next target. As we continued west around Cam Lo there were M48 tanks and some Ontos sitting around. We passed roads heading to places like Con Thien and Camp Carroll. Our convoy was heavily armed and everyone knew that the road had been mined, bridges blown, and once we passed Camp Carroll we were subject to ambush and incoming mortar attacks. We were just south of the DMZ. We passed the Rock Pile and the road turned south to Ca Lu. The bridge there had been blown so we crossed a temporary bridge, passed through LZ Vandegrift, passed Mutters Ridge, next stop Khe Sanh Combat Base and from there to Khe Sanh was really spooky. As we got closer to Khe Sanh, at one bend in the road there is as a unit of the Army's 1st Cavalry, a small outpost, and there was three dead NVA hanging upside down from a tree limb, for our viewing pleasure.

As our trucks were pulling into Khe Sanh past all of the wire, we were greeted by NVA 130mm and 152mm guns firing from Co Roc Mountain in Laos, about fifteen miles away. They were shooting at us, our convoy. That lasted about five minutes. Our guns unhooked from the trucks, everyone else unloaded. We found a scooped-out truck ditch about ten feet deep to put the FDC tent into, below ground. Communications set up beside us, we were east of the guns, everybody prepared for the worst. Then came rockets, then mortars. I'm thinking, "Holy shit, is this their welcoming or is this normal?"

The communication guys were running wire during all of this and the guns were being positioned, unloading and stacking ammo, and we started collecting empty 105 mm ammo boxes to fill with dirt to build a bunker in that hole where our tent was now. For four days I don't remember sleeping, just filling ammo boxes and sandbags with that hard ass Khe Sanh red clay. You dug that shit with your e-tool and packed it in three-foot-by-eighteen-inch 105 ammo boxes and sandbags. We made runs at night down to the Khe Sanh runway and helped ourselves to parts of the runway. We borrowed pieces of twelve-foot-by-three-foot solid steel runway matting for the roof of our FDC bunker. That bunker took a direct hit from a 152 mm artillery round with three of us in it.

In June 1968, the last folks left on the last convoy, Golf 3/12, and guess who gave us a fitting farewell? Those NVA guns that were poking out of the caves in the cliffs of Co Roc Mountain in Laos. Those little bastards hated to see us go. The Battery went down the road about a mile, around the bend and set up the guns on the side of the road and called it LZ Hawk. We had a platoon of grunts from 1/4 for perimeter security plus ourselves. The LZ was indefensible. The ground was so hard you couldn't dig; you had the road on either side, open with a mountain across the road, and behind was straight down to a river. We were screwed. Our mission was to protect those Marines who were left destroying what remained of Khe Sanh, Combat Engineers and grunts.

The NVA fired at us every day from Co Roc, but couldn't hit us because the mountain in front of us prevented the rounds from hitting where we were. The trajectory would cause them to hit the mountain or barely go over us. We did get mortars and some RPGs from that mountain. We finally got the hell out of there to a much safer place, Ca Lu, LZ Vandegrift. Some hot chow, maybe clean utilities and a night's sleep. I'd been sent to 1/4 FSCC earlier as the Op Chief temporarily and went back again. I came back to the Battery because a rat bit Sgt. Jim Larson. He had to go to Dong Ha to get rabies shots, so I was the only other NCO, a corporal to serve as OP Chief in his place in FDC.

I was back two days when Gunny Gaddie came in the FDC bunker and said, "Cpl. Deason, Delta Company got hit last night, the FO teams were flown out by Medevac, and don't think Smitty is going to make it. I need somebody on a helicopter right now, Comm is getting a radio operator, who do you want to send? Any volunteers?" Well, nobody wanted to go out there, and I was the only one who'd been trained. Dunlap humped Lt. Evans' radio when he was a FO and he was on his first extension, been in country fifteen months, so I started packing my shit. I went to Gunny and told him I wanted some more magazines, to get them loaded with eighteen rounds each, a 45 pistol and four grenades. I went back and started trying to get together what I thought I'd need and realized how unprepared I was for the hill and just how shitty the equipment was we were issued. My pack wouldn't hold shit. We had the same stuff from WW II. "I'm about to be dropped into the bush, no maps, not knowing anyone or where I am, oh shit; I need a compass, an artillery compass.... Who are they going to give me for my radio operator? Someone green or experienced?"

I got out to the Gunny and we headed over to the LZ where a bunch of grunts were waiting for a 46 to take us out and my radio operator was a guy I'd seen but didn't know. I asked the Gunny if I could swap him for Big O and he didn't respond, probably didn't know who I was talking about. The chopper came. We had about a fifteen-minute ride and we were dropped off on the side of some pockmarked hill. The CO was waiting for me with maps and filled me in on everything. He took the maps off of Smitty before he was choppered out. It was well marked. I told him I'd not been out before, the radio operator was green, but I'd been in-country for seven months and trained as an FO by other FO's, not by school, and they had tutored me on lots of do's and don'ts, so I'd do my best not to fuck up and I'd ask questions first.

I think he said his name was Delano, but from that day on he was Skipper. He said they were hit last night by ground forces, mortars first, then RPGs hit the machine guns, said the gooks knew exactly where they were. Shrapnel got the FOs and Smitty was hit in the neck and didn't look good. The radio operator was KIA. We would be moving in the morning to Hill 414 and Charlie Company would be next hill over. That night I called in night defensive fires all around us just as I'd been taught. I used two guns and left the set on the fingers and the draws leading up the hill to our position, and I had the batteries fire them every hour that night. I told the Skipper and he had the platoon commanders let everyone know I'd be firing close to our perimeter. I had no complaint about the noise.

25

When we left the next morning and went down the finger of the hill, we found a tennis shoe with a foot in it along with drag marks. On the second night we were on that hill we were both getting hit. I'd already called in night defensive fires and recorded them, so all the radio operator had to do was get the battery on the radio with our call sign and give them the fire mission. Well, the asshole RTO couldn't find anything when the shooting started. He couldn't find his ass, couldn't speak, he was useless. Now I had to find the radio in pitch black darkness with shit flying everywhere as we slid into our fighting hole, grabbing my rifle and map. This was the first time I'd been asleep and awakened in the dark with bullets and RPGs and yelling and who the fuck knew where these little bastards were, maybe in the hole next to me. And I was saying to myself, "Calm down, Deason, get some big bullets on target, get a fire-mission going, do something."

Finally I was on the radio and the first two rounds landed about 300 yards down the hill, exactly where they had stopped firing earlier. I dropped 100 meters and two more rounds landed closer, so I dropped another 100 danger close 100 meters and asked for five rounds, which was a total of ten. Then I shifted right 100 and kept those two guns shooting, then started another mission with two more guns beginning at the same grid as the first two. I brought them up close, shifted them left, then started another mission with the battery's last two guns and brought them straight up the hill within fifty meters of our line right on top of the NVA. I had another battery dropping illumination and then they were gone.

The next day we were picked up and flown back to Vandegrift. I was back at the battery getting another radio operator. I couldn't have David, and I asked again. They gave me another FNG, but at least we got to talk before we went back out. Before I was going back out, I was going on a mission. I was going strolling over through the area where those Army guys stayed. The Army always had good shit and I might just find something unattended. As I walked along, on the ground outside a tent was this aluminum pack frame with canvas straps and even equipped with a waist belt. I grabbed it, did a one-eighty and headed back. Now all I needed was a nice pack for the frame, which I found later.

We went out again and I got another dud for a radio operator. He got mud in the mic. He was terrible on the radio; he was terrible following instructions. I couldn't believe this idiot made it through radio school. At night we were all on radio watch in the Company CP and he decided to fall asleep. It was me that caught him, fortunately. When we got back to Vandegrift, I was back at the Battery, raising hell and finally they agreed to give me Big O. He got that shit-eating grin, he was ready for the bush.

David had been in-country since December 1967, made it through Khe Sanh, seen plenty of incoming and had plenty of time on the radio talking to FOs. I knew he was ready and humping all that gear wouldn't be a problem. We had a few days before the next operation, so we had lots of stuff to go over. David needed to know how to read a map, use a 6400-mil compass, plot a six-digit grid on a map and shoot a direction to a target. If something happened to me, he could help the CO with a fire mission. I also wanted him to always walk two men behind me. Sometimes the NVA shot the guys on both sides of the radioman first. They figured he must be an officer or the FO. I also told him if we get ambushed that I wanted him to get down and get cover as quickly as possible. Our job as the FO team was not to be shooting back with our rifle or pistol. Our first job was, if possible, to get artillery support there as quickly and as effectively as possible. He (David) was to get cover and stay. I would get to him, I would communicate to him. He had a radio with an antenna and the NVA would shoot him and shoot where he was going, me. If he got shot, then I had to carry that heavy ass PRC-25 radio.

Our first operation couldn't have gone any better, Hill 715. I believe it was two tops with a saddle between. Patrols during the day and some night ambushes. We were probed and the grunts fired a few claymores, pop flares threw some grenades, nothing major. I think one of the other companies nearby walked into some trouble and took casualties from a Chinese claymore. Big O did fine. Nice to have a partner who did what was asked the first time and did it well. The worst part of that op was we got socked in and ended up humping all of the way back to Vandegrift. Helicopters couldn't get to us and we were out of food and everything else. Long walk back out of those mountains in the jungle.

The next time we went out, he doubled up on the number of canteens and the amount of C rations he took. I found him a pack that was bigger so he could carry more. One like mine, compliments of the United States Army. No frame, just a "rucksack," as the Army called it.

I believe it was our third operation out that we were in an ambush and Big O did exactly as he had been asked to do. I got to him and he was as calm as someone sitting on a park bench. By the time we got a mission over the radio, they had broken contact and gone. We still blew the shit out of the area, but figured the NVA had disappeared underground. The little bastards lived underground like a bunch of chipmunks. About all you ever saw was muzzle flash. If you saw one, he was usually dead. Every once in a while, a Chieu Hoi would show up, yelling, "Chieu Hoi." That was a program where they would surrender. You would have to watch them until an ARVN or somebody from Intelligence could come out and get them. You had to feed them, give them water and watch them like a hawk. They all smelled like mildew. Personally, I never trusted any of them.

Every time we would go out on an operation, David would carry more and more. Finally, I told him that he reminded me of a pack mule. I never saw him angry or frustrated. I did see him anxious one time. We were at the Rockpile, the firebase, not on top. It was across the road from the mountain or whatever you called that 700 foot pile of stone. We had to hustle out past the Rock to the LP. A Recon Team was running back in, with a shit load of NVA chasing them. They were a couple of klicks out. It was all elephant grass out there and they wanted to see if I could get some artillery rounds between them. I could see the grass moving behind our guys and there was about 200 meters separation. I had a 105 battery from Vandegrift firing white phosphorus and adjusting from behind the NVA. I was ready to fire for effects, which were all six howitzers, when the Battery Six got on the radio.

I had requested fuse VT, which causes the round to explode twenty meters in the air. This was devastating for troops in the open because all of the shrapnel blew straight down on them. The Battery Six was the CO, usually a captain. He wanted to use shell "firecracker" instead and I rogered shell firecracker, battery three, which was eighteen rounds. I had never seen these things, only heard about them. The round popped in the air above the target like illumination rounds and a bunch of parachutes opened, they dropped to the ground, and hundreds of grenades bounced about ten feet into the air and exploded. They sounded like firecrackers.

Well, we fired another battery three and we were right on target. There was no movement out there. All dead or not moving. The recon unit made it in, and the Battery CO wanted a body count. That we couldn't do. It was about completely dark, we were out on the LP and watching for movement out there as light disappeared. It was too dark to get back to the CP, but I damn sure didn't want to be stuck way out there with just four Marines.

Then the Skipper came over the land line to the LP and said, "Arty (Artillery), me, get your ass back to the CP. Intelligence says we're getting hit tonight."

I was asking, "How about making sure they (grunts standing lines) all know we are coming in? We don't have any pop flares so we will put the radio on the company frequency, have the radio on squelch and the mic on his (David's) ear, and we are coming now." I did get a pop flare from one of the grunts on listening post. There was a path that ran along the bottom of the rock to the road and over to the firebase.

As I was walking, David was behind me with his hand on my shoulder and it was dark. We were walking past the area where the Marines who were on the top of the Rock Pile threw all of their trash and garbage off and those jar heads would use a tree branch that grew off the side of the rock as a bathroom and try to hit us with crap for fun. All kinds of shit started moving on my right where nobody was supposed to be. We were in open space between the Fire support base CP and the listening post. I told David to hit the pop flare and I opened up full auto on wild pigs in that pile of garbage. Now we were on the ground, knowing the grunts were about to open up on us. I was telling David to tell them on the radio not to fire, everything was okay, no NVA. There was no telling what those crazy bastards above us might do. So we didn't move. Now flares were going off everywhere and it was like daytime. The "all-clear, get inside the wire in a hurry" came over the radio. I think both of us may have touched a little cotton when we thought those pigs had ambushed us. I caught some shit over that incident.

The next day we got mail and I received a box from home at the Rockpile, about thirty packages of different kinds of chips. The two of us feasted on something salty and crisp, a craving over there; we had to eat them in one day because we moved out the next day, and that resulted in the both of us having the trots the following day. Too much grease.

You get to know someone pretty well when you're with them 24/7 for two or three months. If you served with a Marine infantry or artillery unit in Vietnam, you were in combat, sometimes up close, really close. You get to wear a CAR (combat action ribbon).

David was with me as the radio operator and together we were the FO Team for Delta Company, 1st Battalion, 4th Marines. Our call Sign was "Knife Boy Six Four." Together we humped, slipped and slid, up and down a bunch of mountains, crossed creeks and rivers, cut ourselves walking through elephant grass, were bitten by big ass ants and mosquitoes, dodged centipedes and rats, picked leeches off each other, dug countless holes, filled sandbags, and most importantly provided artillery for the grunts of Delta Company without one friendly casualty.

Most infantry companies had a lieutenant as the FO (Actual) and an enlisted FO or (Alpha) sometimes called a scout. They took turns going on patrols and ambushes. David and I were the only team until a Lt. Andy O'Sullivan joined us in September 1968. We went on every patrol and we were out on night ambushes. I stayed with the Lt. for a couple of weeks, sharing some ideas and showing him things we didn't learn in school. We shared "Big O" during this time. I wasn't sure if I'd be getting a new guy or staying with David. I soon found out because of my experience with Battalion FSCC Op Chief as well as FDC, I was going to the 4th Marines Regiment on LZ Cates as Op Chief in Regimental FSCC. No more humping in the bush. I said my good-byes good lucks, and told David to take care of his new partner. I gave David my Navy survival knife and my 45 magazines. He didn't want the ice pick he'd seen me use on a NVA soldier. I gave him my pack. He could use that aluminum frame to carry even more shit, since I would no longer be needing it.

When I was at Regiment, I found out from a Maj. Frazier that I would be getting some decorations. One was for taking out some mortars that enabled us to get off a hot LZ. We got a direct hit that caused a secondary explosion; the two of us had left the rest of the company to locate those mortars. I asked if David would be getting the same awards and "no" was the answer, even though he was there with me. Not exactly fair. That was how things worked over there. Young men doing their jobs, risking their lives for others without regard for themselves, rarely got more than an "Atta Boy." You do what you have to do, what you are trained to do. We all meet people in our lives who make an impression, someone whom you never forget. I was picked up by helicopter that morning and carried to LZ Cates on top of a hill between Khe Sanh and the Rock Pile. That was the last time I saw David. I left Vietnam in November and figured he would be going home in December or January.

CHAPTER 3

OVIE

Peter "Gary" Smelcer
SGT, 0846, Artillery Scout Observer
Golf Battery, 3/12, Assigned to 1st Bn, 4th Marines

I ARRIVED IN VIETNAM AT DA NANG IN AUGUST 1968, ASSIGNED to Golf 3/12. From there I went to Dong Ha and then Quang Tri. After about a week in Quang Tri, I was assigned to I Corps. I was given orders to join Delta Company 1/4 and replace Larry Deason, the enlisted FO in Delta Company who was rotating back to the world. That was when I met David Ovist. 'Ovie' was my radio man and he broke me in and trained me how to call in a fire mission and how to be an FO in Vietnam. The first thing I noticed about Ovie was that he did not swear, drink, or smoke.

Delta Company was on Hill 715 north of LZ STUD. It had been raining there for days. We were supposed to be extracted by chopper, but it was so socked in they could not fly. So, it was decided that we would walk back to LZ STUD. I do not remember how many klicks it was, but I got my introduction into humping, as we called it. We arrived at Signal Hill sometime around midnight and they called the chow hall to open up and feed us. I could not believe how kicked my ass was. Ovie was packing his pack plus a PRC25 Radio. I do not believe he even broke a sweat.

Ovie and I became fast friends. Right away, I noticed what a decent, kind, patient person he was, and a great radio operator. I don't recall him ever telling me that this was his second tour in Vietnam, but that's the way he was – quiet, never bragged, and when the rest of us were drinking and raising Hell, back at LZ STUD, Ovie could be found in our tent, sitting on his cot, reading his Bible.

As I said, David Ovist and I became close friends. 'Back Alley Bridge' is the name of a card game that is a lot like Spades, played by two teams of two each. 'Ovie' and I were partners and would take on all comers and seldom lost.

To be honest, it has been hard for me to remember. When I came back, the way we were greeted and what I got from some of my 'friends' about 'war stories' and not wanting to hear about it, I put Vietnam away, as far back as I could and covered most of those memories with drugs and alcohol.

I do remember going on operations with Ovie that were Search and Destroy missions in the DMZ, looking for rice caches and weapons. In between times of going on those operations, we spent our time standing lines at fire support bases and the Rock Pile. While we were back at LZ STUD, waiting to go on our next operation, we would usually get a heavy dose of NVA mortars and 122mm rockets. I remember one rocket landing on a Jeep in front of the FDC. It made the Jeep look like a twisted-up beer can.

After a couple of more months, Ovie was transferred from the Bush to FDC. We still saw each other regularly and Mark Abplanalp joined our team as a radio operator in December of 1968.

Like Larry Deason, Ovie and I trod trails all over I Corps on Search and Destroy missions. There is not much I can add about Ovie, my radio operator and friend, that Larry Deason has not described in his vivid account. Ovie was the kindest, most decent, best Marine I ever met, and I wish I could call him on the phone to this day and visit with him or go to Michigan and see him. I guess the good do die young! I think about him a lot.

Mark Abplanalp was more than able to hold his own as an excellent radio operator. Mark and I saw action on two or three Sparrow Hawk missions and Mark was cool under fire. My memory of going into the hot LZ on Argonne is much the same as Mark's, as we were together on the same chopper.

One small disagreement that I have is with Lt. Hunt's hand wound. This is how I remember it: He was in front of us. We were under heavy small arms fire from the NVA, but they were shooting high. I remember Lt. Hunt sticking his hand in the air and having one of his fingers shot clear off and scrambling back on to the CH-46and leaving with them. I do not remember a medevac being involved. On Argonne, for three weeks, every time a chopper came in, we endured NVA mortar fire. Ovie was killed during one of these attacks. We ended up abandoning the fire support base and just walking away after the three weeks.

I was blessed to have the two best radio operators, David Ovist and Mark Abplanalp, while I was doing my tour. Mark and I have stayed in touch over the years and he has helped me remember events that I had forgotten. There was another radio operator who was part of our FO team, who I met when I first arrived, who I remember as Lee Hayden. He showed me a lot about being an FO and being in the bush with a company of grunts. If anybody knows or knew of a radio operator named Lee Hayden from Golf 3/12, please let me know. He had promised to send me a care package when he got home. I got it when we were in Qua Viet on In-Country R CH 2& R. Two bottles of Southern Comfort, numerous other good things like jerky and pepperoni sticks, which I shared. A typhoon hit that night and I woke up and it had blown down one side of the tent. Apple and I both woke up outside in the rain, **sicker** than dogs with wet flaps of the tent over our heads!

That is my story and I am proud to have served with Delta 1/4 Infantry Company and Golf 3/12.

Disclaimer: I am telling this as I remember it. It may not agree with other accounts, but it is difficult for me to recall because I did not talk about it. Mark, 'Apple,' has a much better memory for the names and places than I do. –Gary Smelcer

CHAPTER 4

LONG AGO... JUST YESTERDAY

Bill Black
CPL, 0331, Machine Gun Team Leader
Delta Company, 1st Bn, 4th marines

AT THE TIME OF GOING TO ARGONNE, I HAD JUST BEEN PRO-
moted to lance corporal, and made Fire Team Leader for three
of 3rd Platoon's gun teams. A little backstory of Alpine. We had
been on Alpine probably two or three other times. The fire support
base sat in a valley that runs from Argonne, on the west and pretty
much ran on a southeast course past Alpine and that valley eventually ended up on the north side of Hill 950 and Khe Sanh. Also
northeast of Alpine was LZ Neville with a valley that ran south
of Neville and merged into the Alpine Valley.

So, we were on the hill a lot. One of the guys I came in-country
with was Frank Baldino. He was in 2nd Platoon, and on a dark
November '68 night, his platoon was sent out from the north
perimeter for a night ambush. There was no moon that night and
2nd platoon set up around a clump of trees next to the trail. No one
knew but there was a tiger up in one of the trees above where the
ambush was set up. Around ten or eleven o'clock, the tiger came
down and grabbed Frank, dragged him off and ate most of him.
For those of us who were at the top of the hill, which was probably
about half a mile away, as the crow flies from where they were, we

all heard him scream. The artillery and mortar guys fired off a lot of illumination until they were afraid they were about to run out of them, so they ceased. The next morning, it took the Marines of 2nd platoon about two hours or so to find what was left of Frank. Poor Frank, but those guys having to do that, geez. It was our turn that next night for ambush. We went to the same area and found lots of prints and set off for our ambush site. That was our first experience with Alpine.

Fast forward to March '69

We were at LZ Alpine for about two weeks before we went to LZ Argonne, which we didn't know that's where we were going. We knew we were at Alpine, we only knew what was going on that day. So we were sent out the perimeter, the whole company, to walk around Alpine, which had streams on all sides. We spent basically two weeks during the day in streams, and we would get up at night on the banks and set in, then the next day back in the streams. We did this for two weeks.

On the 19th of March, we were heading back toward Alpine. The company tried to get back in the perimeter before dark, but there was no way we were going to make it. We just couldn't move fast enough, so they had us set in on a trail, which was part of the Ho Chi Minh Trail. The Ho Chi Minh Trail is not one trail, it runs north/south along the border with Laos and then runs fingers west to east from the border with Laos to the coast. It's a massive network.

We all just plopped down on the trail, the entire company, 150 guys. Around 0100, Steve, Robbie and I were awake. That was our Fire Team; me, Steve Eckland, and Robbie Saldana. We just happened to all be awake as Lt. McCormick, our platoon leader, was crawling through the trail, checking lines, and he was finding everyone was asleep. It just so happened we weren't.

When you're out humping around, and you're not getting any sleep...you're not supposed to, but you do fall asleep on watch sometimes. it does happen. if you are caught, it's pretty dramatic, because usually the gunny or your platoon sergeant beats you, severely, about the head and shoulders. then in the morning they send you to Captain's Mast and they read the charges, announce you are guilty and demote you.

And so as Lt. McCormick came through, we were the only guys awake. The lieutenant was pissed everyone was asleep and was vowing retribution in the morning as he crawled through the line.

The next morning nothing was said but there was lots of tension in the air. At first light we saddled up and headed into the perimeter at Alpine. They then told us to square our gear away and stand by. I don't remember if they gave us any food or not, because they were very good at not giving us any food. Then the word came down to get ready, as we were being airlifted to this place called LZ Argonne. We had flown around it a couple of times and dropped north east and north west of Argonne. As we were getting ready, our Fire Team was camped out by one of the larger bunkers on Alpine, all the Command Group for 3rd Platoon, lieutenant, platoon sergeant and squad leaders, were in that bunker listening to the radio traffic and the lieutenant was voicing his displeasure about everyone being asleep. We were being nosey, and we leaned against the entrance to the bunker to hear what was going on. The lieutenant said he was sick and tired of everyone being asleep, and that he was mad that only one fire team was awake. He said that when we got to Argonne, all the squad leaders were going to be dealt with, which really got everyone motivated, as you can imagine. They dismissed the guys, the squad leaders came out and they were all angry. They went about their business of checking all our weapons and gear.

As the radio traffic started coming up on the network, we could tell something wasn't right on Argonne. You couldn't tell exactly what wasn't going, but it sounded like the Z was hot. The squad leaders started setting up the teams for which helicopter they were going to be on and it was 3rd Platoon's turn to be point platoon.

The way that point works is: three platoons in the company rotate who's going to be point, who's going to be in the middle and who's going to be tail-end Charlie. Then within the platoon itself the squads rotate who's going to be point squad, and also within that squad, which fire team is going to be point fire team. The first fire team has three squads. If you do the math, every third time your squad is going to be that, and then three times out of that you're going to be the point fire team. In the gun team's case there were only two teams. You either were or you weren't on point. You were either point gun team or tail-end Charlie. If you had anything to do on a squad-size patrol, you were always the point gun team. That's kind of how that works.

As they set things up, it was 3rd Platoon's turn on point, and Tom Bartlett's gun team, JP Young along with Jeff Forrey, that was the point gun team, leaving on third or fourth CH-46helicopter, and our gun team was probably the fifth or sixth bird. Usually there was a rifle squad between the gun teams as we moved, whether an assault or a move on the ground.

Before the first birds came in the word was passed, "Hey we're going to a hill that's been established before, there's going to be fighting holes, some old bunkers, do not go in them until they've been cleared."

A few minutes later they said, "There might be some people on the hill so think twice before you jump into a hole, but if you have to you have to."

Then about ten minutes, later they said, "The hill's hot. Wherever you got to go to take cover, you go."

So off we went around ten in the morning headed to LZ Argonne. As we came into the hill we headed in from the south, headed almost directly north. That would put us on the west side of Argonne. Looking out the CH46, we could see what was going on, we saw the hill, we saw the smoke from the airstrikes, but the thing we noticed was that there was a UH1H (tail number 68-15340) Huey on top of the hill. We could tell it was an Army Huey. We could tell an Army Huey from a Marine Huey because it was one of the bigger ones they could carry almost a squad. Marine Hueys could carry the crew chief, a door gunner and maybe a stretcher or two. It was on the hill, we later found out, to try to evacuate the Recon Team that was on top of the hill because they'd got shot up pretty good. The Army Huey was on top of the hill and we could tell, looking at our CH46, that the blade was just barely turning, maybe one revolution every five or six seconds slowly moving. So this fouled the upper LZ.

Suddenly the helicopters veered off to the west southwest and went into a holding pattern as some more jets came in. Our team was on the starboard side of our bird, so at times we could see what was going on on the hill, and others we were looking at Laos. Finally it was our turn to go in and as we headed into the hill the door gunners charged their .50 caliber machine guns and we were going, "Oh, crap, we're in for it now."

At 10:26am we were going into the hill, getting closer and closer. I was sitting right next to the right side door gunner, Tom Breeze was next to me, and we were trying to see what was going on and there was all kinds of smoke coming from the hill. And through it all there was that same helicopter still sitting there with the blades slowly turning. We came in and about fifteen feet off the ground they started lowering the rear ramp. Two guys toward the back were starting to head down the ramp, and at the same time everyone was starting to stand. I was between Tom and the door gunner and had no room to stand. So I looked out the window and as I looked up at the top of the hill, I saw a shadow rising up out of a hole. All of a sudden there were all of these muzzle flashes, I don't know, but I assumed he had an AK-47, but he could have had one of those light machine guns they loved. I don't know, it happened so quickly. He opened up and right when I saw those flashes I grabbed Tom by the cartridge and pulled him down.

Tom recalled it as me standing and him pulling me down, which is as plausible as my version. We've talked about it for fifty years and it's gotten to be a joke between us: "I saved your life!" "No, I saved your life!" Either way, I'll tell my version.

I pulled him down and the upper side of the chopper just above and behind the pilot's seat and running back above our window was turned into Swiss cheese. Thankfully, nobody was hit. The helicopter **immediately** dropped the fifteen feet. **Bam**, right on the ground, the two guys on the ramp got knocked down as they started to slide off the ramp. Somehow they grabbed a hold of what, I don't know, possibly the cylinders that raised and lowered the door or whatever, they grabbed onto something. The guys ahead of them grabbed them with a lot of yelling and screaming. The chopper slammed to the ground, bounced right back into the air and the pilot took off. He took off with the nose pointing to the ground, the tail end in the air, as the pilot banked to the left, trying to gain speed.

We were now heading in a western direction then in a south-southwestern direction. It seemed like we were moving very fast as we left the hill and the bird bounced around a lot. I looked back at the hill, everybody on the hill was flat on the ground and under cover. I remember looking at somebody lying right where the helicopter was supposed to land. He was alive as I looked at him and he looked at me. I didn't recognize him and he probably didn't recognize me. It was a good chance he was 3rd Platoon but could have been with the colonel's group. One thing that was seared in my brain from all the things that happened to us, was that when you were past scared and bordering on terror, the mind had a funny way of remembering things.

As the helicopter took off over the valley and the nose kept coming up, it would come up to almost a 45-degree angle and level back out, then come up and level out again. There was a hole in the floor for a hook for slings they called a hellhole. We were looking through the hole into the valley, mostly of elephant grass, some tree line but mostly elephant grass. I saw the elephant grass was getting closer as we travelled for a while. I figured we were going back to Alpine. When I figured we were only about halfway there the nose was still going up and coming back down, going up and coming back down. The crew chief leaned over to me and said, "They shot out the Hydraulics, and the pilot can't control it." I didn't say anything to him since you have to scream to be heard, but my only thought was, "Well, what the fuck am I, a dumb ass nineteen-year-old Marine Grunt, supposed to do about that?"

After a period of time, it couldn't have been more than minutes, the nose of the helicopter rose up, and then it kind of pivoted around the hellhole to the left, so it seemed like it was at a 45-degree angle to the ground. It leveled out and fell to the ground, just like that it bounced a little, the engines went out, and it was just **deathly** quiet. The crew chief said, "Get out!" So out we went. The ramp didn't go down, obviously, since there were no hydraulics.

We exited the helicopter and into the tree line for cover, which was what we were supposed to do. I was the last one out, and as we were running along there was a flurry of activity. The crew chief, the pilots and gunners were swarming all over this thing as I was going, "Oh, crap we shouldn't have run into the tree line." I told everybody to stop, bring everyone together. As we ran back to the helicopter, I looked into the back and the pilot and the crew chief were running around everywhere in there. To me it looked like chickens with their heads cut off, but they knew what they were doing. They had a plan, but I didn't know what it was.

So, I yelled out, "Everyone okay?" and the pilot looked at me and said, "Are you setting up security around the bird?" Aw, jeez. I didn't want to lie to the pilot, so I said, "Well, sir, we're working on it." So Robbie and Steve came up to me and I said to them, "Get a perimeter set up!"

As I walked around to the starboard side of the helicopter, and they were all over there pulling the guns out, the starboard door gunner was just freaking out, thinking he had been hit. He was screaming at me to check him. Their flak vests were like a life preserver type, the sides were open and were fiber mesh, as he was saying, "I'm hit, and I'm hit!" I was looking to see if he was bleeding. I didn't see anything, I told him there was no blood, and he said, "My back, they hit me in the back, I know I'm hit!" So I ran my hand inside his flak jacket. It was soaking wet. I pulled my hand out and saw that it was just sweat.

I told him, "Look, look, you're not hit, it's just sweat!" and he went, "Okay, okay, okay." He, just like the rest of us, was scared shitless. A couple of minutes later, another helicopter landed and dropped off their Marines, the rest of the squad we were assigned to. As they landed the 2nd Squad guys got off and the pilots, the crew chief and door gunners ran on and left us. We had no radios, no officer, we had no corpsman. To say the least, we were a bit lost.

After about an hour, another helicopter landed with very motivated individuals. They arrived and started stripping down the helicopter that had been shot down. Never spoke to us, never said "Boo!" and took the blades off the CH46. They scrambled around, loaded the blades into their helicopter, and disconnected a whole bunch inside the cockpit as they wove this big sling over the helicopter. Around what I guess was the center of gravity near the engines they connected this big hook. Then they turned to the smallest guy (which was Robbie) and they said to him, "Hey, look, when the crane comes you need to get up on top of the helicopter here, the flying crane's (Sikorsky CH54 Sky crane) going to hook onto it and take it."

About 2:30 in the afternoon they finally came and got us and took us back to Alpine. Then we heard all the stories about what was going on at LZ Argonne, that there were a lot of casualties from 3rd Platoon, that some of the people who were supposed to be dead were us! Around 3:30, 4 o'clock in the afternoon, we arrived at LZ Argonne. It was an absolute horrific mess. Everything was burned, and what wasn't burned had blood all over it. It was rather gruesome, as you can imagine, and it was rather solemn. We got up to the top of the upper landing zone where Lt. McCormick and the platoon sergeant, the right guide and some of the squad leaders were. Everyone was absolutely exhausted.

I looked over to Max. I said, "Word back at Alpine is you're dead."

Max replied, "No, I'm not dead yet!"

I said, "Let's go sit over there." We moved a bit. I said, "Look there!"

There were a couple of brains and other body parts lying on the ground. Max picked up one of the brains, and kind of tossed it in his hand like he was holding a baseball, and said, "Well, I guess he doesn't need this anymore!" and he tossed it as far as he could, which ended up being out over the barbed wire, into where we knew there were enemy snipers.

A few words here about my friend Max. He was the first guy from Delta I met when I reported to the company. He was just back from R&R, I believe. I was assigned to the same gun team as him. It was Max, Lewis and myself. Steve Sharp was our team leader. Max was the best friend I ever had. He was twenty-six, so he was quite a bit older than us eighteen- and nineteen-year-olds. We did everything together. He taught me how to be a good field Marine and more times than not talked us out of the trouble we would get in. We even shared a toothbrush for probably four months because he lost his and we couldn't get or steal one.

A few minutes later, the lieutenant said, "Black, get your gun team, 2nd Squad get up here. You had an easy morning, so you're going to go down and get the snipers."

The problem with the snipers was, as the helicopters would come in the snipers would open up on them. The choppers were coming in on a pretty regular basis to extract the wounded, trying to get the dead out and bring in resupplies. The lieutenant, his radio operator, my buddy, Steve McCall, my Fire Team, 2nd Squad and Max, proceeded out through the two rows of wire. They weren't even good rows, just like two rows of concertina. Max didn't need to be on that patrol. He was Gun's Squad Leader and on a squad size patrol it was usually left to the Fire Team Leader. That choice proved to be fateful.

The lieutenant told me, "Split off from the gun team and cover our flank."

Not five minutes later, everything opened up.

There were screams, which we later learned were Max, and several minutes, seeming like hours, went by and the firing became more intense. Then we could hear a gunship coming in. It was a Cobra. At that time, the Army was the only group that had Cobras. We popped smoke and the distance between us and the gooks was feet. His rounds plowed through all of us. Again the gods were smiling and none of us were hit. Robbie and Steve yelled over to me to bring my gun ammo, they were running low. I crawled over with my 400 rounds. They weren't more than thirty feet away. I know it's hard to imagine the terrain, but it was jungle that had been blown up by B-52s, A-4 Skyhawks, and F-4 Phantoms, including artillery and mortars. It was kind of like running through a gigantic set of Pick-Up Sticks while being shot at.

As I arrived, I found out Lt. McCormick and Max had been shot and the gooks had dropped them right in front of one of their bunkers. One of the other guys had been wounded. We evacuated him, but we couldn't get to Max or the lieutenant. Steve was on the radio talking to the FO's at the top of the hill and he was coordinating mortar fire on our position. Doc Allen said he was going after the lieutenant and I pulled him back. I said, "It's suicide and we need you here." (I think he's still mad at me for stopping him. Sorry, Doc.)

Steve and Robbie were pouring rounds into the bunker complex and I was maybe six feet behind them and Doc Allen was next to me about ten feet away. Off to my right several feet away were Tom Breeds and Smith. Sorry, I can't remember his first name. We heard the mortars come in, a sucking sound that chills your bones. As the rounds came in and hit, one landed right behind me. It couldn't have been more than a foot away. There was nowhere to go, it was microseconds away, so I just hugged my rifle and whispered to myself, "Fuck me, I'm dead." I don't know how long it was but my eyes opened and everything was blurry and I thought I was dead. I said to myself, "This is not so bad."

Then things came into focus and I realized I was still alive and still in a world of shit. I still can't forget how pissed I was I was alive. My first thought was, "If I'm alive, that mortar had to have taken off my legs or my back is shredded and I'm paralyzed for the rest of my life." I put my hand up between my back and flak jacket and it was soaking wet. But like earlier in the day with the door gunner, it was sweat. I looked down and my legs were there and they moved. Then I realized I was alive, in one piece and still in the jungle. I yelled to no one but me, "Damn it, I'm alive."

Then I saw Steve and Robbie turn and look at me and Robbie said, "Bill, you're still here. We thought you were blown up." Steve was hit, Doc was hit, Tom was hit, and a bunch of others. We got a dressing on Doc and Steve started yelling for Doc, but he couldn't walk. I went to Steve to help and get on his radio for check fire, but it had a two-inch chunk of shrapnel in it. I got him up and shoved him toward the wire. JP was there and grabbed him and got him to the aid station. I got Doc to the aid station and when I got back, 1st and 2nd Platoon and some officers came down to help. We asked, "What do we do now?" There were so many wounded, we got all but Max and the lieutenant out. The officers told us they were dead at the foot the bunkers and there was nothing we could do. We were ordered to pulled back, as it was getting dark. There weren't that many of us in 3rd Platoon left.

There were forty-two of us in the morning, but we had lost a ton of guys. We didn't think we had enough to cover our part of the perimeter and we had to send out a four-man LP. We were trying to cover a platoon-sized area, and send out a LP. LP (listening post) is like a dead man walking. Go out about fifty yards past the perimeter and radio if the bad guys come. A human tripwire. Like walking point LP is on a rotational basis. It's either your turn or it's not your turn. I don't remember who was on point, then I want to say it was Little John (John Arsenault), Peanut, and two others, but I just can't remember.

Peanut talked to the platoon sergeant, I think it was Jim Cluck. Cluck was the best Marine any of us ever met. Brave as the day is long and kept all of us alive. He told us, "You got to go out fifty yards." Peanut said, "Fuck, we go that far we're going to die." Jim Cluck knew they were going to probably die, they knew they were probably going to die, but being good Marines they got up, followed orders, and started heading out. As they got to the wire, our two wonderful strings of Concertina, some illumination rounds were fired off. As they floated on the wind the shadows moved with the flight of the flares. I don't believe there was a moon that night and the scene to say the least was eerie. They just stood there, ready to go, and everyone on the perimeter who could see them stood out of respect. With the snipers still around, it probably was stupid to stand, but we were all sure we wouldn't see them alive again.

The LP team, Peanut and the others, got to the wire, stopped and looked back at Cluck. They knew they had to go through, but they looked out over the wire, looked back at Cluck. We could hear the LP and one of them said, "Fuck it," and they all sat down. The platoon was all looking at them, and the platoon sergeant was looking at them. We weren't sure what would happen. Normally, if we didn't do what the platoon sergeant said on LP, or we fell asleep, they had a nasty habit of throwing grenades at us to motive us. Cluck looked at them for a moment or two, shrugged, got on the radio, and spoke into the handset. "LP's in position." Cluck was the best.

We all sat down. The LP tried to bury themselves in a some of the bodies in the wire. That was around ten o'clock at night. We could hear the radio start to chatter, and all of a sudden came this helicopter (flying very low), landed right between the wires, the snipers and the perimeter. One of the LP (listening post) guys got up and yelled at the crew chief, "I think you're in the wrong place!" and the crew chief yelled back something. To this day, I don't know what was said, and the helicopter finally took off. I don't know if they picked something up or just took off. I think the snipers were probably as flabbergasted as we were. I don't know why they landed there. All from that point was: "We are all going to die tonight."

The officers spread us all out real thin, but they left our three-men gun team intact. Our other gun team, we lost Jeff, the gunner, and the fire team leader, Tom Bartlett. Jeff was hit coming up the hill with Tom Bartlett and JP. The round that went through Jeff's throat ended up going through Tom's shoulder, and hit somebody in 2nd Platoon. I think they had J.P Young and a couple other guys they had grabbed to help JP. As you can imagine, you get close to people and when they are hit and gone, it ain't easy. The night was to get worse for all of us.

A little bit later that night, the screams started. It was down where Max and the lieutenant were. They started screaming because the NVA (North Vietnamese Army) were torturing one or both of them. The screams would come, and they were blood-curdling, then the gooks would start to laugh. It would continue, screams, laughter, screams, laughter. Then they started taunting us. "Marine, you die. Fuck you, Marine." You know, just your cordial greeting. I started to freak out because I was pretty sure it was Max.

Steve said "No, can't be Max. Can't be." Then Max started screaming my name. **Bill**. I still hear that in my dreams. That made for a fun night. I probably shouldn't say this, but I decided I was going to kill myself that night. Cluck brought down a guy to fill a spot for us, from the artillery unit. He was sitting there listening to all this stuff, and I had my weapon to my forehead and was trying to get my finger on the trigger as Steve and Robbie were looking at me.

"You okay, Bill?" they asked, and I said, "No, I'm not all right."

"Okay," they said. "Do what you got to do."

The Marine from the artillery unit was just freaked out because they were not used to being on the line with the grunts, so he was starting to wig out and make a lot of noise. After a while I heard J.P over in his hole, not yell but whisper forcefully, "Hey, shut the fuck up over there!" and this artillery kid said, "Hey, there's some dumb fuck in here that's going to kill themself!"

And J.P Young said, "Well, let them kill themselves and shut your mouth and quit making noise!" After that it was quiet for a while. I still kept my rifle to my head. I don't know how much time passed, but Robbie and Steve kept whispering to me, telling me to try to calm down and Max kept screaming.

Then I heard JP in a little whisper, "Bill, is that you?" and I said "Yeah."

J.P replied, "You all right?"

I said, "Yeah, I'm okay."

"Okay, I will see you in the morning, right?"

I said, "Okay," as he (J.P Young) yells, "Hey, arty guy, **shut up**." This was one or two in the morning. This went on until about five, all the screaming and everything else.

Then it stopped. Nothing, just the dead silence. A horrible, horrible night. When the sun just barely broke the horizon, the arty guy jumped out of the hole and looked at us and said, "Fuck you guys, you're crazy." Off he went. And he thought his night was bad?

We weren't overrun that night, we thought for sure we would be. That's just the way the jungle went. Horror, terror, complete calm. Not necessarily in that order.

Early that morning, a patrol was formed up to go and retrieve the bodies. I couldn't bring myself to do it. I went to Cluck and I told him I just couldn't go down there. "That's okay," he said. "I understand. Get in here and fill in the lines on the west side." I went over there and they put me in a hole by myself, then the NVA started shooting mortars at us. They peppered the holes on top of the hill pretty good, All around the perimeter there were dead bodies. As a rule, when the mortars came in somebody had to get up and play dodgeball with the mortars to make sure the gooks were not trying to rush the line. I was the only guy in the hole, so there I was.

Mortars will scare you. Mortars come in, you have to crouch with your head just above the top of the whole and you listen for the mortars. You learn to read the sound and drop to the bottom of the hole just before it hits. When I first stood up, I noticed there was this dead, headless gook in front of my hole. He had been there when I got in the hole, I just was so freaked out, I didn't see him. When I popped up the second time, I'm was so freaked out to see him I put a round in him. Finally, the all-clear came. I was told to get back to my side of the hill. As I was leaving, I looked in the hole next to me. A round had landed in that hole, and that was why it was muffled. In that hole was Lt. Col. Sargent, and a couple of other guys. I thought one of them was our arty forward observer, David Ovist, because he was standing near LtCol Sargent when the 82mm mortar rounds hit. David jumped away just in time to avoid being hit by this mortar attack. Normally we had Mark Abplanalp and Gary Smelcer, as our forward observers. "Apple," Gary and I had been together for at least six months. I had met David while hanging out with Apple and Gary on Hill 950. He was a good guy, friendly and fun to be around. We had a soft spot for the FO guys. In the line of march, they were usually right behind our guns teams. So you get to know them well. On the next day David was Killed In Action during another NVA mortar attack, when a round landed near him on the upper LZ. The colonel's hole was a mess. People were swarming around it, so I was sent back to 3rd Platoon's lines.

The patrol found Max and the lieutenant. The word came up to get ponchos down there. Nobody wanted to go, it was hard. The rule was, we're responsible for our own guys. I already violated the rule once by not going on the patrol, I couldn't do it again. I got two ponchos and started heading down there, and as I headed down there, there's an explosion. Come to find out one of the bodies was booby-trapped. One of the corpsman was rolling one of the bodies over. He was told not to touch anything, but he was a corpsman, that was his job. He rolled it over and a grenade under the body went off. Fortunately, the body took most of the blast, but a chunk of something went by Doc's eye and sliced him up pretty good. You get hit in the face, around the eye, you'll think the world is ending from how much you bleed. He (corpsman) came staggering up as we crossed paths. Max was further down the hill from the lieutenant. Turned out it was the lieutenant who had been booby-trapped. He was almost in two pieces. The only thing that was holding him together was about a two-inch wide strip of flesh and muscle from his rib cage down to his hip. The rest of it wasn't there. It was either on the corpsman or in the trees. We had to pick him up. That was a whole lot of fun.

J.P was there with me, so J.P. grabbed his legs, and I grabbed his torso as we got him on the poncho. We start hauling him up the hill. As we got about halfway back up, someone came down and helped. Then Robbie and the rest of the fire team came over to help. Steve and I stayed back and Robbie said he would go with the lieutenant's body to the top of the hill. Then they brought Max up. He wasn't booby-trapped, but rigor mortis had just set in, so he was kind of in pretzel shape. That was a horrible day, I just broke down.

They finally got them to the top and Robbie came down. Robbie came back to the hole an ashen white color. I asked him what happened. He said, "Well, you know, the lieutenant fell out of the poncho, broke in half, and the two pieces went about fifteen feet down the hill." "Oh no," I said, and he said, "Damn." 2nd Platoon came over and told Robbie they would take over from there and get the lieutenant up the hill. Robbie said, "I just couldn't do anymore." There was a lot of that going around. He walked away and went to our hole. We were all freaked out by the events of the last night and that morning.

The next day, they sent 1st or 2nd Platoon out the north perimeter down past where Max and the lieutenant got killed to sweep that little saddle that ran to the next hilltop north. They no sooner got outside the wire, maybe twenty-five to fifty yards, and they walked right into a NVA complex and the NVA were pretty much sitting there smoking and joking, so those guys shot them all up, killed about seven and wounded a bunch.

The third day another patrol went further down the same way and ran into another bunker complex. The initial platoon took about four dead and some wounded and the word came down to saddle up and get down there. There was a pretty intense fire fight, the gooks got trapped in some bunkers and were killed. Finally, we were ordered to pull up to the top of the hill and the lieutenant ordered the whole area napalmed. The napalm was dropped from where Max and the lieutenant died and north, fifty yards to the next hill. 3rd Platoon was ordered off the north perimeter and put us on the east perimeter. All the debris from the airstrikes, all the trees that ended up on the east side of the perimeter, it was all a tangled mess.

So, every day from that day to the day I left, we received incoming motor rounds. Lots of rounds. The only nice thing was that if you've been there a while and you're still alive, you learned to listen for them, hear when they were fired and hear them coming in. They were fired from about three miles away, and they made a little "Thoomp!" If you heard that sound, you knew you'd better find somewhere below ground or you were pretty well screwed.

Our hole was about fifty feet down from where the colonel and all the bigwigs of the battalion were. We were directly opposite from where the mortars were. They always went a bit long on their shots, they wanted to hit the LZ where the helicopters would come in. But a lot went long over to us and the CP Group. They'd usually fly in a northerly route to the LZ. But after a few days they said, "Screw that," and moved the LZ to northern perimeter and eventually they would come in from the east low and pop up in the LZ, drop their stuff and haul ass out. That was because they had pushed the Huey off the hill and set it on fire with diesel fuel and flamethrowers.

By about the fourth day, the gook bodies started to smell really bad. It was just horrendous that smell. There was a working party assembled, and in the Marine Corps, the low end of the totem pole went on the working party. We all had about the same time in, so poor Robbie volunteered to go. They estimated about forty bodies and several body parts they gathered and threw into a bomb crater on the northeast perimeter, a B-52 crater, ones you could make an Olympic swimming pool out of. They threw them in there, put a bit of dirt on them, said, "Well, that looks good," and left. There were arms sticking out, legs sticking out, and the smell was just horrible.

Later that day, we were sitting in our hole, the 2nd Platoon guns squad leader came up and said, "Hey, I wanted to tell you I was with Jeff when he died."

"Really?" we said. "What happened?"

"Well," he said, "Jeff was firing his machine gun, having a duel with the NVA machine guns up on the hill, and a round came up over his forearm and grazed him. It scared him and made him jump up, and another round went through his throat. His fire team leader, Tom Bartlett, was behind him, and the round went into his shoulder. Jeff fell back into his arms and started gurgling. A corpsman came by and said there wasn't anything he could do, and proceeded to move on. He died in his arms."

That was the stuff dreams were made of: bad dreams. He was a good guy for coming and telling us that. We started asking who he knew was dead. We knew a lot of the numbers didn't add up. We had ten dead and a lot of wounded. He told us Max Baer was dead and that the word was we three were dead as well, also the three forward observers, including Apple (Mark Abplanalp) and Gary. We freaked out. That meant Apple, Gary and David. So the numbers were off and we parted company all freaked out and confused.

After he left, I had to go to the command post for something. There was a trail behind our series of holes, that eventually led to the CP. There was this big tree blocking the trail, not Sequoia big, maybe four feet in diameter. I was getting ready to climb over and I saw this guy, and it was Apple.

I said, "You're Apple!" The way things had been going, I was thinking it was a dream and he said, "Well, I know I'm Apple!" and I said, "You're supposed to be dead!" and he looked at me and said, "Well, I'm sorry to disappoint you!"

We started laughing and I said, "I was just talking to a guy from 2nd Platoon who told me that you and Jeff and David were dead!"

Apple replied, "I'm not dead, Jeff's not dead, David is, but you are dead and Steve is dead." It was kind of bittersweet that we were alive. If we were dead, it would mean we wouldn't be on the hill anymore and that wouldn't be so bad. Gary Smelcer wasn't on the hill. It turned out the day we went onto the hill he had a real bad Planter's Wart, and I didn't know any of this, but they sent him back and told him to get it taken care of. Thank God for Planter's Warts!

We stayed on that side of the hill and we got a new lieutenant, Reston, a Naval Academy graduate who was fresh off the boat new. It had to be hard for him. First command and it was being run by a bunch of PFCs and lance corporals. He promoted a bunch of us to corporal, which was really nice. He gave us Meritorious Combat Promotions. He turned out to be a good leader. We got replacements too. One was Steve Effinger, who went to Steve's team.

Because of our marching around Alpine in the streams for those two weeks, I got bad trench foot. It just got horrible. I was peeling all these layers of skin off the bottom of my feet, I had to go on all these patrols, and it was just awful. They decided they weren't going to medevac because the incoming was so bad when the choppers came in, so Doc would paint the soles of my feet with New Skin.

We were trying to train the new guys to replace the old new guys we lost taking Argonne. We made a pact we weren't going to lose any more after we lost three new guys on the same fire team. They were new, but they weren't trained the way they should have been, and we all knew it. That was on us, being the platoon leaders now. We were hard on the new guys like Effinger. They weren't real keen on us being so hard on them, but we told them we weren't going to write any more letters to moms, so they needed to keep their heads out of their behinds.

Every day we stayed on the hill, we had incoming mortar rounds; every time we went outside the perimeter we got hit. The mortars took its toll on people. Hiding in a hole and hoping it wasn't your turn to die. It was a miserable place to die. I guess no place is a good place to die.

We were having trouble getting supplies in safely, so they para-chuted three pallets of food, water and ammo. All three landed outside the perimeter. What a night that was.

There was a stream running north to south on the west side of the hill. We were always hurting for water. 2nd Platoon went a patrol down to the stream and were filling their canteens and sent a patrol further upstream and found the NVA had buried three or four dead bodies in the stream and left them there to contaminate the water. As you can imagine, they were throwing up, not nec-essarily from being sick but from the thought of what they were doing. Argonne was a vicious place.

Alpha Company set out from the west perimeter and was doing recon by fire, where they shot arty rounds ahead of them to clear the area. Several rounds were short, meaning they were defective or the battery calculations were off. Those poor guys took tre-mendous casualties. I believe it was seven dead and twenty-one wounded. They sent a bunch of guys from all three platoons to aid and haul bodies. Another long, deadly night on Argonne.

I finally got medevac'd off with Larry Mercer. I think Larry had bad hemorrhoids. They couldn't risk bringing in so many choppers to move Bravo off the hill, so they had to walk off the hill for about two kilometers south with Bravo Company to an LZ (Landing Zone), and Larry and I and some others got to tag along. My feet were killing me, but I was off the hill.

After I was medevac'd to 1st Battalion's aid station at LZ Stud (later named Vandegrift). I realized I hadn't had more than five showers in the last ten months. The most we'd do was clean up in a stream. They looked at my casualty tag, and at Larry's, and said, "You guys are not coming into our aid station until you get a shower. You stink." They were nice about it, but we did smell bad. Corpsmen were always nice. Off we went in a Jeep and we were taken down to the communal showers. We'd never seen anything like that in the field. The water was treated with a lot of chlorine, it just burned on the jungle rot and the trench foot, but we didn't want to get out. We figured it had been forty-five days since we had any type of "bath."

After they treated us, we were fed and they said, "Hit the rack." We finally got to sleep a full night. What a beautiful feeling. We got to sleep on cots with clean sheets and brand new poncho liners. It was heaven The docs were so cool, and we wished we could have finished our tours in those cots. We were there two weeks. Then back to the bush. But what a godsend those two weeks were.

I think about Argonne and the guys every day. It's on a continuous loop in my head. I still hear Frank scream when the tiger got him. I still hear Max scream. And the smell, the smell of death, my God that is the worst. And I'm not a big fan of noise and darkness, especially at night. I sleep with a night light and ear plugs. I have for the last, I don't know, forever? Flying still isn't much fun, but Kat and I like to travel, so I have to suck it up. Business Class helps. So, what do all the docs say? It's okay to think about it, just don't relive it.

Okay, Doc, whatever.

I've had a good life. I promised I would never complain. Almost never. I have a great wife, Kathy (Kat), a great son, Jason, daughter-in-law, Jamie and two absolutely wonderful grandsons, Jonah and Jacob. A great brother, Jim and best friend, Dwight. Plus a bunch of great friends who over the years have taken it upon themselves that, if by chance I wander off the mental reservation, they are there to smack me literally and figuratively upside the head. I still talk to Mark, J.P., Steve McCall, Tom Breeds and Max's widow, Charlene. I call J.P. and Tom every March 20 and sing them Happy Birthday. Which is always worth a laugh. Steve Ecklund passed in 2015. We lost track of Steve over the years, but Apple found him in 2014. We were able to talk and swap lies like the old days. Apple and Joanne have done more than anyone to find us and connect us all. Not sure where Robbie is. Tom Bartlett passed a few years before Steve. He had become a lawyer. We've all coped reasonably well. Some days are pluses and some are minuses. What did that Chinese philosopher guy say? A long journey begins with one step. He sounds like the docs.

It was an honor to earn the right to become a United States Marine. There's not a better feeling.

Semper Fi.

CHAPTER 5

GUNS UP

James Patrick Young III
L/CPL, 0311, Machine Gun Squad
Delta Company, 1st Bn, 4th Marines

*Note: What follows is a record of what I personally witnessed
and participated in as a member of 3rd Platoon, Delta Company,
1st Battalion, 4th Marine Regiment, 3rd Marine Division.*

MY MEMORIES OF THE EVENTS THAT OCCURRED DURING MY
involvement have softened somewhat in the past fifty-one/fif-
ty-two years.

Background:

My tour with Delta 1/4 began 8 August 1968 and ended when
I rotated back to the US on 24 August 1969.

Delta was in the field on Operation Scotland II when I and
other replacements joined the operation. Initially, I was assigned
to Delta's 1st Squad, 3rd Platoon. 1st Squad was made up of a
couple of combat veterans, Cpl. Marcum and L/Cpl Graham and
several of us replacements. Mike Leonard, Steve McCall, John
Arsenault and I made up the "new guys." Once greetings were
exchanged, the first thing I remember was having my "skivvy
drawers" ripped from me while still wearing trousers! My first
lesson of many about life in the jungle.

Delta Company seemed to be moving almost constantly from one hilltop (mountain?) to another. Crossing small streams and also rivers. Elephant grass over your head that had sharp edges. We new guys saw our stateside skin become a mobile food source for every flying and crawling creature in that part of the world. Snakes, leeches, mosquitoes, foot-long centipedes, rock apes, and more than I care to remember. Up one side of a hill and down the other. I adjusted to life in Northern "I" Corps, knowing I had the better part of a year ahead of me, and of course...the enemy.

Days became weeks and weeks became months. We went from hot humid weather to hot wet, then cold wet weather when the monsoon season set in, and then back to hot and humid! It was tough to remember what day it was. We did know when a week was up since we were given the **big** anti-malaria pill in addition to the daily pill.

The terrain we operated in was very rugged and we had quite a few casualties due to falls, rockslides, and heat exhaustion. We'd hump all day, climb a last hill before dark, clear fields of fire and dig fox holes before setting in for the night. If you were in a two-man hole, you knew your sleep time was limited. If you were on LP (listening post) duty, you likely didn't sleep at all!

Why? Because you and two or three other Marines were out in front of the lines... "listening" for the bad guys. Lots of time to think about being nervous!

It wasn't all bad. I have fond memories of Delta Company being on "Sparrow Hawk" duty at LZ Stud/Vandegrift Combat Base. Sparrow Hawk duty was being a reactionary force on standby and having your gear packed and ready in case a unit in the field needed reinforcements. We had a daytime reaction time of fifteen minutes and nighttime reaction time of thirty minutes. We were housed near the airstrip with multiple helicopters, with air crews staged and ready to go.

So, we did have some downtime. John Arsenault (aka "Little John") and I had noticed that near the airstrip on the other side from our location was the chow dump. We weren't sure what exactly was stored in the dump, but there was more barbed wire fencing around it than on the perimeter of the base!

I never seemed to have enough to eat, or maybe I just burned it off climbing all those hills, but Little John and I hatched a plan. We waited for nightfall and then slipped out of our company area and eased our way closer to the chow dump. We decided to split up and meet back up at the same start point. We each made it through all the barbed wire (and there was a lot!) and fanned out in search of "goodies." High on our list were dehydrated steaks and dehydrated shrimp. We were also on the lookout for peach pie filling, apple pie filling, and anything else that looked like it might make an epic dinner. As the night progressed, we had a "mini chow dump" forming. It was about that time the MPs showed up and we were caught red-handed. The MPs brought a Jeep around, made us load up the spoils from our evening, and drove us to our area near the airstrip. The MPs met with our Delta Company CO (Lt. Caldwell), who chewed us out and turned us over to our "Gunny." The Gunny really chewed us out and bellowed that he "ought to make you eat every goddamned can you stole!" Which was what he did and what we did! Of course, there was plenty of good stuff to go around. Delta ate well that night.

Our Sparrow Hawk duty did have us called to action a couple of times, but our last time was to deliver radio batteries to FSB Neville. Since the 1st and 2nd platoons were on other missions, 3rd Platoon along with Delta's CP group went to Neville as a reinforced platoon. The monsoon season was upon us and so bad that visibility was about zero up in the mountains and no re-supply by helicopter was taking place. Our mission was to land in the valley below Neville and hump up the mountain with a fresh supply of batteries for all the radios up there. We started up from the valley floor, ascending as we humped. The slope was steep and the vegetation was thick. Weather was a mix of rain and mist and it felt colder than it probably was. About halfway up, our man on point, Roger Howard, turned and said to his squad leader (Cpl. Berry), "There's gooks up here."

Roger was told to keep moving and keep his eyes open. He took one step and took a burst of AK47 fire in his chest...killed instantly. We had just walked into an ambush that resulted in the point element being hit and the rear element being hit at almost the same time. We hit back and were able to break out, but at a cost of one dead, and several wounded, including our company commander, Lt. Caldwell. We treated the wounded, rigged a stretcher from tree branches for Roger's body, and continued our climb up the ridge leading to FSB Neville. It was a tough climb both physically and mentally. We made it to the top, which was totally "socked in" with heavy clouds. We had casualties that needed medevac, but nothing was flying. We were told that the word had been sent out to USMC aviation that emergency medevac was needed for Neville. A lone Marine CH-34 "Choctaw" helicopter crew volunteered for the mission. Neville FAC (forward air controller) talked the pilot up the slope since visibility was **zero**. Once the '34 was above us, he was talked down ever so slightly. Eventually we could see one of the '34's tires.

While hovering, we were able to boost the wounded above us, and with the help of flight crew get them inside the '34. Roger's body was a bit more difficult to hand up for loading…there were others helping me.

A week or so later, Neville was overrun by NVA during the February 1969 Tet, or "mini-Tet" as we called it.

Operation Purple Martin/ LZ Argonne
Date and Time: Early Morning, Thursday, 20 March, 1969
Location: Northwest Corner, Northern "I" Corps, Republic of South Vietnam

Typical start of a day for ongoing search and destroy operations. Move out at first light in the direction of that day's objective (OBJ). The past couple of days had us in and out of a sizable flowing stream as we searched an area near LZ Alpine, looking for signs of enemy activity. It did not take long for all of Delta Company, 1st Battalion 4th Marines, 3rd Marine Division, to be wet, muddy, and miserable. In and out of the stream, up and down sloping hills, hacking through the jungle. All of us had done it before and this routine was all too familiar, but things were about to get interesting.

About mid-morning, our direction changed and we soon left the stream and headed toward the relative safety of LZ Alpine.

Delta had been to Alpine a couple of times in the previous months and it was a familiar place. As we made our way to Alpine, some of us began to wonder why the change. Pretty soon wondering turned into rumor sharing. Rumor sharing turned into increased radio communications. By the time we reached our designated OBJ, we had learned we were being re-directed to stand by for resupply and helicopter transportation. An obvious change in mission! We learned a Marine recon team had met strong enemy resistance at former LZ Argonne.

Delta Company was now broken down into various groupings such as command groups, platoons, squads, fire teams, etc., and it wasn't long before CH-46 Sea Knight helicopters brought in our resupply. Typically, we received c-rations, mail, personnel, supplies, etc. This time, however, all we received was water and ammunition, and plenty of it. Those of us who had "been around" noticed this and we felt something big was coming and we were all in the middle of it.

Delta Company was assigned the task of attacking LZ Argonne from the air and 3rd Platoon was to be the lead element. This would be a "vertical envelopment of a fortified position" operation. We were now huddled into our various squad formations and our squad leaders broke us down into heli-teams. I was in the M-60 machine gun squad's first fire team and I would be in the third helicopter along with Squad Leader Max Baer, Tom Bartlett, Jeff Forry, and George Becker. Also included in our heli-team were Marine riflemen from first squad. Other Marine riflemen would join heli-teams for 3rd Platoon CP group and Delta Company CP group that made up the first two heli-teams. Our second machine gun fire team would follow on another CH-46. The rest of 3rd Platoon followed, as did 1st Platoon, followed by 2nd Platoon and 60mm mortars. Mixed in on each of the remaining heli-teams were H&S Company Marines, 81mm mortars, 106mm recoilless rifles, artillery, and on and on. The entire battalion was headed to Argonne.

We formed into single file lines as our helicopters came in and we boarded immediately. As each helicopter was loaded, it immediately lifted off and flew to an altitude and circled Alpine in an increasing circle as more loaded CH-46s joined the circle. By now, a number of Huey gunships had joined us and we flew westward but not directly to Argonne. As we flew and circled and flew some more, we eventually were in the final approach to Argonne and Argonne's upper LZ came into view. I noticed a single Huey gunship had landed on the upper LZ and its main rotor was still turning. I yelled to one of my team members that the LZ was either really cold or really hot. About that same time, bullet holes tore through the thin metal skin of our CH-46 and answered my comments about cold or hot. The burst of fire was about eight inches above the heads of the Marines opposite where I was. Our CH-46 banked and we began our descent at the same time our crew chief yelled we were going in hard and fast and would only be on the ground for a matter of seconds. We either got off or we'd go around for another try.

All of us were standing when we hit the lower LZ on Argonne. We hit the ground hard enough that many of us were knocked down. The crew chief was yelling, we were scrambling, bullets were flying, and adrenalin was pumping. As we exited the CH-46 via the back ramp I noticed Lt. Hunt(?) standing on the LZ at the base of the ramp. Lt. Hunt was pointing up the hill as the direction for us to go and in an instant his right index finger disappeared. Gone! Shot off his hand. Everyone was trying to get off our CH-46 at the same time and we all expected NVA mortar rounds to start hitting us. As I started down the ramp there were a couple of Marines in front of me not sure which way to go. I took a hard right and was off the ramp. Our CH-46 was still on the ground and seemed to be at full power when it just lifted and it was gone.

I was on the LZ, no cover, bullets flying, incoming rounds, up the hill I went. Crawling, low crawling, praying but I was moving. As I made my way upward, I noticed what a brilliant day it was. Bright sun, deep blue skies, just a magnificent day. At that point an automatic burst of AK-47 rounds impacted the ground about a foot up from my right hand. Now **that** was a reality check! I knew I was in someone's crosshairs and I started moving faster and zigzagged my way toward the top. As I continued to move upward, I came upon a couple of old bunkers that had no roofs (probably blown off when Argonne was abandoned earlier). In one of the bunkers was our 81 mortars Forward Observer (Townsend?). He told me to keep down, there was a sniper nearby. I yelled back that I had already run into him but never saw him. Townsend had only his .45 and wanted to use my rifle to take a couple of shots at the sniper. I was still lying out in the open and tossed my rifle to Townsend, but he could not get a clear shot. He threw my rifle back and I continued my way to the top.

I finally made it to the top of the hill where active fighting was going on in several places on or near the top. I found Max and the rest of our fire team and they were already returning fire, but ammo was running low, I gave them my ammo and off I went to find some more M-60 ammo. Heading off towards the downed Huey that crash landed on the upper LZ before our assault, I learned there was ammo aboard it. I was also told it was zeroed in by the NVA mortars. I had passed Lt. McCormick (3rd Platoon CO) and Steve McCall (the lieutenant's radio operator) and was told to keep down due to snipers and an NVA bunker dug in near the LZ. I made it to the Huey and saw that it had been shot up pretty bad and that pilot and co-pilot likely did not survive. I located the ammo and carried all I could (four cans) and worked my way back to our gun's position. I found a fighting hole to get in and joined the fire fight. We were directing our fire to the right (bunker near the downed Huey) and to the finger leading away from the upper LZ.

The gun was working but was getting really hot, but we had no extra barrel. Gunner Jeff Forry slowed his rate of fire a bit. To Jeff's left was Tom Bartlett acting as A-gunner and spotter. I was on Tom's left. We were crammed together in that hole pretty tight. There was a slight pause in our firing, when all of a sudden I heard coming from behind me in a loud, gravelly voice, "Do you know how to make that thing talk? Because if you don't I sure as hell do!" I turned around to see a crusty old Marine with an M-16 and crossed bandoleers. It was our battalion commander, Lt. Col. G.T. Sargent. We **all** opened up, he nodded, smiled, and off he went.

We needed more ammo, so off I went to scrounge some more. I found a couple more ammo cans and made it back to our position.

I was now upright but stooping as I handed the ammo down, and I looked to my left where my position once was. Some other Marine had moved into it and I started bitching. I glanced to my right and saw Jeff Forry slumped over the gun. Since I was still somewhat upright, I assisted with helping ease Jeff off the gun. He had been shot through his neck. The shot entered just below his right ear and exited on the left side of his face. He had swallowed once and blood poured from his wounds. I was now looking to my left at Tom Bartlett. Tom was acting kind of funny and favoring his left shoulder. Blood was now running down his left arm. We got Tom out of the hole, took off his flak jacket and applied a field dressing. I took a quick look at his flak jacket and noticed the bullet hole. It made me wonder if Tom had been hit by the same bullet that killed Jeff.

With the loss of our gunner and A-gunner, and the need for immediate first aid, our gun was temporarily out of action. I took Tom Bartlett to the lower LZ (where wounded were gathered for medevac) and headed back up the hill. By the time I made it back to our gun position, Sgt. Jimmy Cluck had taken our gun, moved forward about ten feet or so and resumed firing it. I asked him if he needed me to A-gun and he said, "No, but keep the ammo coming." Cluck continued firing until the gun starting acting up after it had made a weird sound. After that it would fire, but only single shot. He could cock it, the ammo belt was intact, the gas piston was free, but it would only fire single shot. Cluck gave up and moved to find another gun. We also had just learned that the CH-46 with our other gun team had been shot down and had not made it to Argonne.

The call went out for all dead and wounded to be moved to the lower LZ. Jeff Forry was still in our position, so I moved him down the hill. As I carried him down toward the lower LZ, I noticed about six H&S Marines bringing the 106 recoilless rifle up the hill.

I was able to put Jeff on the CH-46, with a silent prayer, and started my trip back up the hill to rejoin what was left of our fire team. Up the hill I went. By now the 106 was in place and the crew was aiming it to take the NVA bunker out. The first 106 gunner was taking a shot with the spotter/ sighter gun when he was hit by fire from the bunker. A second 106 gunner jumped into position and attempted another shot. He too was shot. A third gunner jumped up and instead of using the spotter/sighter gun, he opened the breech and bore sighted in on the NVA bunker. A "beehive" round was loaded and fired. The bunker was maybe twenty-five yards away from the gun and the 106 round must have been set for muzzle blast, since the devastation was immense. The bunker was completely destroyed. No survivors. The ground between the 106 and the NVA bunker looked like it had just been plowed.

After the 106 fired, it became relatively quiet in the immediate area. Most of us started picking up pieces, getting organized, checking who was hurting or needed assistance. There was a fair amount of interest in the NVA bunker. An intelligence officer showed up and was looking for assistance to clear the bunker or what was left of it. He was interested in maps, equipment, communications, and other G2 information. He asked another Marine(?) and me to give him a hand. I did not really want to have anything to do with that bunker, but I didn't mind helping the lieutenant. So, we started pulling bodies and body parts out of the wrecked bunker.

Up until Argonne, I had been a Marine grunt in the field for eight months and had seen firsthand plenty. Nothing prepared me for what I encountered while pulling the NVA bodies from that bunker. I was amazed at how young they appeared to be. I was also amazed at the destruction the beehive round delivered. Flesh was shredded. Some body parts were unrecognizable. I pulled one body from the bunker using his foot to pull on. Once the body was free, I was able to hold him upside down using only one arm. He must have weighed less than 100 pounds. It was then I noticed his brains had fallen from his head and were lying at my feet.

We continued working until the lieutenant was satisfied he had all the available intelligence. The next question was what to do with the bodies. We were instructed to throw them down the hill not far from our gun position. Then there was the question of what to do with the brains that had fallen out. I kicked them in the direction of the other Marine who was helping and he kicked them back to me. An impromptu soccer match started.

It was now mid-afternoon or so, and our shot down heli-team had been retrieved and brought to Argonne. We were glad to see them and they were glad to see us. One good friend, John Arsenault, found me and we were both relieved to see each other. While we were catching up, I noticed blood running down the right side of John's forehead just above his right eye.

"You've been hit," I said, as we fumbled to get his helmet off. I saw more blood, but we could not tell where it was coming from. It turned out John's helmet actually belonged to fellow Marine B.J. Cammage. When John and BJ landed on Argonne, BJ was wearing his helmet and John was wearing a soft cover. Bullets were flying around and BJ was hit in the head. His helmet did its job and no doubt saved his life, but was knocked off BJ's head. John, wishing he had a helmet, stumbled across BJ's helmet after BJ had stumbled away from it. When BJ learned John had his helmet, he wanted his "good luck charm" back.

Soon our attention shifted to getting defensive positions ready. My attention turned to getting our disabled M-60 to function again. I field stripped it and looked at everything associated with the operation of the gun. Everything was intact and all the individual parts were okay. I had figured the problem had to be gas system related. I was looking really hard at the gas cylinder, gas port, and gas piston for a problem area, but everything looked as it should.

I had remembered Sgt. Cluck coming up after the gun stopped working. He had scrape marks on both sides of his forehead. I said something to him at the time I noticed it and he waved me off. I started thinking about those forehead marks and the gun. I went inch by inch down the barrel from the flash hider to the chamber. Nothing stood out. I did the same thing a second time, but from a different angle, allowing more sun on the parts. Bingo! There was a split on the small connecting tube/port between the gas cylinder and barrel. Looking at the split, it looked like something hard had hit it. Bingo, again! Sgt. Jimmy Cluck may have been the luckiest Marine on Argonne that day. I believe an NVA was shooting back at Sgt. Cluck and the incoming round hit the gas port and split it in two pieces and each piece scraped his forehead. I shared my findings with Sgt. Cluck and he just laughed and shrugged it off.

During the assault on Argonne, it became apparent that some of the NVA defenders were falling back and taking up positions on the finger leading down the slope from the upper LZ. Plans were being made to push down the finger and eliminate any resistance encountered. The heli-team that had been shot down earlier, and included our second gun team, was to be part of a reinforced patrol to sweep the finger. Squad leader Max Baer had been actively involved in the assault on LZ Argonne. We saw him throughout the day, and he was busy helping everybody. At some point during the assault, Max's M-16 jammed and became useless, so he picked up an AK-47 and continued to fight with it. He was now out of ammo for the AK. Max needed a functioning M-16 for his use while accompanying our second gun team on the sweep and came to me for mine. Initially I refused to give him my rifle, but Max suggested that if I didn't give him my rifle, then I would take his place on the patrol. I saw the light and gave Max my rifle!

The patrol formed up on the edge of our perimeter and included Lt. McCormick, radioman Steve McCall, gun squad leader Max Baer, fire team leader Bill Black, gunner Steve Ecklund, rockets Tom Breeds, plus other riflemen, medical corpsmen and others I cannot remember. The patrol started slowly and cautiously, but ran into concealed NVA positions almost immediately. A fierce fire-fight developed between the dug-in NVA positions and our patrol. Supporting fire from Argonne was directed into the area of NVA concealed positions. Small arms fire and 81 mortars from Argonne were used. An Army Cobra gunship provided 30mm canon fire from above. We could see some of the action clearly from our positions on the hill. The patrol was receiving NVA small arms fire and grenades.

A reactionary team was quickly formed and left the perimeter to assist the patrol. I was there (with no rifle) along with Mike Lewis from 3rd Squad plus others. By now survivors from the patrol were met by our reactionary group. Steve McCall was still yelling, "Check fire, check fire," into his handset, but his PRC-25 radio had been blown off his back. Mike Lewis and I saw Tom

Breeds stumble and fall as we got to him. He appeared to have shrapnel wounds in his lower back. We carried Tom back to our lines, where a hasty aid station had been set up. I don't remember the total number of wounded from that patrol, but I do know that Lt. McCormick was killed, as was Max Baer. Several additional Marines were wounded, including radioman Steve McCall. Unfortunately, Lt. McCormick and Max Baer were left where they fell, but would be recovered the next day.

It is now late afternoon. The wounded were being treated and awaiting medevac. Every time a helicopter approached Argonne, we would receive enemy mortar fire. We'd hear approaching helicopter noise and almost immediately hear mortar tubes thumping. Some helicopters would make it in, bringing replacements and supplies and taking out wounded. Others would be waved off because of mortar fire. Close air support was pretty constant but could not stop the incoming mortar fire.

Defensive positions had been defined and improvements to them were taking place. Our position was now slightly forward and slightly left of where we'd been earlier in the day, but we still lacked a new barrel for our M-60. George Becker and I would soon have a couple of replacements joining us and we'd be digging a deeper and larger foxhole. We now overlooked the finger where our patrol was ambushed. Once we were settled in and had our replacements helping us, we discovered that our position was directly above the spot where the dead NVA bodies had been thrown earlier in the day. They were maybe twenty feet or so downhill. Our other gun team was farther to the right, covering a different finger.

Pretty dark now and we still had wounded who needed medevac. To avoid incoming mortar fire during medevac, it was decided there would be a night medevac. The medevac LZ was to be in front of our lines to the right of our foxhole. We heard the approaching CH-46 and braced for incoming. None. The CH-46 was now almost overhead and still no incoming. The helicopter was now hovering but not touching down. Then, in the pitch dark, he turned on his landing lights! I think everybody on the hill 'puckered' on that! Luckily no incoming and the '46 landed okay and the wounded made it aboard and had a safe departure.

We were on 100 percent alert throughout the night and could hear NVA on the finger in front of us. They must have been doped up since they were almost laughing and made enough noise that everyone could hear. A couple of thoughts came to our minds. One was that they were likely booby trapping the bodies of our two fallen Marines left at the ambush site. The second was they might be trying to get to their fallen comrades lying in a pile about twenty feet from our position. At one point during the night, one of our replacements realized there were NVA in front of our position and started to freak out. We asked him where he was seeing the NVA and we realized he was describing the pile of dead NVA. He finally calmed down, but none of us slept that night. Partly because "Puff, the magic dragon" was circling overhead and would fire its mini-guns, sending the long bursts of fire down to suspected NVA positions. The loud bursts would sound like a long "buuurrrrrpppp." We felt better knowing Puff was overhead and working.

Early Morning, Friday, 21 March, 1969

The word had been passed that we were heading down the finger in front of our platoon's position to recover our fallen Marines. 3rd Platoon Marines were involved, as were Delta Company Marines from other platoons. A new lieutenant (?) was in charge, but our Sgt. Cluck (our acting platoon commander) was right there with him. I was there too, but toward the rear of the column. Our movement was slow and deliberate since we knew the NVA had been out during the night. We fully expected contact or boobytraps or both.

Our column came upon the bodies and was halted for discussions on how to proceed. Sgt. Cluck felt positive that the bodies were boobytrapped and wanted to attach lines to each fallen Marine and give each a pull, just in case they were boobytrapped. The lieutenant in charge disagreed and ordered the Marine closest to the first body to move up and roll that body over. The Marine followed the order, moved into position, and rolled the body. The grenade under the body exploded and seriously wounded the

Marine. There was some yelling and the lieutenant reluctantly said, "Okay, Cluck, now we'll do it your way." The second body also had a grenade under it but no other Marines were wounded. Our column returned to our perimeter with our fallen Marines without further incident.

At some time during our recovery mission, our battalion commanding officer and another officer were killed and others were wounded by an enemy mortar attack. The battalion CP was located behind our position on Argonne and in among the few trees still standing.

Friday was a rough day. Our position was changed and we were now in front of the battalion CP. We were on the bullseye and kept digging our foxhole deeper. One man dug while the other rested or was on work detail.

Due to enemy mortar activity whenever a helicopter came near, and with helicopters taking evasive action, our resupplies often did not make it to our position. Water was especially scarce. Air drops by parachute were tried but the bundles often missed our drop zone and likely ended up in enemy hands. Air strikes against known NVA positions were regular. I remember one airstrike that was so close to our position that we **had to** take shelter in our foxholes. On another airstrike, the F4 Phantom pilot (Marine) was so close to us, when he pulled up after dropping his 500-pounder, I saw him look back over his left shoulder and flash the peace sign!

There was not much to laugh about, but one thing that was sort of humorous was the day the paymaster showed up on Argonne to pay us (in MPC/military payment certificates). Most of us had never seen that happen before. Payment was usually in the battalion area at LZ Stud/VCB.

Saturday-Sunday, 22-23 March, 1969

My factual memory of the 22nd and 23rd has pretty much blurred into just memories. New guys coming in, some guys going out. Helicopters and incoming mortar fire. Digging foxholes, sleeping in foxholes.

Several months earlier, John Arsenault and I decided we had enough field time and we'd sign up for every perceived easy job that came along: MP duty, Recon, Chaplain's assistant. You name it and we signed up for it. CAP (Combined Assistance Platoon) was another one we both signed up for. Well, I received word on Argonne that I was selected to be considered for CAP. I was instructed to be at the LZ to board a CH-46 and work my way back to battalion HQ. Sgt. Jimmy Cluck was on the same helicopter, as well as a few other Marines. We made it off Argonne without incident and it felt great. My journey was back to LZ Stud/VCB and then on to our rear area at Quang Tri. I had an interview with an officer and was selected for CAP.

I now had second thoughts about leaving Delta Company. What to do now crossed my mind. My father, J.P. Young Jr, (Lt. Col., USMC Retired, WWII and Korea) is someone I always looked up to. I wrote him a letter and asked for a little guidance on my future. I shared my thoughts with the interviewing officer, who gave me five days to make up my mind. I was either going to CAP or back to 3rd Platoon Delta. I was back with 3rd Platoon on the fifth day.

Final thoughts:

My dad (Pop) was with the 4th Marine Division in WWII and made all four of their landings (Roi-Namur, Saipan, Tinian, and Iwo Jima) and was on the front lines the whole time.

In the 1980s I was traveling with my dad and I was doing the driving. We had been small talking for a bit and we were both just sort of talked out. After a while I looked at him and asked: Pop, does it ever leave you? He answered without hesitation: Not for a goddamned minute! We didn't say anything more for a half hour.

What a true statement...

All of it is with me, every day and night!

Semper Fi

CHAPTER 6

EMERGENCY MEDEVAC

Jim Berg
1st Lt, 7562, Helicopter Pilot, Ch-46
HMM-265, 3rd Marine Division

The following is the text of a cassette tape sent by helicopter co-pilot 1ˢᵗ Lt. Jim Berg, USMCR to his parents in San Antonio, Texas, recounting his accounts of the day of March 21, 1969 when his CH-46 flew two or more emergency medevac missions into LZ Argonne, which took 5.8 hours to complete.

TODAY IS THE 21ST OF MARCH AND IT MAY SOUND LIKE I'M talking in a room of some sort, but I'm talking from underneath my covers – now getting my electric blanket turned up to six.

I came back today from flying the medevac mission. And, uh, I'm really pooped ... it's about 10 PM. I'm ready for the rack!

I'm miffed — I mean, we came back to no hot water after a long sweaty day. Hot water is our only luxury. But, even so, when you don't get it...you get kind of ticked. Something has gone wrong with these hot water heaters. So, we're told that the hot stuff will be back on tomorrow. Right! Give us some hot water! But tonight, no hot water, so therefore no shower.

Today was the day of all days. It was my turn to fly the (dangerous emergency) medevac, again. I am through with it for about at least another week now; it was a very, very bad day.

We launched out in the morning and immediately flew up to Vandegrift. I sent you a letter, by the way, on the 19th showing you pictures of Vandegrift Combat Base. It had layouts and how it works. So, I mean, you know what Vandegrift is now.

It's recently doubled in size as to what it is right now. And, at any rate, the base supports two US Marine regiments with two command posts. They are really running a big operation and supplying all these outlying combat bases.

In northern I Corps, well, the gooks are really on a big push. We understand that they're in some sort of a third phase of their offensive right now. Last night they shelled Da Nang again and for the first time, they also hit Chu Lai — that's the Marine air jet base south of Da Nang.

They got twelve jets sitting on the line out there and at about $3.0 million apiece, I'd say they got $36 million worth of aircraft. They completely totaled them with rockets. But so far, we've been quiet here in Phu Bai. We've had some penetrations and mortaring of the perimeter, but nothing anywhere near the scale as Da Nang.

When I had the duty overnight, Phu Bai went on full alert and everybody went to their bunkers. We thought we would be taking incoming mortars. But as I say again, nothing — beyond the perimeter — happened to us.

(Berg notes: Marines always said amongst themselves: "Phu Bai is OK" 'cause we didn't get rockets and mortars within the perimeter like Da Nang).

I don't think anybody got injured last night...but in Phu Bai it gets tense when we're called out of bed to hit the bunkers and grab a rifle.

But as I was saying, this morning we flew to Vandegrift's field hospital and we didn't have to wait there long before we launched out to evacuate about nine or ten emergency medevacs from an LZ in the extreme northwestern corner of South Vietnam. It's maybe two miles below the DMZ and about three klicks (thousand) meters from the Laotian border.

Yesterday they took a company of Marines out there and an artillery company as well. That started the trouble.

They lost many Marines and lost the hilltop. So they decided to go back there again with reinforcements. In order to get the hill back, they had to take it the hard way – with Marine grunts. So, they took the hill and took some more casualties — I'm sure. And now they are on top of this hill and call for medevac helicopters.

Well let me try to explain what this LZ looks like. It's on the bottom, if you can picture it, of a sharp ridge line, which is not very high. The zone itself is 4,500 feet high and the mountains around it go up another two or three thousand feet from the valley floor. So, the mountains themselves — their tops — are at least six or seven thousand feet up there.

Now, that's high for our overloaded helicopter. But once our underpowered helicopter is filled with a crew of five – two gunners, a crew chief and two pilots, plus fuel plus wounded grunts with their stuff...now we have a problem even hovering at 4,500 feet.

So this little zone was 4,500 feet. It didn't really have too much strategic value and from what I could see, it was hard to find or defend. But for some reason or other, somebody in Command loved that place. So, Marines went back and they took it and set up their artillery.

But from the time they were there to the time that they were extracted for emergency reasons, they were just being battered to hell. By the time we got there, it was combat chaos.

The first time we got our airborne briefing from Dong Ha DASC (Direct Air Support Center) of what was occurring on the ground, we were told we'd have no gun cover except for two OV-10s. That proved to be worthless.

The Marine grunt or FAC (pilot-Forward Air Controller) in the zone with the medevacs said, "You can expect incoming mortars and anything else when you come in." Then he said: "...our perimeter is fifty yards wide...anything beyond twenty or twenty-five yards either side of your airplane that is moving is not ours — it's theirs."

Both of us in the cockpit were sweating now with the prospect of this emergency medevac with gooks nearly in the zone itself and only two OV-10s to suppress fire. We called this a **Hot Zone**.

So that's how small the zone was we had to spiral into. We were at six or seven thousand feet. My HAC (helicopter aircraft commander) is real good and an experienced pilot. He radioed the FAC: "Okay, we're coming in...pop a smoke."

He downed the collective to initiate the rapid autorotation to the small ridge line, the zone. As a relatively new pilot in Vietnam, I had never seen any helicopter react as it did today. He made the helo do a couple of things that I had never seen or imagined it could do at that elevation. No doubt we overstressed the engines/ blades and airframe tremendously to descend and decelerate into that small zone — I thought. But it didn't seem to have hurt the aircraft at all. For a short time the rotor RPMs were about 7 or 8 percent above the maximum limit. But at any rate, we landed in the zone.

Our rate of descent was two or three thousand feet a minute. So from the time we were over the zone to setting down was sixty seconds or so. Despite that high rate, we slowed our forward speed tremendously to hit the zone perfectly — not under or over shooting it – that's deadly. On the way down I told both gunners on our .50 cal machine guns to start firing on my command and to **not** stop until our departure from the zone. Well, the HAC did a beautiful job.

Immediately we got these six emergency medevac's aboard... six or seven. I can't remember what the exact number was, and while this is going on right in front of us...three mortars exploded about twenty yards away. And if they had been smart they would have, you know, walked them to us. But they didn't.

Then, surprise — one more mortar in front of us; then another closer; finally one more closer still. But the walking of the mortars in the same hole in front of me was probably an illusion. Anyhow, it was time to get out of there. Uh, looking out through the windshield the guy in front of me looked like a priority medevac — not an emergency. A priority is less than an emergency. In other words, he can live for a couple of days without hospitalization. He's not critically wounded. He got out of his position to try to get on the helicopter. When he stood up, we saw him fall down. I found out later on that he was killed by one of the mortars that was aimed at our helo.

So, anyway, we got him on the helo, wounded or not. We were taking heavy weapons fire from all directions around us. The HAC pulled the aircraft up into a hover. We could hardly break ground – we were too heavy. Even a one-foot hover was tough to maintain. So we inched over to the sheer cliff on the north side of the lower zone and fell off.

Our RPMs had decreased to 82 percent! Only our high altitude saved us from crashing and burning. Below 88 percent we lost all our electric power and stabilization equipment to safely fly under control...we were at 82 percent and falling, dropping out of the sky — fast.

The good part was our increased airspeed got our RPMs back to normal. We could make a safe running landing on the airstrip at Vandegrift or Quang Tri.

Well, we got out of there in one piece. It seemed like we must have flown over at least an entire NVA battalion on our way out. And to our amazement, we did not even take a hit on the airplane. We took scratches from shrapnel, but nothing very serious at all.

The NVA are either poor shots or, more likely, my directions to our gunners kept the gooners' heads down, but rifles up firing at the noise of the helo.

Well, I was very relieved. I said, "Thank God I will never have to go in there again." But, to my surprise, we were ordered back to the same medical battalion emergency field hospital at Vandegrift, back to the combat surgeons who reported to us on our bleeding cargo: "They all lived." We shut the aircraft down in the hospital's zone and ate lunch.

Dong Ha DASC radioed again after we got to Vandegrift. Same zone (Argonne) had another thirteen emergencies medevac's. Oh no.

Well, I'm sure by this time you will read about LZ Argonne, and it will prove to be one of the very poorest mistakes of the war.

Worse still, we heard it was overrun. That's all there is to it. Off we went — this time with three helo's. Our aircraft was the lead 'cause we could more easily find Argonne.

After we spotted the zone again, an Army major in a Huey behind us took the lead now and his Huey gunship was like ones are over at Ft. Sam Houston. He radioed that he was going to take out any wounded that we couldn't lift out. Then we heard on the radio: "I'm sorry; there were seventeen emergency medevac's." Seventeen! They were really getting battered. The major went down and took ten out and we went down this time again and we got fired at as well — again.

It was just incredible. The only thing that we heard transpired between the morning extract and the afternoon was a tremendous air strike with F-4s loaded with bombs and napalm to try to burn out the gooks.

Well, I don't know who went in there, how many planes or jets. But when we came back there was a full-fledged forest fire all around the area and we could hardly see for the smoke. There was no more enemy, I thought. The fires are still burning up and down all these ridge lines and everything like that — the whole area was being burned out. And if there is anything in there, it's dead. That was all there was to it — just crispy critters. Wow.

We didn't want to fool around with this anymore — no more mortars! They must have hit the mortar position. Maybe they did. Maybe they didn't, but at any rate – we had no more incoming mortars at after this second extract at Argonne. But we did take small arms fire. And they just threw it at us again. Gunfire and forest fires: our whole world was lit up with fire. You could just see fire coming from all over the place.

I hadn't seen anything like this. I could see muzzle flashes. I could see them from everywhere. I said to myself, "Wow, this place is going to be a mess." This time we took out somewhere around seven to ten more casualties and flew them back to Vandegrift where we could also check our helo for damage.

And again, they didn't even hit the helicopter once, not even once when one of the things that bothered me about the entire flight is that we were called in to extract emergency medevac's under fire. And none of these guys turned out to be emergencies. They could all have waited a couple of days until the free fire out there was suppressed and the zone was a little bit more secure. But someone called them emergencies. So, off we had to go and it really sort of bugged me that we were risking our lives and that of the three crew plus the aircraft for non-emergencies. Our flight of three made it in and out without getting shot down.

I can understand that these grunts were not able to fight and they knew that Argonne was not going to be holding its own for too much longer. So, because of these tremendous casualties we had to take them out there.

Every time they would hold position like Argonne, many more helicopters had come in to evacuate casualties. And every time a helicopter would come in, the NVA would try to get it. They knew each '46 would make so much noise that the people on the hill would never be able to hear from where a mortar had been launched and they wouldn't be able to track it down and kill it.

So gooks would wait 'til the helo came in and they'd shoot their mortars – suppressing return fire on them and exposing helo's and crews to destruction. In this second extract we must've gotten the bad guys with the airstrikes. It saved us, I'm sure.

Later that day we heard that Argonne lost its commanding officer, who was a lieutenant colonel. That'll probably make your news. He was killed by a mortar that hit two feet from him. It blew him apart. An Army Huey was shot down in the Upper Zone. This Army Huey was really hit too, and I mean that Army Huey was really hurting. And it got both pilots right through their windshield. Better them than us.

Unfortunately, the HAC was killed and the co-pilot wounded. Small arms fire got both. The pilot was shot because I am told he flew an approach across the enemy lines — the exact opposite way he was warned against. They told him to come in one direction and he did the opposite. A deadly error. By contrast, we never let them even take a look at us and the result was we didn't even take one hit, except for two minor shrapnel impacts. Maybe they weren't even mortar shrapnel.

Wasn't too long before the phone rang at Vandy. Dong Ha DASC: Non-emergency medevacs at Heritage 14 on the Laotian border. We didn't know quite what to think of this. It was about three miles south of (the abandoned Marine outpost in 1968) Khe Sanh. We had no trouble finding it. We had good OV-10 cover and four Huey guns. We were the leader this time. We went down first and we took no fire at all.

The zone was horrible. It had trees sticking up in it. And we could only rest our two rear wheels on the ground, leaving the nose wheel up in the air. We hovered over the ground so that we wouldn't bring the front blades into the trees. No doubt, the blades would have taken the trees down anyway.

When I heard the blades hitting the smaller trees, I was not too worried. But anyway, there were trees and bushes all around. But all told, we took out four emergency medevacs. These guys were really hurt. And these were not shrapnel wounds. Boy, these were bullet wounds. I can't understand why we didn't take fire, but we didn't. I think from what we understand, they were on patrol and they finally grouped in one place to make this LZ ... made from a finger bomb to clear trees for a possible helicopter landing site.

Well, because we had a hard time getting all the other men back into this one group of nine medevacs, they only gave us four of the nine. We were quite ticked off that they didn't give us the other five and that another helo would have to expose itself to possible fire. So our wingman went down, picked up the other five, uneventfully.

Well, we had some hurting guys on board. We had a guy who was shot through the jaw. He was bleeding really badly. He had a bunch of bandages strapped around his head and they were all blood-soaked and dripping on his trousers. When I looked back, there was another guy who had his arm blown half off, and I understand, he had bled so badly he was in shock and from what I understand died en route. Near the ramp there were a couple of guys with small arms bullet wounds and were definitely emergencies, but not as hurting as these other guys.

Well, that was the day today!

I tell you, I'm more convinced that what we're doing is so wrong and just so horribly wasteful. And it's just got to end soon because the culminating thing of all today was that those two companies that were put in Argonne yesterday, only yesterday, the decision was made to pull them out...an emergency extract... pull them out — everybody. What was left of them, from what I understand, I heard they were overrun, what was left of them. And all their equipment was left behind. The heck with the equipment.

This was just before dark, because we left there at five o'clock and everything was all right. I'm sure about six or six thirty a whole squadron of '46s assembled to pull what was left of the 4th Marines out. That meant they left all of their howitzers and everything else there. But those men were going to be overrun tonight, I'm sure of it. They couldn't hold off the NVA in the daytime. How were they going to hold them off at night?

I kept hearing the gooks would come down right around their perimeter and they'd start talking really loudly just to tick the Marines off. They knew that the Americans wouldn't come outside their lines because they'd be butchered. So, they'd talk real loud to taunt our guys.

Boy, I'm not going to be flying this mission for a long time again. We're going to let everybody else share this job before I get it again. I was really scared today, really was. Never really for myself as much as for the others. The aircraft was a charmer and was not hit. That's the hardest thing of all to believe. The two .50 cal gunners kept a lot of heads down. Well, I'm going to go to sleep now. That's all I'm going to say.

Tomorrow. I'm flying with the (squadron's commanding officer) colonel. I don't know where we're going. We're not going to be doing anything dangerous, though. Probably flying resupply. So that's all.

(Berg: the colonel and I were shot down the next day by an RPG while on our way to Vandy...flying at 100 feet at 150 mph. We made it to Vandy and didn't fly the rest of the day).

Well, today's the 23rd of March. We've all been listening to Radio Peking, which is almost a nightly affair sometimes. Mark Steves, a fellow pilot/good friend of mine picked up a real fine radio at the PX for $27. Mine cost twenty-five and only has an AM FM bands, you know, a small, little portable. He picked up AM/FM and shortwave model for $27 and it can work off electricity or batteries. And it's really a fine radio made by Panasonic. Mark got the better deal. I'm jealous.

I guess the last time I talked to you was the night after Argonne. Well, as it turned out, they did not evacuate Argonne that night. They sent in an emergency resupply. The next morning, they sent in a company of men and put them on the bottom of the hill and had them work up to the top of the hill, killing everything on their way until they got to the top.

But Argonne is still under siege, and it's a real big mess out there. People are getting killed all the time. And they just lost a helicopter today. I don't know whether or not the pilots were killed. I understand that one was shot in the head. And that was from HMM 161 out of Quang Tri and I think Joe Black, one of my roommates from Pensacola, was the co-pilot.

I understand the pilot was hurt, though, not the co-pilot. Uh, things are really hanging out there. It's really rugged country in that valley up there — in the corner of Laos and the DMZ. The trouble is that they've got all the weapons and all their ammo and their supply lines from North Vietnam and Laos. All their supplies are very close to Argonne. All they do is just keep pumping more stuff in there. That's why the NVA won't tolerate us there.

Argonne has been number-one priority for air strikes and everything else for the past couple of days now. They're going to hold it for some reason or other. After we flew the mission to Argonne, the next day two lieutenant colonels and two majors flew medevacs there. They lost an engine in the zone due to dust. It was the same zone we flew into. They managed to restart the engine. The clogged filters saved the engines from the ashes from airstrikes and underbrush.

The same thing happened to a helo on our mission today... in fact, to our flight leader. He was lifting out of the fuel pits of Vandegrift when he lost power in his number one engine for this very same reason...too much dust and dirt.

He immediately pulled the barrier filters and the engine just went back to full power. But they had too much weight, so they dumped fuel, offloaded medevacs and restarted the engine. They finally got out.

Well, a lieutenant colonel, who was the operations officer for the group, decided that was it for the (HMM-265) Alpha model CH-46s in these high zones and hot weather.

So, that was the last medevac mission HMM-265 will ever fly. Yeah, I flew the next to the last one. So that's it. I will fly air taxi service, you might say. The high-altitude medevac action is finished for our squadron. Now all we're doing is being a taxi service and carrying meatloaf from one zone to another. Not too exciting, but you know, I'm feeling safer. We'll continue resupplying units at lower altitudes and replacement troops too. I don't really care. I've seen it all now. After Argonne — I saw it all there.

The HAC who commanded the helo...whose fantastic approach got us safely in and out of Argonne, is now up for the Silver Star. He only has a couple more weeks in-country before he goes home. I guess the pilot of the other plane (helo) is going to go up for a DFC. And I guess that's what they're going to put me up for and they're going to put the copilot of the other plane up for too.

You know, I monitored things for him and it took two of us on the collective as we descended out of control. Once when I thought he was making a mistake with his over-stressing the aircraft, I helped him keep us in one piece. But he did all the flying into the zone the first time.

We should be going aboard ship now – LPH-2 USS *Iwo Jima*, at the end of June. And when that happens, we'll be in Fat City and out of a lot of dangerous stuff.

That will be good duty and will be away from mortars, which incidentally hit us recently. Yesterday morning Phu Bai took fifteen rockets out near the landing strip — coming over the Army side of the field toward us.

Incredibly, I was up and getting dressed and I could feel the ground shake and hear the noise of them going off. Yet there was no siren. And I just stood by, knowing that we were under attack and I said to myself: "That's no big deal." No siren.

Because Phu Bai had little in the way of incoming in the three months I had been there, I was a virgin to enemy rocket fire. In any case, the rocket attack was over after lasting about two minutes.

The gooks unloaded what they had left from their mortar attacks around Da Nang and used them on us. We've taken some mortars now, in and around different parts of the base. They are definitely stepping up the war. There's no doubt about it. They're sticking around and fighting.

When we have a battalion exposed out there, I'm sure right now at Argonne in that valley, the NVA is sticking around for some sort of an offensive in northern I Corps. We've heard no specific news about what's going on down south. Nothing like the overall picture you get on the (NBC's) *Huntley-Brinkley Report*. You'll get the Army news, you know, and what operations were launched. But you don't know exactly what you do. You know pieces of the story, but it's hard to get a full picture of it all.

I got my watch back from Da Nang a couple of days ago, and it's working better than I ever needed it to. A little cleaning out and now it's keeping perfect time. I took the GI watch and put it in my file cabinet, hopefully never to use it again. I always had to wind it and it was jammed with dust.

As I said, now I'll be going to a jungle survival school either on the 13th or on the 20th. I found that out when I saw Del today. He was up in Quang Tri, but will be returning to Phu Bai. He's also going to school on the 20th of April. So he and I and another guy who I came over here with named Chuck Perriguey.

(Berg: Perriguey after Vietnam flew police helicopters for the LAPD. It was his helo whose camera followed OJ Simpson's white Bronco on an LA Freeway, which the nation viewed in disbelief in June 1994).

We intend to stay there at least two weeks. So, we're going to stay out of country for just as much as we possibly can and have a good time.

That's it.

CHAPTER 7

WHEN THE SMOKE CLEARED

Jesse Villanueva
L/CPL, 0351, Infantry Assault Man
H&S Company, 1st Bn, 4th Marines

MARCH 17, 1969, I RETURNED TO OUR UNIT AT FIRE SUPPORT
base Russell from our base at Quang Tri, with the mail, STPs, a
package of personal effects, and beer, reporting to our section
leader, Marcelino Anguiano, who informed me that we would be
pulling out the next day to LZ (Landing Zone) Argonne at 0900
hours and to inform the squad leaders.

"Oregon, that's great, I can walk home to Washington," I
exclaimed.

He said, "Not Oregon, Jesse, Argonne!"

I told the squad leaders about the next day's events and gave
them a few cases of beer because we couldn't take it into battle
with us. Besides we were loaded for bear (bare essentials).

As I made my rounds through the base, a fresh-faced Marine
asked for the 81's section. He looked like a kid to me, young and
inexperienced, but in actuality he was four months older than me.

"You're looking at it," I replied. He introduced himself as PFC
Sam Gatlin. I handed him a beer and said, "Welcome to Vietnam,
Sam! What part of the world are you from?" I asked.

"Grapeview, Washington," responded Sam.

"Where's that?" I replied.

"It's near Seattle," Sam answered.

"Then we're homies. I'm from Toppenish, Washington, near Yakima."

To my surprise, he knew where Yakima was but had no idea where Toppenish was. Very few people out there knew where Yakima was, so I was happy about that. To us in Vietnam, far away from the World (USA), anyone who lived anywhere in our state was a home boy. It felt like that person was from our neighborhood. I introduced Sam to his squad leader and told him to have fun and get a good night's sleep because we would be pulling out tomorrow at 0900 hours.

The next day at dawn, I woke up the squad leaders and told them to have everyone ready to roll and be at the LZ by 0830 hours, where we would wait for the next few hours. The Marine Corps has this thing about making us hurry up and then having us wait. However, this time we were actually okay with waiting; we were in no hurry to get there. The choppers arrived early afternoon. We loaded up on the chopper and off we went. As we were approaching LZ Argonne, our section leader, Cpl. Marcelino Anguiano looked at me, and without uttering a word, I knew we were going to have our work cut out for us. Marcelino was the only corporal section leader in the battalion. The rest of our section leaders were sergeants and above.

The LZ was still hot with heavy incoming fire: there were enemy small arms, rocket propelled guns, and 82mm mortar fire. Cpl. Anguiano knew I didn't like getting off the chopper last, after what had happened at LZ Loon. I had fallen off the chopper at about forty feet, so he ordered me off first to lead the 4th Section to where we were to set up our guns, telling them to be careful not to step on the bodies and to watch out for the live ones. I still remember smelling death and burning flesh in the air caused by white phosphorous and napalm. Although we had a few small arms fired at us, it was light.

The upper part of the LZ had better cover because the enemy mortar 82s are unable to reach that far; however, my section was assigned to protect the lower part. To increase our anxiety, an empty downed Huey Chopper had been shot down, and had been stripped of all weapons and ammo. The Huey sat at the top part of the landing zone.

Anguiano and I spoke about the guns sites. We were not happy about setting up on previously dug gun pits and requested to dig new ones. However, the XO Executive Officer overruled, and we were to set up our 81s at the same location where the previous guns had been. We feared that if we set up in the same location, the enemy would have the site zeroed in. We dug in rapidly, setting up our mortars and clearing our bunker of booby traps. Some fox holes had grenades strung to them with trip wires. We disarmed them. Meanwhile, jets were flying overhead, clearing out areas of brush and the enemy with napalm, as we settled in the landing zone.

The sergeant major approached me and asked me why I hadn't written to my mom. He told me that the Red Cross had contacted him. He scolded, "Don't you know your mom worries? You better write to her so she at least knows you're alive. I don't want to hear from the Red Cross again. If I do, you will be in deep shit with me!" Previously, after I had fallen off the chopper, which had fractured a vertebra in my back, I had been writing to my mom often because I was on light duty. Since I didn't want her to worry, I hadn't told her that I was injured or on light duty. Now I was in the field, I didn't have many opportunities to write. But that night, I wrote a letter to my mom on a C-rat top, and it was ready for me to send out in the morning. Later that night, we slept in our bunkers while Delta and Charlie Company were on perimeter watch.

The next day at daybreak, while the squad leaders, gunners, and A/gunners were fine-tuning the 81 mortars, and aiming stakes, I took all of our boots (rookies) to retrieve 81mm shells, which were still at the lower point of the LZ near our gun pits. We had made quite a few trips retrieving 80-pound boxes, which contained three 81 shells. We would pick them up at the LZ, carry them on our shoulders to a bomb crater, which was about twenty to thirty feet from our gun pits and fire direction center (FDC) while our section leader and our two 81 gun crews were still cleaning and setting up the mortars. All of a sudden, I heard *blup, blup,*

blup, blup, the sound of mortar fire. It was the first volley of 82mm mortars, coming directly over our heads. I don't remember who hollered, "Incoming," but our entire work detail hit the ground. All hell broke loose when those 82 mortars shells hit the ground landing between the FDC and our gun pits. As we had predicted, they knew our location, which was why Marcelino and I had requested to move the gun pits and FDC. The mortar shells were landing in five-foot intervals as if they were walking them one after another toward the FDC, instantaneously, in only a matter of five seconds from the blupping sound to the mortar shells landing. Our troops had very little time to react. Lt. Col. Sargent (Sargent is his last name), our battalion commander and a lieutenant were standing in front of the FDC. After I hit the ground, I lifted my head and watched, horrified, as each mortar shell exploded on the ground. The first shell landed in front of the lieutenant colonel and lieutenant; Sargent and the lieutenant's body were full of shrapnel. They were both killed instantly.

Approximately ten others were also wounded from our section, including my good friend and section leader, Cpl. Anguiano, who had been hit by the first volley, and had serious injuries. Shrapnel had riddled through his hand, and all over his back. As he tried to get to cover and ran toward the bunkers, he was shot several times on the back of his legs and fell to the ground. PFC Mark Abplanalp and I went to his aid. We each grabbed an arm and dragged him to the bunker. Once we were inside, Marcelino groaned, came to, and looked at me.

"You're now in charge," he gasped.

"You can't do this to me."

"Jesse, you are ready."

As I left him inside the bunker, my first thought was to return fire. Running to our gun pits, I adjusted the mortar to fire back. Gary Protanic joined me in the pit, and we began to fire back. We must have launched over forty mortar shells over the span of twenty to thirty minutes. We were firing at locations that had any movement, smoke, or fire flash, buying time for our work detail to bring the wounded to cover. This silenced enemy fire for a short time. I rounded up the remaining six Marines from our unit and assigned three of them to each gun pit, directing them to fire in the general direction of the enemy. As they were firing, I headed back to the FDC to help load our wounded on the choppers. Mark and I assisted Marcelino to the chopper, which was about 100 yards away, and loaded him in. I then returned and loaded another Marine. On my third trip to the FDC, I picked up my good friend, Tom Parker, who was covering his face with his hand. He pressed his hand tightly against the upper portion of his face as blood poured out from both sides of his pressing hand. I tried to evaluate the extent of his facial injury but Tom, a Goliath of a man who had played football in college, was in too much pain and much too strong for me to remove his hand, As I took him to the chopper, I remembered the letter I had written to Mom and put it in his front flak jacket pocket.

"Make sure the letter gets sent to my mom," I urged.

He whispered, "Yeah, I'll make sure it gets sent."

We continued and I hoisted him up into the chopper with both hands, but before I could let go of him, he violently jerked backwards and blood splattered in front of me. Those SOBs just shot him in the chest. There was gunfire all around, but that was the first shot I heard that was in close proximity. After that shot, bullets flew all around me and ricocheted off the ground three feet away from where I was standing. Since Tom was inside of the chopper, I took off for cover and ran uphill toward our gun pits. The sound of gunfire and the volume of bullets increased. It was probably the fastest 100 yards I had ever run in my life, but it felt as if I was in slow motion. I could see the gun pits and dove over our sandbags. As I dove over the sandbags, an 82 shell exploded right behind me. The grunts continued to fire mortar rounds and M-16s for about five minutes, until the enemy stopped firing. When the enemy attacked, they did not attack for a long period of time because we could zero in on their location. They seldom attacked at night because our troops could easily locate their gun fire. It was getting late and the enemy had stopped firing, so I told my men to get some rest but to be alert. I also confiscated all the marijuana from my section and told them I would give it back once we got off Argonne. When I went to my bunker and sat down, my leg felt wet. I was wondering if someone had spilled a canteen of water, so I lit up some beeswax, which we often used for candles, and looked at my leg. To my surprise, it was covered in blood and began to burn. I had been hit by the shell that had exploded behind me.

Rather than resting, which I had anticipated doing, I had to get up to go see the corpsman. The corpsman was unable to extract the piece of shrapnel that was embedded in my leg and said to just walk it off and that it should eventually fall out. Later that night, I realized I was responsible for the lives of the unit's remaining members and the grunts we were to support. That was a terrifying thought, but thanks to Cpl. Anguiano's leadership and training, I had the confidence to take over the role of section leader.

When the smoke had cleared, there were seven of us left in our section, down from seventeen. Most of them were new to combat conditions. We had three men per gun, a gunner, A-gunner and one ammo man. For the next few weeks these guys, my fellow Marines, fired those mortars with the upmost professionalism. The following day we relocated the gun pits, the FDC, and our bunkers. This time I did not request permission.

Normally when we moved on from a battle site, we left enemy bodies where they lay, but since we were going to be there for a while, we had to gather bodies on the first day we were there. We had cleared the area, and someone had dumped two or three North Vietnamese Army bodies into to trash dump. We had set the trash dump on fire to get rid of all the trash. Boy, did we live to regret that! Think of being on a hill with the stench of burning flesh and decomposing bodies for three weeks.

We needed to order more 81 mortar ammo because we were almost out of shells, but receiving our ammo was difficult because the enemy would fire at the LZ every time the choppers would attempt to land. Finally, the choppers loaded a pallet with mortar shells on a net and slung the pallet toward us. However, the chopper missed its target and the ammo landed in the trash dump, which was still on fire. We hurried before the ammo was damaged and formed an assembly line with grunts and mortar men to haul the ammo to the gun pits and ammo bunker. At this point, I had no idea how long we were going to be there, but this became routine for us. As soon as we knew the choppers were coming to deliver supplies, we would start to fire at the enemy while the chopper would quickly sling us our supplies. We never knew when we would receive supplies, so we began to ration our food and water.

On March 19th (day 2), we were down to seven Marines, so I walked to the other side of the hill to talk to our platoon sergeant, who was on the upper area with a fully staffed section. I didn't really blame him for being on that side. Hell, I wanted to be on that side too! But my responsibility was to protect the lower LZ and keep my men alive. I requested men from the other section. He said he couldn't do that.

He continued, "Jesse, you're doing a great job; you'll get a medal for this."

I was pissed! I said, "I don't want a medal, I want men!" and I walked back to join my six men.

For the next couple of weeks, it became a routine that the enemy would fire upon us and we would fire back until they stopped.

On March 28 (Day 10), I went and talked to the platoon sergeant and told him I knew the general location of our enemy and suggested a plan of attack. Since they were in a 200 by 200 yard area, we coordinated a united attack with the other section using a strategy that Marcelino and I had practiced with our section. Command enhanced (and enhanced is an understatement) fire power by adding artillery, choppers, and jets. The attack would commence toward the end of the day at sundown.

The plan of attack started with my squad, the 4th Section, attacking the upper two corners and walking our mortar fire toward the middle. The 2nd Section started from the bottom two corners and walked their mortar fire toward the center. The artillery and air attack filled in the gaps made by our mortars.

On April 2 (Day 17), preparing for the attack, I had ordered our squads to have the 81s out of the canisters, ready to fire, and have the increments adjusted (increments determine how far the mortar shells travel). I gave my men the deflection and elevation for our mortars. We were set and ready.

I gave the order to fire a Willie Peter (round made of white phosphorus) to a mark a location. Between the two sections, we had marked the four corners of the zone to fire on. I then gave the order to fire for effect (blast the shit out of them). We were in full-attack mode and in complete control of this battle. I had never seen such an awesome sight in my life.

Jets flew and swooped in from above, blasting streams of bullets, and dropping napalm one after another. I'm not sure if the jet pilots were showing off or if they were using techniques that they were taught to use, but the way they flew was spectacular!

On the ground, we felt vibrations of explosions, jets, and helicopters. The sky was lit with fire and smoke as if it was a chaotic 4th of July on steroids. Helicopter gunships were doing their part of the show as well, shooting rockets and lighting it up with machine gun fire. Our artillery covered the ground with their 155s (big rounds) to put icing on the cake. The part of the hill where the enemy had been was transformed into a mound of devastation and death. I was proud of my entire unit, specifically Sam, because he had just joined our unit the evening before, and had not practiced with us. What a first day on the job. We no longer had any boots on that hill. They all became seasoned vets.

On April 3rd (Day 18), we received the report that we had taken on an entire NVA regiment, annihilated eight 82 mortar gun pits, and the entire regiment had been killed or retreated. The area had been completely cleared. Artillery, Delta, Charlie Company and our 81 mortar sections' professionalism was why we were successful in defeating the NVA at Argonne.

On April 4th (Day 19), the battalion's objective was complete, and we received orders to move out from Argonne. The seven of us humped back together to Fire support base Russell, along with the rest of the battalion. On our hump I thought about my friends who had been injured, specifically Marcelino and Tom. I also felt proud, relieved and grateful as a section leader that not one of my men were injured or killed.

A few weeks later at LZ Russell, I received a worrisome letter from my mom. The letter I had written said, "Mom, I'm okay. Please don't write the Red Cross anymore because the sergeant major will get after me. Don't worry I'm doing fine. I'll see you in June when I come home." Her letter stated, "Your letter had blood all over it, I'm praying it's not yours." My first initial thought was, "Damn it, Parker!" Then I remembered that I had placed the letter in his flak jacket, and when I had loaded him in the chopper, he had gotten shot right above his pocket. It wasn't entirely Parker's fault and I knew I could count on him to deliver. I only hoped he was still alive somewhere.

Additional Information:

Sam Gatlin: Sam contacted me in 1981. It was the first time I had seen him since 1969 in Vietnam. I consider him one of my best friends, and we have remained in contact to this day.

Tom Parker: The last time I saw him in Vietnam was when I helped him to the chopper. I was finally able to contact him in 1989 over the phone, and after twenty years he recognized my voice. He came to visit me and my family. One of the first things Tom said, was "Jesse, I lost my eye in that battle and now have this glass eye." We talked about our time in Vietnam, the day in Argonne and our injuries. He thanked me for helping him. He made it very clear that he delivered my letter for me. I said, "Yeah, I know you did because my mom freaked out when it had blood all over it. I do appreciate that favor you did for me because I knew what you were going through." We went to visit each other a few times, but I lost contact with him. I'm still trying to find Tom and consider him a very dear and close friend.

Marcelino Anguiano: The last time I saw him was in Argonne. Sam Gatlin found him through social media and contacted him in 2011. In 2012, I invited him to be the main speaker at the Korean/Vietnam Memorial for Memorial Day. He accepted, and I finally saw him after forty-three years, since the battle for Argonne. We picked up where we left off and visit each other every year. In 2018, it was an honor to be his best man at his fiftieth wedding anniversary. We remain best friends to this day.

CHAPTER 8

"RTO"

Steve McCall
L/CPL, 0311, Infantry, carried Field Radio
3rd Platoon Delta Company, 1st Bn, 4th Marines

ON MARCH 20, 1969, I REMEMBER BEING ON ALPINE AND waiting for the word. Being Lt. McCormick's radio operator, I usually was kept informed about the goings on in the platoon. The lieutenant came to me and said we were being lifted into a hot LZ. Later I learned it was Argonne.

The lieutenant and I had become pretty good friends since his arrival to the platoon a couple of months previously.

We loaded onto the first CH-46 helicopter, being the last two on board. Sitting directly across from me was Lt. Col. Sargent and two or three of his officers. We flew toward Argonne, which was northwest of Alpine, and started circling the hill. I looked out one of the windows and saw a UH-1H Huey helicopter on the upper LZ with its blades slowly rotating. Eventually we headed in to land on the lower LZ. Bullets started ripping through the helicopter and at least two Marines were hit. They both dropped to the deck. The ramp was going down and one of the Marines slid off the ramp and landed on the LZ. The other Marine just lay where he fell on the deck.

We exited the helicopter and the lieutenant proceeded up the hill and I followed him. I have to say right now that Lt. McCormick was one brave Marine Corps officer. Continuing our way up the hill we were taking constant fire and the NVA were slowly moving back to the top of the hill. We were doing our best to move, return fire and not get hit. It was so hot and with our seventy pounds of gear on our backs it was very tough going. We probably got about halfway up the hill and I had to stop and drop behind a bunker. I was so exhausted; I thought I was having a heart attack. The lieutenant stopped about ten to fifteen feet ahead of me behind another bunker.

He said, "Let's take a few seconds here to catch our breath," because he was just as beat. All the time the NVA were firing down on all of us. I looked down the hill at one of the bunkers without a roof we had passed, which we thought was empty, and an NVA jump up and out of the bunker and took off for another bunker with a roof a few yards away. I shot him three or four times and killed him. I remember then switching my M16 from semi-automatic to full auto and then two more NVA popped out of the same no-roof bunker and opened up on me. Their rounds hit an engineering stake next to me and a splinter of metal hit me in the leg. I opened up on them full auto and shot them both. This all took no more than twenty seconds. The lieutenant saw what had happened and came back to me and had the two of us drop grenades in the bunker. The lieutenant signaled to a Marine coming up the hill to enter the bunker and check it out. He found two more dead NVA soldiers.

I'm not sure what happened next, but we continued up the hill, still under fire, and doing our best to return fire and stay in one piece. This went on for a while as more Marines were landed and the NVA were pulling back to the top of the hill. We were able to get pretty good shots at them and I killed two more and then we kept shooting, and I'm not sure how many hits we got.

We reached the top of the hill and I was totally exhausted. We were on the top right of the hill and two Marines, I'm not sure who, were moving up and to the left and the NVA shot them in the head. I know Sgt. Jimmy Cluck tried to help one of them, but they were both gone. We were trying to locate where those shots came from. Someone, not sure who, located the bunker the rounds were coming from. At the same time, I looked down the hill and saw my good friend, J.P. Young coming up the hill.

I yelled "J.P., what are you doing?"

And he replied, "I'm looking for ammo."

I replied, "Well get down, we are under fire."

J.P. must have found ammo because he bent down, picked something up, and headed back down the hill. A few minutes later a shot rang out from that bunker and went through Jeff Forrey's neck and into Tom Bartlett's shoulder. They were manning the M-60 machine gun. Instead of attacking that bunker, the lieutenant called up the 106 Recoilless Rifle Team to take out the bunker. I'm not sure, but I think one or two of the 106 crew were hit before the rifle was fired and took out the bunker.

Sometime later the lieutenant came to me and said, "We are taking a patrol out to get the snipers shooting at the incoming helicopters." It was the lieutenant, me, Max Baer, the guns squad leader, my good friend Billy Black, and his gun team of Steve Ecklund, Robby Saldana, Tommy Breeds and his rocket team. The rifle squad that was with Billy (Black) and Tommy (Breeds), their CH-46 helicopter was shot down earlier in the day. As we started down the hill, we got about fifty yards outside of the wire and the NVA opened up on us and shot Max and he screamed. It was the most bloodcurdling scream. The lieutenant veered off to the left a little toward the sounds of the firing. He had me call in a mortar fire mission. A spotter round was fired, and we tried to correct from that round. The lieutenant got up and proceeded a little farther down the hill and the NVA opened up on him and killed him. At that point I felt like a lost sheep, the lieutenant was gone, and I was just sick. I was behind a small tree when a mortar hit behind me and slammed me into the tree. I got hit with shrapnel in my butt twice and my arm. The one in my arm punctured my artery. I called for Doc Young, but he was wounded along with several others.

Billy Black came over with Doc's kit and bandaged my arm. More mortars were coming in and Billy helped me up and I took off for the aid station at the top of the hill. At this point I was having a very hard time walking and was dizzy and numb. J.P. met me at the wire and got me to the aid station. The doctor there said along with my wounds, I probably had a concussion. Just as nightfall was approaching, I was medevac'd to Quang Tri. I think on the third medevac helicopter out. I found out later that I believe it was J.P. Young and Billy Black who examined my radio and found two or three large chunks of shrapnel in my radio. They were about five to six inches long.

At Quang Tri they took x-rays and said, "You're going to the hospital ship *Sanctuary*." I think they sewed my arm up at Quang Tri, but with all the drugs, I just don't remember. I was out for a long time and in the morning they sent me to surgery for my hip. Seems the shrapnel in my butt did damage to my hip. Several days after the surgery they did a skin graft on my butt. I stayed on the hospital ship for two months. I spent another couple of months in the rear at Quang Tri.

They finally gave me some options for the rest of my time, about one-and-a-half months, and I chose to go back to 3rd Platoon. I was glad to see those of my friends who were still alive.

CHAPTER 9

I STOOD WITH MARINES

John Arsenault
L/CPL, 0311, Squad Leader, M-79 Grenade man
3rd Platoon, Delta Company, 1st Bn, 4th Marines

IT WAS STILL DARK IN THE MORNING, BUT MOVEMENT BEGAN
in our position near FSB Alpine. Our platoon commander, 2nd Lt.
McCormick called for the squad leaders to huddle up for a mission
brief, so L/Cpl. Ralph DeSavilla, the squad leader for 1st Squad,
3rd platoon, Delta Company went to meet with the platoon HQ for
our instructions. L/Cpl. DeSavilla came back and passed the word
that we were going to helo-lift to an LZ/FSB near the border with
Laos. A Marine recon team had landed during the night and was
in great peril, several dead and almost all wounded. We moved out
of the jungle and into the elephant grass, which wasn't too high,
only about three feet tall. Here we formed into helo-sticks for the
lift out. Lt. McCormick had me help with the platoon getting ready
for the CH-46s. I counted the Marines on each helo-stick and
helped fill in who would go where on the lift-out. My count was
thirty-five Marines in 3rd Platoon and several additional Marines
from Machine Guns, Rockets and Comm. About forty-five, plus or
minus, total for our section. We were instructed that 3rd Platoon
was going to be the "lead" element for the vertical envelopment
into FSB Argonne. I was running around the makeshift LZ trying

95

to help organize the Marines getting ready to fly into Hell. I'm not sure if any of my efforts helped, but I was busy, and then a Navy Corpsman runs up to me and asks if I knew where L/Cpl. J.P. Young was, because he had a pair of prescription glasses for him. I told him I knew J.P. and took the glasses from the Doc and promised to get them to J.P.

I need to spend a moment here and talk about James Patrick Young III (J.P.), a son of a WWII Marine officer who landed at Iwo Jima and led a machine gun platoon throughout the bloody battle. J.P. volunteered for the Marines and had to sign a waiver to serve because he was legally blind without his glasses. As an example, he could not see the **big** "E" on the eye chart without glasses. And of course, he was assigned an infantry billet! We became close buddies early on, when shooting the bull one night we discovered that our fathers had both served together in the Marines, at Headquarters Marine Corps, at the end of each of their careers. My dad was also a Marine WWII and Korea veteran. I could spend several pages describing my experiences with J.P., who would lose or break his glasses and then hang onto my ruck-sack sometimes to get through the triple canopy jungle, and yes, I actually started fires using a lens from his glasses. I consider J.P. to be the bravest Marine I have ever known. Going to war is tough enough, but going into war without the ability to see is way past brave. Just picture Stevie Wonder with a M-60 machine gun. Jim was just crazy brave. Okay, maybe just crazy, but there Jim was, serving his country. He never refused to go on a mission, because of the fact that, well, he was legally blind.

So, back to getting ready to lift into Argonne, I put J.P.'s glasses in my shirt and fell in on my team. We loaded up and took off for what we could only imagine as being pure hell and it turned out to be just that, pure hell. In the air, everyone was stone quiet as we rode to the LZ/FSB. I was sitting at the very rear of the CH-46 on the starboard side and looking straight across to L/Cpl. Ralph DeSavilla. We would be the first ones out of the bird when we landed. The crew chief came back to us and shouted that there was heavy fire coming from the ground at the LZ/FSB and one chopper had been hit. I really don't know for sure which number our helo was in the lineup for the landing, my guess is we were the second helo to land. There might have been one ahead of us that was shot down. Anyway, as we came in on final to land, I could hear bullets going through the CH-46, pieces of aluminum were flying around the inside of the helo. At this point I expected to die in the air or as soon as I got on the ground. I began to pray as best I could and soon realized that this would not be adequate, because I knew in my heart that I was not smart enough or clever enough to know exactly what to do once we landed, so I just thanked the Lord for the twenty years of my life I had been given and asked to be accepted into His kingdom. This will sound crazy to most, but I never asked to be saved from death during the fight. In my heart, I knew there was no chance for that, I just asked to be forgiven and taken into the Lord's hands. As I looked up, I saw Ralph looking straight at me, and I remembered a time several months prior when we were on a company patrol and our squad, 1st Squad, 3rd Platoon was the lead element for the company and I was walking point in a stream bed. Here I found a food wrapper from a NVA outpost and very fresh footprints leading away from this position down the stream bed close to the stream bank. I fell in on his trail, figuring that it wouldn't be booby-rapped. After about seventy-five meters, I came to a place where I could see where the NVA soldier had climbed up the bank into the jungle. I stopped the column and looked for any other signs of enemy activity and determined that this just didn't look good at all. I suspected something was ahead. I asked to recon the area to find out if there was any NVA waiting for us around a bend in the creek where there was a rock wall on one side and thick jungle on the other. After a couple of minutes, on the radio, instructions came back to just "move out."

At this point, as the point man my fate was now set forever. If the NVA was there, as I figured they were, being the point man, I would be the first person to get cut down. Here I turned to Ralph and asked him to send a message to my parents. Then Ralph looked straight at me and said, "Little John, you will not die alone, I will walk with you, at your side and we will both go down together." And that was what he did, walked right next to me. In war there are many acts of courage that are not recorded, and I want this one to be recorded for all to know. In my small world, this was the greatest act of courage and sacrifice I had ever personally experienced, Ralph was willing to give his life so that I would not die alone. We both had that really bad feeling in our guts as to what was ahead. I stood up, Ralph moved up next to me on my right, and we moved out.

After we walked about twenty meters, the world exploded all around us. The NVA machine gunner opened up from my left on Ralph and me, with the first rounds hitting in front of us, then the next rounds hitting behind us. How could they miss, we were less than ten meters from their ambush position. This fight was ferocious with NVA machine guns, AK-47s, hand grenades, and a Chi-Comm claymore mine. We were in the "kill zone" along with 1st Squad and the machine gun team, which included J.P. Young. When the smoke cleared, L/Cpl. Ralph DeSavilla and I were the only Marines left in 1st Squad, 3rd Platoon, Delta Company.

So now I was sitting and looking at Ralph as we approach FSB Argonne and we had our new squad behind us. I decide to attempt to return the gesture to Ralph, because now he would be the first one out of the helo, so I stood up, looked at Ralph, our eyes met and we nodded and turned toward the rear of the aircraft. This was the last time I saw Ralph. We ran out the back of the helo together. I was on the starboard facing the rear and closest to the summit of the hill. As I exited the helo, I looked to my left and saw high ground and not a single Marine to be seen anywhere, so I just started running toward the high ground and felt my soft cover get shot off of my head (I chose to not wear a helmet*). About thirty to forty meters from the aircraft, I came upon Lt. McCormick and his radio operator in a small crater.

This was where the "fog of war" jumped in like a hippopotamus into a wading pool. I was looking for Marines and there were none to be seen, other than the lieutenant and radioman. I shouted as I ran, "Where are they?" Meaning: where are the Marines? The lieutenant warned me the NVA were up on the top of the hill, but I only heard "up on the hill." And I dashed up the hill as fast as I could lumber along with seventy pounds of gear on my back.

I instantly understood what Lt. McCormick was saying when I came within about five meters of a bunker and saw a NVA soldier shooting franticly at me with an AK-47. Bullets were going everywhere and I was trying figure out what I could do. The terrain was really steep where I was, there was no option to jump up with all of my gear and take out the bunker. I was just screwed as I danced around, dumping my ruck, then bullets shot my ruck in mid-air and then all my ammo was shot off me and I just hit the dirt.

This will sound crazy to most people, but in the middle of all this I felt the presence of the weight of a hand on my back, pushing me to the ground — hard and pinning me in place. Lying there, bullet impacts were striking all around my body, to the point that I just disappeared in a cloud of dust from bullet impacts. I just froze there, watching a small tree stump a couple of feet from me disintegrate from bullet impacts, face on the ground and rifle in my right hand lying next to me. I knew I only had one magazine in my rifle and no others, so I had a total of eighteen rounds of ammo to my name at this point.

I guess the NVA assumed I was dead, so they turned their attention to other Marines on the hill. So there I was, close enough to almost spit at the NVA bunker, playing dead and I looked up with my right eye and saw the perfect silhouette of a NVA solider against the light of the rising sun behind him and decided to do something really stupid. I raised the barrel of my rifle with my right hand and guessed where the alignment was and fired one round. It hit low, but close enough to quickly adjust and fire again, twice striking the NVA soldier, and I watched him fall back into the bunker. My rifle muzzle blast kicked up a lot of dust, so now the SOBs knew I was a shooter, and again bullets struck everywhere.

One bullet took off a piece of the heel of my boot. And again I felt the weight of a hand on my back, but there wasn't anyone there. Then the NVA figured they got me good this time and they let up again. This procedure repeated four more times as I fired three rounds each time, and watched another NVA soldier fall back each time. And after each time I fired, the NVA threw hell at me. I took out the bunker with five NVA soldiers, shooting only fifteen rounds, leaving me three rounds in my magazine. During this period, close air support screamed in with F-4 Phantoms delivering ordinance on the top and back of Argonne. On one of these F-4 runs delivering napalm, I looked back and saw the F-4 release the napalm tanks, way, way, way far away and watched them tumble in the air toward our position. It looked like they were going to land right on me, but went right over my head and hit near the back edge of the summit. The blast was unbelievably huge, shock wave, heat and wind blowing.

About this time, I saw Sgt. Cluck running from the left flank to the bunker in front of me and he cleared the area. I got up and went back down the slope to join Lt. McCormick and other Marines who had landed. This was when I discovered part of the napalm strike had blown back over me and landed on a couple of Marines behind me. I didn't see serious injuries from the napalm, but my observation was very limited and many could have been seriously wounded without my knowledge. I turned and went back up the hill and joined with Marines I could find. I didn't know where my squad was at this point, so I just moved forward to help push the line over the top of the summit of 1308. The flat summit was secured, but on the east side there was another bunker that had shot several Marines. Their bodies were lying just over the edge, going down the other side. The NVA soldiers were shooting Marines right in the center of their helmets, with the rounds going straight through. At this point I ran into J.P. and gave him his glasses, which he immediately pulled out of the box and then shouted, "Sun glasses, fucking sunglasses, what am I going to do tonight?"

We both moved out to different locations on the hill, I moved right next to the machine gun team with L/Cpl. Bartlett, the machine gun team leader acting as the A-Gunner, helping L/Cpl. Jeff Forry running the M-60, directing fire. There was so much noise I never heard the shot hit Jeff in the throat and then land in L/Cpl. Bartlett's shoulder. I was only one foot to the left of L/Cpl. Bartlett, and when I saw what happened, helped pull him back away from the sandbags they were behind. A corpsman arrived out of heaven and took L/Cpl. Bartlett away to the LZ for medevac.

The L/Cpl. Jeff Forry was KIA and taken also to the Lower LZ. I didn't know where the NVA bunker was, just that it was close. I picked up some ammo that was thrown up to where we were and passed it out to Marines in the area.

Somewhere along this time the NVA bunker was located and nothing seemed to work to knock it out. And out of nowhere, a 106mm recoilless rifle showed up with a team of Marines to operate it. The 106 was set up on a tripod and the gunner opened the breach and just looked down the barrel to aim the rifle, and when he was satisfied a round was loaded and fired. Direct hit on the top of the bunker, but the round didn't go far enough to arm itself, so it was just a big piece of steel hitting the bunker. It did some damage, but the NVA were still fighting. I moved over to the right flank of the summit and then found Marines from my squad who were there. I don't know if they were there and I joined them or I was there and they joined me, but what was left of 1st Squad was now together. I was informed that L/Cpl. Ralph DeSaville was hit real bad right after getting off the helo, and no one was sure if he would make it. Also our newest Marine, PFC Daniel was KIA and B.J. was shot in the head, but alive. This now made me the 1st Squad leader.

We were in a pretty good position, with some cover to stay behind. Then a Marine I knew only as Frenchie ran out in front of my squad in an attempt to flank the bunker from the right, and immediately drew fire from the NVA. I saw his leg swing up in the air and guessed he was shot hard. I looked at my Marines and thought about sending them out to help Frenchie, but just jumped up myself and ran to his aid. We were behind a downed tree and I looked at Frenchie's leg and saw that the knife he carried strapped to his leg had been shot off. His leg was injured pretty bad, so I told him to get back to the doc for help, and covered his movement with fire until Frenchie was clear of danger from this bunker. Now I was out front all by myself and decided to stay there and move down behind another downed tree, which would take me to a much better flanking position. So I moved to within ten meters of the NVA bunker and was trying to figure out what kind of miracle would save me this time. Then my miracle arrived with a thud. It was Sgt. James Cluck, sliding into my position.

Jimmy Cluck was a real "John Wayne." He ran into the ambush I described earlier in the middle of a complete shit-storm of explosions and gunfire and directed our return fire, helped the wounded and ran up to Ralph and me at the very front of the column to make sure we were okay. It took Jimmy about five seconds to come up with the plan to take out the bunker. He would take a hand grenade and just run up and drop it into the bunker. And that was what he did, except the NVA soldier threw it back out at him. Jimmy got far enough away to avoid getting hit. Then the next Marine came sliding into our location, It was Lt. Col. Sargent, the 1st Battalion, 4th Marine commanding officer. So here was the situation: three Marines out in front of everyone, conducting an ad-hoc flanking operation. Myself, Jimmy Cluck and the battalion commander, Lt. Col. Sargent. Jimmy grabbed another grenade and made his run again at the bunker. At this point my M-16 crapped out on me, single shot fire with me having to slam the forward assist after every round, and now the battalion commander, Lt. Col. Sargent was firing his 1911 Colt, laying down the real covering fire for Jimmy. The NVA threw the grenade back again. On the third attempt to clear the bunker with a grenade, Jimmy let the "spoon" fly halfway to the bunker and he slowly lobbed the grenade in and it exploded almost as soon as it landed, bunker cleared.

After this, things got kind of murky. For the life of me, I can't really say what happened after we cleared the bunker. I know Marines charged down to the bunker and made sure all was secure and I walked back to my squad, but I can't remember what we did right away.

The next thing I remember is helo's landing 105mm howitzers on the top of the hill behind us. We hadn't cleared the hill yet, but arty was put in place on the top of the hill. The arty gunners went to work right away, getting the tubes ready with the front line of our cleared perimeter only fifteen meters in front of them. They were working out in the open, getting everything prepared for a fire mission. It was inspiring to me to see the arty Marines setting up their guns without any regard for the danger they were in.

About this time, 1st Squad was moved over to the north side of the perimeter, east of the summit. I think there was only about five to six Marines left in 1st Squad, and no one knew how many Marines were left in the platoon. I went back to find Lt. McCormick and check in with him. I found him on the top of the summit of Argonne, going over the perimeter defense with other officers. When they broke up, I walked over to Lt. McCormick and talked with him about how we would set up our defense. I looked down and saw that the mail had been delivered in the middle of the battle and Lt. McCormick was very broken up over the fact that so much mail was piled in his lap for Marines who had just lost their lives. This was the most stark, heartbreaking image of war I can remember: all of these letters from loved ones, that almost, almost made it to the Marines before they died in combat.

I need to add this fact: Lt. McCormick was the best Marine leader I ever served with. His dedication to his Marines made us want to bust our butts for him. He would always stand up for us and protect us from the ravages of higher command. He was a motor transport officer who was leading an infantry platoon because there was a shortage of infantry officers, mainly because 2nd lieutenants would lead their Marines from the front and were often WIA or KIA within minutes of contact with the NVA. So a motor transport officer was assigned to lead the infantry, our 3rd Platoon, Delta Company, 1st Battalion, 4th Marines. Lt. McCormick didn't come in with a textbook of strategy and theories to beat us over the head, he just asked us to explain to him how we were fighting this war, up in the north western I Corps/DMZ/Laos border region. He then found ways to improve what worked and we were thankful he was our platoon commander. He would soon prove his true strength, sacrifice and merit as a Marine Infantry officer.

We were assigned a section of the perimeter facing the north/northeast. There was a steep drop-off in front of our position, which is always a good terrain feature when in defense. We took over an old Marine bunker from when it was last occupied by Marines, and as luck would have it, I found a discarded paperback book from one of the last Marine occupants, I carried this book with me for the next month and read it when I could, tearing off the finished pages and using them to start fires. As the day wore on, more napalm runs were delivered to our surrounding areas and more Marines arrived on the hill. There was a short respite in the fighting, and we used that time to secure our positions. What was left of 1st Squad had two positions next to each other. I think we had about six Marines left in our squad. One of the horrors of war was right next to my position: a pile of dead NVA soldiers. They had been dragged over and placed along the perimeter to clean up the area inside FSB Argonne. Anyway, sitting there looking to my right and seeing these dead NVA soldiers about fifteen feet away was a reminder of the real cost of war. War is an endeavor that has no "do overs" or timeouts, rest periods as in sports. This is mortal combat. It is simply kill or be killed.

I can only guess about the time of day, but I think it was around 1600hrs (4PM) when a patrol was formed to sweep the ridge leading northeast from Argonne. From my position sitting on top of my newly recaptured bunker, I could see down on the area that was to be patrolled very well, and I set up my position to support any way I could for the patrol. The patrol had L/Cpl. Max Baer, Lt. McCormick and several Marines from other squads. I really don't know if a particular squad was assigned or this mission was made up of Marines from several squads or volunteers. Anyway, I had a ringside view of their movement sweeping down the hill on line with L/Cpl. Baer on the far left and Lt. McCormick to his right, then other Marines on line to the right of them. They moved slowly and deliberately forward, scanning for signs of NVA occupation.

As they moved about thirty to forty meters in front of me, there was a single gunshot and Max fell to the ground. Lt. McCormick, without any regard for his personal safety, jumped over to where Max was and was shot within seconds. Lt. McCormick crawled up on Max to protect him and that was where they both died. The NVA position was in the triple canopy jungle somewhere within three to four meters from where Max and Lt. McCormick were. At this point all hell broke loose and Marines fired into the jungle to suppress the NVA, but it didn't work. Their position was heavily concealed and protected. A fire mission was called for from the

81mm mortars on the hill and they fired a couple HE (high explosive) rounds. These mortar rounds fell on the Marines near Max and the lieutenant.

This caused a lot of confusion and the need for more medical support. I remember L/Cpl. McCall carrying one of the wounded Marines back up the hill and I think McCall was also wounded. One of the wounded was Tom Breeds, who still had his weapon in his hand and wouldn't let go of it. As I met them, Tom gave me his weapon and asked me to take care of it "Cuz it was a good one." I took Tom's M-16 and kept it for my own and later it would prove to be just as Tom said, a "good one." I went back to my position and looked on helplessly as the carnage lay before me outside the perimeter.

I have no idea what transpired next, if volunteers were asked for or I was ordered to join a rescue group to help at the ambush site, but the next thing I knew, I was there, down as near as we could get to Max and the lieutenant. We were maybe thirty meters away from them, but might have been a mile, because getting to them was impossible from where we were. I then volunteered to attempt a flanking movement from the north, coming back uphill to where Max and Lt. McCormick were. I set off by myself and figured I could crawl up to Max and Lt. McCormick. I crawled and crawled on my belly with my M-16, a couple of magazines and no hand grenades. I got real close to them, maybe only a couple of meters away, when I had a rifle blast go over my head from only a few feet away. This kind of knocked out my hearing and I knew I was real close to the NVA because I could feel the muzzle blast on the back of my head. (BTW, still not wearing a helmet, which is another story.) I just lay there, unable to move because of being so close to the NVA position and still couldn't see it.

At this point in my life, I was completely out of ideas and had no thoughts of what to do. This situation lasted several minutes and the NVA fired a couple more shots at me and I felt each muzzle blast going over me. I can only guess as to why they didn't shoot me, but my best guess is that there was a tree limb that blocked them from lowering their AK-47 enough to shoot me. So then the craziest of things one could see in combat happened.

PFC Murphy saw my predicament and jumped up and started running around in the open, yelling and swearing at the NVA, which immediately caused them to start shooting at him in earnest. This gave me the ability to roll over and slide away from the NVA position, get cover and move back to the rest of the Marines. PFC Murphy wasn't hit and stayed with us for the rest of the mission on Argonne. He was another hero who remained unknown to all except those of us who saw him use himself as a human target to get me out of that jam. By now it was getting dark and word came to us to return to the perimeter, and we would attempt to recover the bodies of Max and Lt. McCormick the next day.

That night was a month long it seemed, dark and still as we all waited for a counterattack. Sometime around 2200hrs (10PM), a medevac helo landed in the wrong LZ. They landed in front of a position facing the southeast/east. The helo was sitting in the field of fire between our positions and the NVA in the woods. For reasons I don't know, they didn't get fired on and lifted off to fly over the overside of the hill where the "lower" LZ was. All of us stayed awake all night and were ready for the worst to come. When morning broke, we got up and started moving around. There was on and off mortar fire on the hill for several hours. Then we got the word that the HQ took a direct hit with an 82mm mortar and killed Lt. Col. Sargent and one other officer.

Sometime in the morning of the second day, the rescue team was formed to retrieve the bodies of Max and Lt. McCormick, and I was going to be part of the security for this, just another gun to help if there were more NVA. We set up around the ambush site and I was towards the north, near where I was the day before. Then all of the Marines were instructed to don gas masks because there was going to be some CS gas and smoke, to be used as a screen to move to the KIA Marines. We put on our masks and the CS gas was thrown and I think a smoke grenade, then two Marines ran out to grab Lt. McCormick, who was on top of Max. For reasons I can't explain, I jumped up and ran out also, so we could have three Marines to pick up and carry him. I was the last to arrive, so I grabbed the lieutenant around the knees. The next Marine had him at the waist and the first Marine had him at the shoulders. We lifted and started to move and then the explosion went off.

The NVA had placed what we call today an IED (then it was a booby-trap) on Lt. McCormick. I'm not sure what the charge was, but it was significant. I was blown back about ten feet and was unconscious for a short period of time, maybe ten seconds, and woke up to Marines screaming from their injuries. I had only superficial wounds but was covered in blood and flesh from Marines, which I scrapped off with my hands. I was taken up to the medical area and tended to, scratches and cuts. All in all, I was okay, and I didn't think I needed any other medical help. We were very short on Marines by this point.

Later in the day, our squad was moved to the other side of the hill, facing the south on a steep decline, and where the recon Huey was pushed off the hill. It was lying down below us. Here we had two positions that were blessed with a good field of fire and very steep terrain below us that would slow down NVA assaults. We started working on our fighting positions as soon as we got moved, because the NVA had our hill "dialed in" with their 82mm mortars, rounds landing all inside our perimeter and striking direct hits on Marine positions. My squad built up a fighting hole and turned it into a small bunker with a short trench leading into the bunker.

Every time a helo got near the hill, mortars started flying toward us. The distinctive "thump, thump, thump" of the NVA mortar round launching gave us about ten to fifteen seconds to find cover. I have to give credit to the NVA on their mortar skills, they really understood the value of their 82mm mortars as a stand-off weapon that can fire from defilade, hit targets from two klicks away, and come straight down to impact and detonation with a twenty-five-meter blast radius. These last two features were what we all feared the most, because a 82mm mortar round could come straight down into your foxhole. Their accuracy on Argonne was very impressive. They hit next to the water buffalo up on the top of the hill and wiped out our water supply. Many of our bunkers were direct hits and they also landed rounds inside our own 81mm mortar pits. Because of this NVA mortar fire, helo's stopped landing on the hill and attempted to air-drop supplies to us with parachutes. Not a single one landed inside the perimeter and they were abandoned out in the jungle. We were pretty pissed off, watching our resupply drift through the sky and into the NVA-controlled areas.

I can't track the days from this point, because it all was just a blur of mortars, close air support running bombing and napalm missions, patrols going out and making contact with the NVA, and trying to get the most precious commodity of all: **sleep**. On one afternoon I had actually taken my boots off for the first time in about two weeks and lay down with my trusty poncho liner under my poncho made into a hooch, and was just falling asleep when another helo resupply attempt was coming in to try to land on the hill. I remember lying there and just saying to myself, "I just don't give a fuck what happens, I'm staying in my little hooch and resting."

At this point, my team leader, L/Cpl. Booker, came and grabbed me and dragged me down into the bunker. This was a determined mortar mission by the NVA, lots of incoming landing very, very close, as I sensed from inside the bunker. We had dirt flying around inside and shockwaves rumbling through the little bunker. When it was over, we all went outside and assessed the damage. I went to my little hooch and it was just some strands of poncho blowing in the wind. An 82mm round had hit one foot to the left of where I was lying down. Our bunker had taken a direct hit and two near misses (one meter from our position), and if one of those rounds had landed in the trench, the blast would have gotten us all. They missed the trench by a couple of feet.

I wish I could put all of this in a neat timeline, but I can't. All I remember is trying to keep my squad alive, day after day of incoming NVA mortars, no sleep and always being very thirsty because we couldn't get water.

Somewhere after we had been on the hill a few days, maybe a week, a patrol from one of the other platoons or even another company was engaged in a firefight a couple of hundred meters from the perimeter on the north side. 1st Squad was part of a reaction group to go and help with the fight. We moved down to where the patrol was engaged with a bunker complex and it was a fierce firefight. We linked up with them and I was directed to move my squad to flank the NVA. I had my Marines form up and start moving toward the flank of the NVA. Apparently they were expecting this, because we only moved about thirty meters and hit NVA fire.

There is good and bad about being in the triple canopy jungle of this region of Vietnam. The bad is that you can literally walk up on an NVA position and not see it. We had been in a firefight going up to FSB Neville that started with 3rd Platoon point man only five feet from them, and he never saw them. Now this same situation was working for us, because they couldn't see us, only hear our movements, and fired in the general direction of us. None of my Marines were hit or injured in this exchange. We couldn't see more than two to three feet in this thick jungle, so we fell back and linked back up with the rest of the Marines.

So now I got another bright idea: use LAWS rockets on the bunker and knock it out. I yelled for "rockets" and a couple of LAWS rockets were delivered to me. So now I crawled out from the jungle into a clearing made by a napalm strike and found a big tree to get behind. I pulled the pins and extended the tube and aimed the rocket at what I wanted to strike, took a deep breath and fired. To my anger I missed completely — it was high and the rocket went past where I wanted it to hit and blew up about twenty meters past my target. So I crawled back and got another LAWS rocket and proceed to do the same thing again, and this time the NVA knew where I was positioned. As I got the next LAWS round ready to fire, I got the pins pulled and extended the tube and started to swing around the side of the tree when a bullet struck about three inches in front of my head and the wood chips and bark struck my face so hard that I thought that I had a bullet injury. The bullet went so close to the side of my head that I yelled back to Sgt. Cluck and asked him if I still had my right ear, I just didn't have the guts to put my hand to my head to find out. He just laughed and said I was okay.

At this point I grabbed my LAWS rocket again and took aim again and fired. And much to my disgust, I completely missed again, with my round exploding twenty meters past where I wanted, and right were my last rocket had landed. All of a sudden there was a terrific volley of fire from the Marines down the line in the jungle and then movement into the area in front of me, right where my rocket rounds had landed. The Marines moved thought the bunker complex and secured the area. I went back to my Marines and Sgt. Cluck. Then a couple of Marines from the other platoon came up to thank us for the LAWS rocket fire that knocked out the NVA bunker with two direct hits on the bunker. As you can expect, I never admitted that I missed my target by a country mile and just accidentally hit the NVA bunker exactly where it was needed. Sometimes being lucky is better than being good, and this was one of those times.

The rest of my time on Argonne just passed like a recurring nightmare of being trapped on a mountain along the border with Laos and just south of the DMZ, with no way out and no one coming to help. I knew the other companies of 1/4 were actively moving all around in the mountains in the vicinity of Argonne. They didn't have bunkers or barbed wire and were in great danger. I had a deep gut feeling of despair about how we were going to get all of these Marines out, or where were the other battalions, which would be needed to really pursue the NVA to Laos. There were no other battalions coming, so we were going to do the best we could with what we had.

After several weeks, I can't really say, the word came that we were going to leave Argonne soon. We started to work on the loading out of all the unnecessary equipment by helo. After a few days we had the hill pretty much packed out, all of the arty was gone and the supporting heavy arms gone also. Then other companies loaded up on helo's and flew out, leaving Delta company on the hill by itself. We packed up and left in the early morning just at dawn, to the north. We were going up into the DMZ. I can't explain why I thought this was okay. We just all accepted that this was our piece of ground and we were going to stay with the mission. I guess we might have felt that we had paid a very high price for this mountain and we didn't fear staying and walking out instead of flying back to a rear support base like LZ Stud (Vandegrift Combat Base). This sounds crazy, but I wasn't upset or fearful of walking out to the north to the DMZ, and none of the other Marines were either. We knew this was our "joss," to use Chinese slang for luck.

At this point in my short Marine Corps career, I felt like I was in my element, in my true place in war. We had adapted to the Vietnam War. This might be called going native in current language, but we now built tree huts, using vines and branches to build a structure off the ground, and stayed dry as we moved to the DMZ. The journey north took several weeks and included a re-supply perimeter in one of the valleys and a patrol base on a high ridge. While we were at the re-supply location (grid # 677644**), I was able to participate in one of life's smaller luxuries. I was on a water detail, so we went to a stream close by and filled canteens for the platoon. While there, I brushed my teeth. From before we landed on Argonne, I had only one toothbrush and my choice was to brush my teeth or clean my weapon. As you would guess, that wasn't even a question. I cleaned my weapon with my only toothbrush and went, by my guess, about five weeks without brushing my teeth. And now I just brushed and brushed. It was the most pleasant thing I experienced in months.

After we were re-supplied, Delta went up a steep ridge line and established a patrol base in a small saddle along the ridge (grid# 679640**). Here, my squad was assigned a sector of the perimeter that was very easy to defend, because from our position, a rock face dropped straight down a cliff for about twenty meters. The bad news was the ridge line was so narrow and had knife edge-like rocks jutting up, there was no place to establish our squad location. There were a couple of small trees rising from our spot, so we went to work and made a "tree hut" about one meter off the ground, just over the top of the rock formation. We made a little ladder to climb up and pitched our "poncho-hooch" on top of this woven platform. The entire structure was made of tree limbs and "wait a minute" vines used as rope to lash a frame to trees, more vines to make floor webbing and then brush woven into this for the floor. We were "high and dry." Our watch position was located in the rocks and was very well protected from any fire. All of our squad gear was stored under our structure and stayed dry and was next to our fighting position. I mean, we were living in the "Beverly Hills" of the jungle in I Corps. We received several resupply missions here and the pilots did a simply remarkable job of landing a CH-46, rear wheels on our ridge line, with the front of the chopper hovering over a cliff. After a week or so in this patrol base we moved again, down the ridge to the valley then north, heading for the DMZ just over a klick away.

This part of the Argonne mission lasted three-plus weeks, maybe a month. As we moved up towards the DMZ, I started to have some real difficulties with the new platoon commander, who replaced Lt. McCormick for 3rd Platoon. When the new lieutenant showed up, about a week after we landed on Argonne, the first thing he said to us was, "Stick with me and we will all go home with lots of medals." I couldn't believe what the hell I was hearing. We had just lost most of the platoon and he was talking about getting medals. This USNA grad was focused on his own career and he needed medals. No need to name this individual, it has been over fifty years, I just butted heads with him at every turn. Our disagreements on how to lead and deploy Marines came to a head when we (1st Squad) were assigned to go back to our position from the last night to capture or kill a NVA solider that had been spotted and shot at by Marines in company "D". They were on high ground and could look down on our old encampment and saw an NVA solider rooting around our old perimeter.

The 2nd lieutenant joined us, and we also had a machine gun team that included J.P. Young and my squad. The 2nd lieutenant placed our machine gun on the edge of the elephant grass clearing facing the direction we would be going, then took us into the elephant grass, which was a foot or two over or heads. Basically we couldn't see crap in any direction. The new lieutenant directed me in the elephant grass, giving me bearings to follow with hand and arm signals, and after about ten to fifteen minutes we broke out of the grass, dead center on J.P.'s machine gun crew. We had walked in a complete circle and came back to the starting point. Only the discipline of J.P.'s M-60 team allowed us to live another day. I now just said, "Follow me," and off we went toward the old Delta Company bivouac site. As we arrived at the old encampment, the

2nd lieutenant started shouting instructions to Marines to move out fifty meters and establish a perimeter. There were only seven of us and we were in short elephant grass on the edge of high elephant grass and any movement more than five meters would put Marines in over their heads in the grass, which removed all sense of direction and blocked our vision so much we couldn't see anything more than a couple of feet in front of us, to include our fellow Marines. This would most likely cause a blue on blue firefight or get us completely wiped out if there were any other NVA in the area. All of the Marines had taken a position in a semicircle as we arrived at the site. Now they just stood and looked at me and waited for my nod.

I grabbed the 2nd lieutenant, walked him a couple of meters away and informed him to be quiet and watch what was going on, he could learn something, and I was running this operation. The words I used might not have been very polite and contained multiple words of profanity Marines commonly used, but this was the gist of my short conversation with him: "I'm running this, shut up and watch." I didn't wait for his answer, just turned, instructed the Marines to drop to a knee where they were and I stepped toward the direction of the last sighting of the NVA solider. After moving only six to seven meters and looking down a ten-meter bank to a small river, there was the NVA soldier. He saw me and brought his weapon to bear, aiming his AK-47 at me. I fired first and hit my target with Tom Breeds's M-16. Yes, Tom, your M-16 was a "good one." When this was all over, the new 2nd lieutenant was really pissed, really, really pissed at me.

Several hours later, after rejoining the company position on the top of Hill 650, the new 2nd lieutenant went to the Delta Company commander and demanded that I be brought up on charges for a whole list of things, to include disobeying a direct order from an superior officer on the field of battle and even mutiny. I was standing nearby, ready to give my brief to the CO and heard every word. My company commander, 1st Lt. Rabbit, listened and then sent the 2nd lieutenant back to the platoon and waved me over, then asked me, "What the hell happened?" After I told him what transpired, he nodded and said don't worry. 1st Lt. Rabbit just saved my skin from the brig and a sentence of probably three years hard labor at Portsmouth Naval Prison, in New Hampshire, which was the norm for these things, back then.

If you could ask Sgt. Jimmy Cluck, he would be informative on this subject. Jimmy came to 3rd Platoon as a private with over three years' time in the "Corps," and we were his third tour in Vietnam. He was what would be called today a "subject matter expert" on the subject of Portsmouth Naval Prison and a three-year sentence of hard labor, which also included "bread and water" rations if the prison staff deemed it necessary. As the story went, Jimmy was a sergeant at USMC Base, Quantico, VA, after his second tour in Vietnam when a bright and shiny new 2nd lieutenant didn't like the way Jimmy saluted him and stopped him and was instructing Jimmy on the proper way to salute an officer. Jimmy gave the 2nd lieutenant a proper hand salute and a broken jaw as a bonus, and ended up in prison. After I think it was a couple of months in prison, the Marine Corps offered him an early release from prison if he would return to Vietnam for a third tour of duty, which he accepted. At this moment in time, as I was standing on Hill 650, Jimmy had gone from private to sergeant in six months and now had a Sliver Star from Argonne, two Bronze Stars and four Purple Hearts, and had been reassigned to the 1st Battalion, 4th Marines, Headquarters at Quang Tri. This didn't end well for Sgt. Jimmy Cluck. Eventually he went home a private, with only a single four-year hash mark stripe on his Alpha uniform sleeve. You see, Jimmy Cluck was the real deal, the real John Wayne, the real Marine. He ran into hell with only a hand grenade. He was what we respectfully called a true "Mud Marine." Just make sure he was never taken out of the field and all was good.

We helo-lifted off Hill 650 and went back to LZ Stud (VCB), and when we landed, I felt totally out of place. There were Jeeps, tents, noise, roads, trucks and wire, things I hadn't seen in months. What was unnerving, I felt more comfortable out in the jungle than at LZ Stud.

I want to provide my final thoughts on the story of Argonne. The new 2nd lieutenant found a way to get his revenge on me. I was put up for a combat medal for valor (Silver Star) by many of the Marines in 3rd Platoon for all of the combined actions I took on Argonne and was also meritoriously promoted to corporal during the combat on Argonne. But the new 2nd lieutenant derailed the submission for the medal and busted me back to lance corporal and removed me from 1st Squad leader on Hill 650, just before we extracted back to LZ Stud. I finished out my tour as a lance corporal, M-79 "Blooper Man."

I have no regrets as to any of my actions on this mission. I led Marines as best I could, fought as hard as I could and protected Marines with all the energy I had. None of my Marines in 1st squad were KIA or WIA from the time I took over on the first day after Ralph was hit on March 20th, until I was removed as squad leader on Hill 650 as we readied to be extracted to the rear in late April.

In conclusion, a bit of my history: I spent over two months aboard the Naval Hospital Ship, *USS Repose*, from October to the end of December 1968, where I recovered from Dioxin poisoning, or Agent Orange as it is known today. I rejoined 1st squad, 3rd Platoon after getting out of the hospital, getting back to the field in early January 1969. And now I can tell the one thing that has always pulled very heavy on my heart, caused much pain in my life during all of these years. Of the Marines in 1st squad, 3rd Platoon that I rejoined with in January 1969, I was the only Marine not killed or wounded.

This is my story of "LZ Sitting Duck, the fight for FSB Argonne," March and April 1969.

Semper Fidelis

L/Cpl. John "Little John" Arsenault

I ditched my helmet in September, 1968. I found it to be of little use in dense, triple canopy jungle. I could see, hear and sense danger much better without one. Because of the triple canopy jungle, most of our contacts with the NVA were at very close range, sometimes only one to two meters apart. In my opinion, a helmet provided little benefit and was an excellent target for the NVA. The helmet looked like a big turtle popping up when we tried to look over a log or around a tree. For most of my tour, I wore a soft cover or bush hat.

* Map sheet 6242 IV, Ngoun Rao, Vietnam:Laos, stock # L701463424

CHAPTER 10

BIG SHOES TO FILL

Mark Abplanalp
PFC, 2531, Field Radio Operator, Artillery
Golf 3/12, assigned to Delta Company, 1ˢᵗ Bn, 4ᵗʰ Marines

GOLF BATTERY, 3RD BN, 12TH MARINES, FURNISHED ALL THE forward observer teams for all 1ˢᵗ Battalion, 4th Marines. Dave Ovist and I were the radio operators for Delta Company 1/4. I knew I had some big shoes to fill as David's replacement; he was a big, husky guy and could carry a lot. He was just a dandy fellow, from everyone I ever talked to. Nobody ever said a bad word about him.

I was David's replacement. I didn't get to know him. The way it worked at that time in the Marine Corps was that the artillery units provided forward observer teams for the companies. We were both in Golf 3/12, and David had just finished his full tour and extended, having just come back from leave in a deal that he would be under Headquarters Company and not have to serve the field anymore. It didn't work out all that good for him.

Argonne is about 1,500 meters to the east of the Laotian border (grid coordinates 675.573, elevation 1,308 meters). U.S. Marines had been there before in November 1968 and abandoned LZ Argonne mid-December 1968. There were old bunkers and concertina wire left over from then. When we went in, I was on one of the early CH-46 helicopters, though I don't know exactly which ones. We had to use the lower LZ because there was a Huey that had been shot down on the upper LZ.

When we approached the landing zone, it was the hottest LZ I had flown into. I really don't remember a whole lot about the approaching flight. I guess ignorance is bliss. I couldn't really see much from where I was sitting. We had stuff flying around in the cabin of the CH-46 we were in. I wasn't smart enough to figure out it was from someone shooting holes in the side of the cabin. The flight crew really wanted to off-load in a hurry. I can't say as I blame them. I thought at the time they wanted to get back to the rear with clean sheets and cold beer, but I really would not want their job. It takes some brass ones to do their job.

When I came out of the CH-46, I fell down and landed in the concertina wire. I cut my face on it and bled profusely. Not bad enough to get a Purple Heart, but that's all right. I lost my helmet. I hated wearing the thing before, but now, the only time I ever wanted it, I lost it. So when I got out—I recollect the back end of the helicopter that I exited through was facing south—I ran to a depression on the north side of the helicopter and got down in it. I remember looking over and seeing Lt. Col. Sargent charging over the hill with a pistol in his hand like John Wayne.

Over to the left of me, Lt. Hunt, who I believe was the executive officer of Delta Company, got shot through the hand. Seems like it took a while for the corpsman to get to him. He had a short stay, since he got medevac'd out. I remember there was a mortar pit not far from me and I remember there was a wounded man named Marcelino Anguiano with an Army flak jacket. Gary Smelcer and I, the enlisted forward observer, helped pack him down to the medevac landing zone and I acquired his jacket. The Army flak jacket was much more comfortable and lighter than what the Marines issued and was highly sought after by all.

We went back to our area, and I was debating whether to keep the Army or Marine flak jacket, and Lt. Walker, who was my FO officer said, "Well, it didn't do Marcelino any good, so I wouldn't do that." So I laid it back down. The next day, I saw him wearing it. I guess he decided he needed it worse than I did. That's okay, though.

I remember taking a patrol around because a helicopter had dropped a pallet of mortar rounds off to the side of the hill where we couldn't get to it; we had to go with a few engineers to blow it up in place, since we weren't going to be able to pack it out. I was snooping and trying to be as quiet as I could, but I had a bit of a cough, and every time I'd start to cough, Lt. Walker would turn around and give me the death stare. I didn't want to make any more noise than *he* wanted me to make.

Wasn't long after that I'd heard David Ovist was killed. I remember telling Smelcer and he looked like I'd hit him between the eyes with a two-by-four.

I remember Cpl. Blaney, the company supply sergeant at the time, was going to put me on a work detail. I kindly told him in Marine Corps fashion to "kiss my ass" and I reminded him that I wasn't in his chain of command. Besides what was happening there, I received a letter that my mother's cancer had returned. Lesson number one: do not piss off the company sergeant. I thought we were going to starve so I apologized later on. He didn't say much, but I think it was a work detail that would have been disposing of the dead NVA soldiers.

The battalion chaplain came out to us and held a service in a hole caused by a mortar round. His coming out to Argonne, which was never a secure place, impressed me. I believe his name was Chaplain Alread. He reminded me of a regular old-time southern preacher...a good man.

I remember the jets strafing and dropping napalm. They were close enough we could feel the heat from them and could hear the 20 mm cannons. They were coming at us in a way that compressed the sound. It was the weirdest noise I'd ever heard. The napalm was close enough it felt like it was going to singe our eyebrows.

Every time we had helicopters coming in for resupply or to take out the medevac's or anything, it just brought mortars down from the NVA, mostly from the north, and our guys were firing back at them. We had more people than I remember at the time, but I remember sharing a hole with Lt. Walker. We used whatever we could to cover our hole, and we used a rubber lady to cover ours. A rubber lady is what we called the inflatable mattresses that we used when we could get them. It had been filled with dirt to cover the hole. We felt pretty good about it.

I was sitting on the edge one day with the radio outside and I heard three rifle shots that couldn't have missed by very much. I got back down in the hole. When we'd get mail call, Lt. Walker got a lot of pictures, but would never share them. So one day when we were taking fire, I took a look when he wasn't around, and the pictures were all Charolais cattle. I'm a farm boy and would have been interested in them, so I don't know why he didn't share. He also had a flask of whiskey that he'd never offered to share. Don't know if he ever knew that he shared that day, but I had a sip, not that I was a whiskey drinker. We walked off April 4th, 1969, and we noticed the lines had been marked with rags by the NVA, which were about to overrun us.

Years afterwards at a 1/4 reunion in French Lick, Indiana, I was in the hospitality area visiting with Jesse Villanueva, who was in the 81 mm mortars section on Argonne, and I asked him, "Who was the man Gary and I carried down to be medevac'd out?" Jesse raised his arm and pointed across the room and said, "That guy over there!"

When dinner was served, we all sat at the same table and caught up with each other. I learned that Marcelino Anguiano had stayed in the Marine Corps and served a tour as a drill instructor, retiring as a master sergeant just short of sergeant major. We got into telling stories on the "other" side of basic training and I laughed so hard I almost lost my dinner contents!

CHAPTER 11

THE SMELL OF DEATH

Wayne Marxen
PFC, 0311, Infantry Man
Alpha Company, 1st Bn, 4th Marines

I WAS A RIFLEMAN WITH ALPHA CO. 1ST BN 4TH MARINES during Operation Purple Martin in late March and early April 1969. These are the events that took place on or around FSB Argonne.

Argonne was a mountain in northwest Vietnam, less than 2,000 meters east of the Laotian border and about 8,000 meters south of the DMZ. I had been with the company, as a member of 3rd Platoon, for about five weeks. We had seen considerable action in that time, but nothing like what was to happen in the next few days.

March 20, 1969, we were at Vandegrift Combat Base for a few days between operations when we got word that we would be taking part in Operation Purple Martin near the Laotian border. On the 21st we were flown out to FSB Alpine, which was about 7,500 meters southeast of Argonne. Argonne had been taking mortar fire from across the Laotian border for a few weeks and had taken many casualties. Our part in the operation, along with Charlie 1/4, was to go into the valley West of Argonne and put an end to the mortar fire. Charlie was to sweep the north part of the valley while we went into the valley from the southwest.

March 23, 1969, we set out on patrol out of Alpine and up to Argonne from the southeast. I don't remember much about that day, but the fact that it was very hot. I guess my mind was preoccupied with what was to come, going into that very active area. We were told to expect numerous casualties.

March 24, 1969, we spent the night on Argonne, which was occupied by Delta 1/4. They had come in and reclaimed the hill after it was abandoned and had a very fierce battle to chase the NVA off the hill. All I remember about that night was taking a few mortar rounds and that it was unbelievably dark. We sat on the west side of the hill and watched the lights reflection in the sky from the trucks coming down the Ho Chi Minh Trail, knowing they were carrying supplies to our enemy for the next day. It was said that the trail was only about 3,000 meters to the west. In the morning we humped off the hill and headed for the Argonne Valley, west of the firebase. The second half of the day I walked point. I had some experience walking point but not in a hot area. At 6'4" I made a big target. We didn't see any action that day, but I knew tomorrow would be different. We set in a defensive perimeter for the night about 1,000 meters from the valley floor. With an eerie feeling about this place, we dug our fighting holes extra deep.

Just before dark a chopper came in and dropped off a scout who was to walk point the next day. His name was Dennis Orbino, an E-5 from Syracuse, New York, who had two tours and was about three weeks into a six-month extension. We had set in early that night, so we had a little time to kill before watches started. Three of us sat around and talked with Dennis for about a half an hour. He told us he was with the scout platoon and they had attached him to us to walk point because we were going into an area that was crawling with NVA. He carried a sawed off 12-gauge shotgun and a .45 pistol. I noticed that he had a white plastic c-rat spoon in the pocket above his heart. Immediately I thought about my squad leader telling me, when I joined the company, to never give the enemy any kind of a target. The night went by without incident. Again, it was very dark and there was an eerie feeling, because we knew they were out there.

March 25, 1969, we set out in a column march from our night time position at about 8:00 AM. My platoon had point the day before, so we were last in the column. Everyone was quiet, the old salts had an idea of what was to come and the young guys were just scared. I was somewhere in the middle, but more on the scared side. I remember someone saying, "This place smells like death." It wasn't even ten minutes and a firefight broke out on the trail; the front of the column had been ambushed with automatic weapons. There was a quick exchange of fire and then just a lot of screaming, hollering and then calls of, "Corpsmen up." We weren't even in the column yet and I was leaning back on my 100+ pound pack. Then we were up and running on the trail.

Soon we came upon a machine gunner from 1st Platoon who had been shot many times in both legs. I knew him pretty well; his name was Jim Brannon. We were both from Eastern Iowa and had come into country at the same time. He was lying along the trail with both legs riddled with bullet holes. I can remember talking with him when the column stopped for a few minutes. The corpsmen were working to stop the bleeding and stabilizing him. He was turning gray and going into shock quickly. Since that day, every time I see someone with leg injuries, I remember Jim and his face while he was fighting for life. We got word a short while later that he didn't make it. That was the first I had witnessed someone that I knew dying in combat. It didn't hit me right away because of the situation we were in.

When the column started moving again, it was only about twenty-five feet when we came upon Dennis Orbino, lying along the left side of the trail. His flak jacket had been ripped up by bullets, just under that white plastic spoon. To this day when I see a white plastic spoon, I can remember him lying there. He never got a chance to get off a shot. The marksmanship indicated that we were dealing with some NVA soldiers who knew what they were doing. Because of the turnover in troops, most of the time we dealt with inexperienced kids. Not this time.

About 9:00 1st and 2nd platoons were engaging the NVA in a fierce battle on the valley floor. The enemy had retreated to a fortified bunker complex just across a large stream. The casualties from the initial contact had been staged on a small flat area on the west side of the hill. There were two KIA and about a half dozen wounded. The number of wounded was increasing as the battle continued below. Our platoon set up a security perimeter around the casualties. We had staged our packs and other gear near that spot and a guy who was supposed to go home in a few days was put in charge of watching them. My fire team leader positioned me under a rock outcropping, just under the casualties, and facing the valley. As I mentioned, the NVA was in a bunker complex, so we called in artillery. I think it was coming from FSB Neville, which was about fifteen klicks east of Argonne and they would be firing right over the top of us. When arty rounds go over they whistle in flight and stop whistling when they are ready to hit. We heard the first two rounds whistle above us and they hit near the target They called for an adjustment for the third round. We heard the round coming and when it got to us it stopped whistling. There were a few scary seconds when I knew something bad was going to happen. It landed right in the area of the casualties and those caring for them. It exploded just above me, about ten feet away. The noise was deafening and the concussion knocked me over. Because I was below it, I got showered with dirt, rocks and other debris. The shell killed four more guys and wounded numerous others. My fire team and squad leaders were badly wounded. I never heard if it was 105 or 155 artillery, but when they land on top of you, it doesn't matter.

On March 25, 1969, around 10:00 A.M, it was decided the casualties would be moved to the top of Argonne to be medevac'd, as it was impossible from our position because of the canopy and the nearby battle going on. 3rd platoon and what was left of the mortar platoon were to carry them halfway up the hill, where Delta Company would meet us and take them to the top. The short round had killed four more and wounded numerous others. I knew three of the KIA and several of the wounded. Two of us were to load a guy from mortars in a poncho and carry him. The round had hit at his feet and he was a mess. He was like a 160 pound mass of bloody jelly. I think the blast had shattered every bone in his body. I remember picking up a severed arm and a hand and putting them with the body. This was in my memory for thirty-five years, until discussing that incident at an Alpha Co. reunion, with other guys who went through it. I learned that I had also picked up his severed head, but through VA therapy my mind had blocked out what really happened. Since then, I can vividly remember picking up his head. This bothers me all the time and I see it in dreams. My only consolation is that he died instantly and didn't have to suffer.

It took about an hour and a half to carry them up the very steep and heavenly vegetated hillside. It was only about 2,000 feet, but the heavy load made it tough going. It was well over 100 degrees and very humid. I was completely soaked with sweat, scratched up from the vegetation and in bad need of a drink of water. The poncho ripped open twice and we had to load him in a different one. We met Delta Company, made the exchange and hurried back down the hill to join the fighting.

As mentioned before, the NVA had taken refuge in a fortified bunker complex and the artillery had done nothing to take it out. Air strikes had been called in with the same result. They dropped a 500 pound bomb that hit the complex, which was followed by napalm. When napalm explodes it creates a burning gel that is dispersed through the air. The heat from the blast is tremendous and it consumes the oxygen in the air around it. One bomb landed about 100 feet to the right and front of me. I could feel the tremendous heat and it sucked the air out of my lungs and I almost passed out. The NVA were running toward Laos and we were shooting at them. The blobs of napalm were hitting them as they ran. I could see one gook, out of shooting range, get hit in the back with a blob. He went down and lay there screaming as the napalm burned through his body. After the napalm, things were quiet except for a few sporadic shots, as the NVA had fled into Laos.

Later in the afternoon we went to retrieve our packs and equipment and found that all our canteens were empty. It was suggested to carry four one-quart canteens, and I always carried at least twelve. The guy watching the gear had no explanation and the mystery was never solved. It was getting late in the afternoon and it had been over 100 degrees all day and I had not had a drink or anything to eat since before the action started. We humped to the north along the side of Argonne until it was decided to dig in for the night.

It had been a long day and everyone was exhausted. We found a suitable spot to spend the night and had formed a perimeter. We had just dropped our packs and were preparing to dig our fighting holes when the NVA began firing at us from above us. I dove behind a log facing the valley. I couldn't tell where the fire was coming from. They only fired for a couple of minutes. Bullets were hitting everywhere and I had a half a dozen hit within six inches of my legs. They fired hundreds of rounds and miraculously only hit one guy, a gunnery sergeant who stood up to direct fire. He was about ten feet to my right and took three rounds in the back. I can still see the look on his face when he went down. After the firing stopped, it was decided the whole company would carry him to the top of the hill. He needed a medevac and it was too dangerous to spend the night there. It was a steep 4,000-foot climb in total darkness and thick vegetation. It took over two hours and it was after 11:00 PM when we got to the top. All hopes of getting a drink of water were dashed when we found out that Delta Co. hadn't been resupplied and didn't have any to spare.

On top of the hill, it had been a long, hot day and I was totally exhausted and thirsty. I did have a c-ration meal, but it was hard to get down without water. It was so dark it was hard to tell what the fire support base looked like. I could see the shell of a burned-out chopper sitting on the upper LZ. We were near the lower LZ and I could just make out the poncho covered KIAs lying in a row. The Gunny needed an emergency evacuation, so we carried him to the lower LZ to wait for the medevac bird. I counted seven poncho-covered bodies and we had only carried up six that morning. I assumed that one of the wounded hadn't made it. The KIAs would spend the night on the LZ until a larger chopper picked them up the next day. When the Huey came in, the Gunny was loaded aboard. When they were ready to take off one of the crew members noticed that one of the ponchos was moving. It was my fire team leader, who had gotten mixed in with the KIAs. He had laid there for over twelve hours, most of that time in the sun, and it was over 120 degrees on top of the hill. He had a collapsed lung and numerous other injuries. How he had survived wrapped in a poncho and lying in that hot sun all day, I'll never know. He did survive and spent five months in Guam recovering.

The Marine Corps, in all its infinite wisdom, sent him back to the company to finish his tour. He had less than a month left and he was frightened stiff at every noise. I was good friends with our platoon sergeant and our new lieutenant, and when I told them his story, they made sure he didn't have to go back to the bush and could spend his last month in the rear. We didn't have to stand watch that night and I collapsed into a deep sleep for about five hours.

March 26, 1969, back on top of Argonne, I woke up soaked in sweat. It must have stayed over 100 degrees overnight. The hill looked so much different in the daylight, a lot of damage from the constant mortar barrage experienced over the past weeks. The largest feature was the command bunker, which had been used by the NVA as a hospital after we had abandoned the firebase. Guys from Delta told us that when they had retaken the hill, they found two nurses and a number of patients that were housed in the bunker. From the hill, to the west over Hill 1154, we could see into Laos, to the north toward the DMZ and to the east was Tiger Tooth and Fire support baseNeville. The one feature that really stood out was a burned-out UH-1H Huey helicopter, that sat near the upper LZ. I never heard the story about it, but it was evident that it was the victim of a mortar attack. It was an eerie sight, to say the least. We still didn't have any water, so it had been over twenty-four hours since my last drink. I remember opening a can of c-ration beef slices in juice and drinking the salty liquid. Our c-rats were WWII surplus that were packed in 1941, but even after twenty-eight years in a can there was still moisture. They flew in a water tank that afternoon and we all got less than two canteens of warm, stinky water. It was tempting to drink it all at once, but we didn't know when we would get more.

It had to be the hottest day I had ever experienced. There was a thermometer hanging in the burned-out UH-1H Huey helicopter. I don't know how accurate it was, but at about 2:00 PM it registered 140 degrees. We had eleven heat casualties that day that had to be medevac'd. I saw a guy lay his hand on a bunker frame and hit it with a 2x4 three to four times. There were two other guys who poked holes in their skin with a P38 can opener, to make it look like they had been bitten by a rat. I don't know if they knew the treatment for rabies at that time was twenty-two shots in the stomach over a three-week period. Some guys were willing to do that just to get out of this piece of Hell.

That night we helped man the lines and my hole was located on the west side of the hill. We could see the headlights glare on the supply trucks coming down the Ho Chi Minh Trail. I heard that it was only a couple of miles from Argonne. What an eerie feeling, knowing they were resupplying the NVA that we were to fight in the coming days.

March 27, 1969, the day started out hot and promised to get hotter. Our platoon commander, a 2nd lieutenant, volunteered us to go on a patrol down the side of Argonne and toward Hill 1154 and the Laotian border. We had received mortar fire from that direction since we had been on the hill. We were supposed to scout around on Hill 1154 and see if we could find any signs of where the mortar fire was coming from. It would be a welcome relief from the heat to be in the triple canopy of the jungle for a while. We crossed the stream and searched a few hours with no sign of the mortar position, but we did find plenty of signs of enemy activity. There were bunker complexes everywhere, but no signs of the enemy.

Before we started back to Argonne there were mortars fired from farther west and heading for Argonne. It was getting too late to check out where they had come from and we had to get started back. When we crossed the stream on the way back, the plan was for everyone to fill some canteens, but when we reached it the word came back not to drink any water from the stream because it was contaminated. There were three dead NVA soldiers, with head injuries, lying in the water. They were probably killed in the fighting of the 25th, because they were bloated and dark in color. You could tell they had been placed there because they were in a line with their heads in the water and there was no way they just fell that way. This taught me a lot about how the

NVA honored their dead. The column stopped for a break just as I got to the stream. The NVA soldiers were lying in fast moving water and were about ten feet across from me. Another guy and I filled twenty canteens. Looking at those bloated bodies almost made me sick, but water is water. Nobody ever got sick from the water, so I guess it wasn't contaminated. We reached the top of Argonne just before dark and had to man lines again, but at least we weren't thirsty. Word got around that the whole company would leave in the morning to patrol Hill 1154 and beyond to find that mortar position.

March 28: On the 26th, a supply chopper landed on Argonne with resupply of food and water, and also a few replacements for the ones we lost the day before. I got to talk briefly with a twenty-year-old PFC, who was from Maryland, and this was his first day in the bush. He had been in-country for about a week. What a place to start his tour. We saddled up on the morning of the 28th to head west to find the mortar position that had inflicted so much damage at Argonne. We didn't know how long this patrol would last , so we had to pack enough food and water for a few days. We were to carry a full load of ammo, which for me consisted of twenty-five loaded M16 magazines, 200 extra M16 rounds and 200 hundred rounds for the M60 machine gun, tenty hand grenades and a claymore mine. We moved in a column, as usual, ten to fifteen feet apart. We moved down the northwest corner of Argonne and crossed the stream. The three dead gooks were still in their position at the edge of the water. What a disgusting sight. For those who have never witnessed it, the smell of rotting human flesh is the worst smell imaginable. As a matter of respect, we usually buried the dead gooks that we found, but no one made an attempt on these three because they were most likely booby trapped.

It was another very hot day and that ever-present smell of death was in the air. By early afternoon we had made our way to the top of Hill 1154, which was a ridge line that stretched for several hundred meters. Rumor was that we had crossed the border into Laos, which was against the rules of our politicians and our higher up leadership. They could stage troops and attack us from there, but we couldn't shoot back or cross the border. We had seen plenty of signs of gooks, bunker complexes all over the place, but had not made any contact. It wasn't long when our point came across an indentation in the ground that led to a shallow cave. This was the mortar position, but the gooks had heard us coming and fled with the mortar tube. They had left the baseplate, and in checking the cave we found over 100 mortar rounds and other ammo, gear and food. We placed everything in a pile on top of the hill and called in an airstrike. From a distance we could see a Phantom jet come in and make a direct hit with the first bomb. All that stuff the gooks had humped down the Ho Chi Minh Trail and through the jungle to this place was all gone in an instant.

We waited around a while in case of retaliation, but nothing came. They were saving that for later. It was getting late, so we would have to stay on the hill for the night, which didn't seem like a good idea, but we couldn't make that hump back in the pitch black darkness. We started to move to the north to find a good spot to spend the night.

Night of March 28th. We found a good spot and set up our perimeter over the top of the ridge. Digging our holes was tough because the soil was rocky and hard. We had to dig them deep, because we knew we would be attacked as soon as it got dark. We also cleared the brush in front of our holes seventy-five to 100 feet. The smell of death was stronger than ever. My hole was on the north end, just off the west side of the ridge line. 1st Platoon sent out an LP about fifty meters to the north of the perimeter. An LP was a listening post placed out in front of the perimeter to be an early warning of any movement. They were to phone in the movement and get back into the perimeter. They were not sup-posed to fire unless fired upon. The new guy I had talked to when he arrived was sent out on that LP. I can only imagine how scared he was, this being only his third day in the bush.

When darkness came, it was sudden and pitch black. After about thirty minutes, the LP reported movement. We could also hear movement in front of us and we knew this would be a no sleep night. The LP requested to come in and were told to stay in place and monitor the movement. A few minutes later they reported that the movement was getting close to them. They were ordered to take them under fire and then hurry back to the perimeter. My hole was about 150 feet from them, and I could see the flash and hear the explosion of an RPG. After that, all hell broke loose, the NVA was firing everywhere in front of us. We didn't fire but threw grenades, so as to not give away our positions with muzzle flashes.

I had what we called a chi-com land next to my hole. A chi-com was a primitive grenade, an explosive packed with nails and any small pieces of metal they could find, wrapped around a stick with string. Some kind of a primer was placed in the end. The grenade had to land on the end to detonate. I was lucky it landed wrong or I would have been wounded. Without thinking, I picked it up by the handle and threw it back out and it exploded. I guess it was my lucky day again.

We continued throwing grenades and then firing at muzzle flashes, which were very bright in the total darkness. Planes dropped illumination canisters that lit up the whole place. And then a Spooky Gunship came in and worked over the area outside the perimeter. The gunship was armed with machine guns that could cover the size of a football field, every six inches, in about six seconds. This put an end to the contact, but we had to stay on 100 percent alert the rest of the night. There was no movement or contact the rest of the night. I think we had pretty well wiped them out.

The LP had taken a direct hit and had one KIA and two wounded. The KIA was the kid I had befriended when he got off the chopper two days ago. He took a direct hit from the RPG and didn't have a chance. He didn't make it through his third day in the bush. At the time I really didn't know what had happened out there, only that they were hit. In talking at a reunion with the guy who was in charge of the LP, I learned they had put the new guy in the first spot along the trail. After repeatedly asking to come in, they were told to take the enemy under fire and then come in. He stood up to fire his M16, but it wouldn't fire. He didn't have a round chambered. The guy in charge threw him his rifle and he tried to fire again. Nothing happened because the safety was on.

Then came the explosion that hit him and the other two guys were shot while running in, but they made it. Everything was wrong with that LP. You never send a new guy, with no bush experience, out on an LP in a spot crawling with NVA. And he never should have been put in that position in the LP. Quick decisions have to be made in that situation, and experience is needed. An LP's job is to be an early warning for the perimeter and is not supposed to take the enemy under fire. 2nd Platoon also had one KIA on their LP and there were other wounds around the perimeter and they all got evacuated that night. I had been here for less than two months and it was seeming more all the time that I would be very lucky to make it through the next ten.

The morning after (March 29th) was another no sleep night. Each platoon had to conduct a damage assessment in front of their holes. Out about 120 feet we found a young NVA soldier with a chunk missing out of the side of his head. He was just a teenager and was dressed in new fatigues and boots, an indication that he had just arrived from the North. Our Cho Hoi scout told us that in the North they take the boys from their homes when they are fifteen, give them a couple of months of training and send them south. A Cho Hoi was an NVA soldier who had defected to our side or been captured, who was rehabilitated and trained to be a scout. They were attached to our company for operations. Some of them you could trust, but most of them would lead you to where the enemy was and when the shooting started, they would turn and run. All the young NVA had on him was a worn billfold, which contained a few pieces of paper Vietnamese money and a picture of a young girl. The girl was probably his girlfriend and it was sad to think that she would never know what happened to him. We buried him in an unmarked, shallow grave.

There was blood and a lot of drag marks everywhere, indicating that the survivors got rid of the bodies. This was a common practice of the NVA, so we wouldn't know how many we had killed. We found a like-new Chinese canister machine gun lying close to the young soldier. It was partly covered in cosmoline, a sticky substance that weapons were packed in for shipment. I don't know if it belonged to him or if he had ever gotten the chance to fire it. A little later we found fourteen NVA knapsacks, just up the trail from where the LP got hit, that they had staged before the attack, and never made it back to get them. Another indication that we had killed a lot of them. In the packs were pictures, money, canteens and food. The food consisted of maggot-infested rice balls. Our Cho Hoi told us that the rice was boiled with fish parts, mostly heads, and when it got sticky it was packed in balls, about the size of softballs. He said that a week's ration was two rice balls and two canteens of water. We thought we had it bad with c-rations.

There was also a corpsman pack that was filled with an assortment of drugs and syringes. There was a big package of heroin, which one of our guys took and put inside his shirt. He said it would be worth a fortune back in the World. We put everything in a pile and blew it with C-4, a powerful plastic explosive. That afternoon we headed back to Argonne. We never encountered any enemy activity, but a lot more abandoned bunkers. It had been a long, exhausting five days, and those of us who made it through felt lucky. We had taken eight KIAs and numerous badly wounded, who weren't lucky.

During the final days back on Argonne (we would stay for another four or five days), we manned the lines at night and ran small patrols during the day. Sometime on Hill 1154, I had lost a large filling out of a bottom molar, and the pain was killing me. A couple of other guys also had dental problems. They couldn't afford to medevac any more men, so they arranged for a dentist to be flown in. When they unloaded, they had a chair and a big drill, which was run by the assistant pedaling. The doctor looked at my tooth and said he would put in a temporary plastic filling and I would have to have it taken care of at a later time at a proper facility. He gave me a shot of Novocain, and with his assistant pedaling he cleaned out the tooth and put in the temporary filling. Almost a year later when I got home and went to my family dentist, I told him the story and he said he was afraid to see what was under the filling. When he took it out, everything was good under it, so all he did was put in a permanent filling. He said he couldn't believe that the field dentist had done such a good job under those conditions. Fifty years later, I still have the tooth with that filling in it.

Late that afternoon, we were manning the lines on the northeast side of the hill. We started hearing radio transmissions from a recon team that was surrounded and taking casualties. They had requested an emergency extract by rope. They were in a valley about 1,500 to 2,000 meters east of Argonne, and with the rough terrain between us it was impossible to get to them in time to help. The chopper arrived, and under fire, extracted the five-man team by rope. They got them out, but I never heard if they all made it alive.

One morning on patrol on the east side of Argonne, we saw a large bulldozer that had rolled down the hill and landed right side up. The story was that it had been dropped on insertion when they were first building the fire support base in 1968. Every piece of metal, wire and glass had been stripped off the wreckage by the NVA. Some of it probably ended up in chi-coms they threw at us. That old dozer sitting in the jungle looked strange and eerie. Another casualty of the hill called Argonne. A little later we found a clear mountain stream and we could see large fish swimming around. A major food source for the NVA. One hillside was loaded with orchid-like flowers. Such a beautiful and peaceful place in the midst of a war. It was hard to imagine all the fighting and death that had taken place on top and on the other side of that hill. For a short while the smell of death was not present. Then it was back to the top of the hill and back to the reality of the war.

On April 2nd or 3rd, we moved out of Argonne for Fire support baseGreen, which was about 8,000 meters to the northeast and had just been built. I said goodbye to Argonne, which had been the most horrifying and deadly place I would experience in my tour. Many had been killed or wounded for life, both physically and mentally. I had been one of the lucky ones. I was twenty and many were younger than me. We had signed up to defend our country and had done our best despite terrible conditions, a formidable enemy and the restrictions that had been put on us by our own politicians. I look back on it as a very difficult time loaded with many memories, both bad and good.

CHAPTER 12

BOOT ON THE GROUND

Sam Gatlin
PFC, 0341, Mortar-man
H&S Company, 1st Bn, 4th Marines

MARCH 19, 1969, ON LZ RUSSELL WHILE CATCHING UP AND
relaxing, Jesse Villanueva said, You can finish your beer, but don't
drink too much. We're going to another hill, LZ Argonne, in the
morning. Find a place to sleep and be ready at first light."

A landing zone, LZ, can be any place where a helicopter can
land. The term in this case meant it was not a fire support base
but rather a hill that can be supported from the nearest firebase.
This one happened to be just at the edge of accurate fire support.
"What did *that* mean?" I wondered. "Oh well, I guess I'll find out
tomorrow."

As I bedded down, rolled up in a poncho liner, a light camou-
flage blanket on the ground, the artillery began firing a barrage that
lasted the rest of the night. This was to prep the LZ we were going
into in the morning. Officially the artillery was used to "soften up
the target," but was more like knocking on the door and saying,
"Y'all want'a come out and play."

"I don't have a good feeling about this," I thought, but managed
to sleep just fine. Maybe a little beer and a couple tokes helped.

Jesse had been in Vietnam since the end of May of the previous year. The Tet Offensive may have been over, but the war wasn't.

In 1968, the nation was in turmoil over the war in Vietnam, Richard Nixon was elected President and had promised to end the war. "Peace with Honor" was what he said. In 1969, that meant the re-supply line from North Vietnam had to be severed. LZ Argonne was located eight klicks south of the DMZ and 1,700 meters east of the border with Laos and many miles northwest of the Khe Sanh valley.

Delta Company lifted in early in the morning along with Charlie Co. They found heavy resistance from the enemy, who were dug in around the hill. A UH-1H helicopter had gone down on the upper LZ with several casualties. It had brought in a recon team at the beginning of the insertion; the pilot killed and co-pilot possibly killed.

We went in on the third wave. We were loaded on to a CH-46 for the flight in; just before landing the door gunner locked and loaded his .50 caliber machine gun. I noticed Jesse and Cpl. Anguiano exchange knowing looks, like, "Oh shit, here we go again." As the helicopter touched down the door, the gunner yelled, "You got three seconds to get off this bird and two of them are already gone, now move, Move, MOVE!"

This was a hot LZ; we were coming in under fire. We piled off and a thought went through my head that this was just like hitting the beach with John Wayne and "The Fighting Leathernecks." That thought didn't last very long. This wasn't a movie, this was for real. "Get down," shouted the grunts. "Snipers."

Jumping from hole to hole, we regrouped and set about getting the mortars set up. The downed UH-1H Huey helicopter on top had to be moved for re-supply. It was pushed off the side into a garbage pit on the north side along with the dead bodies of the NVA. A flare was tossed in to burn it up. With the helicopter made of magnesium alloy, it was completely consumed along with the NVA bodies. The odor of burning human flesh filled the air. The hill had been occupied before and they told us to set up in the old gun pits. Jesse, who was the ammo corporal, didn't think that was such a good idea since the NVA knew where they were and had the hill zeroed in. As we worked, heavy fighting continued on the sides of the hill. There was a bunker a hundred meters or so outside the perimeter on the north side. Jets hit it several times with napalm, flying in low and slow dropping long silver canisters, which tumbled through the air and exploded with a very impressive ball of fire.

When the smoke cleared, they returned fire with their AK 47s. The hole they were in was built with an A-frame in it made from branches from the surrounding forest and filled back in with dirt up to ground level with an opening at either end. I think Charlie Company assaulted the hole. *If it was Delta, please forgive me.* A platoon lieutenant laid down covering fire while a Marine got next to it and threw in a frag; an extremely courageous act. Problem solved. In another bunker was an NVA nurse, they tried to take her alive but she kept throwing Chi-Com (Chinese Communist) grenades at the grunts. She had to be eliminated. That evening someone said it was a darn shame; "We could've had some fun with her." He was about half kidding. "Yeah right," I said.

Don't misunderstand, military discipline has a purpose. We all have a thin veneer of civilization; shatter that shell and what emerges is a barbarian who is capable of incredible violence and deprivation. He must be controlled, and when he has a deadly weapon in his hands, discipline is all that stands between the animal within and a man.

The Marine Corps requires and demands a high level of discipline of its men, and an even higher level of its officers, who can ill afford a charge of conduct unbecoming an officer and a gentleman. The punishment for a breach in discipline can be quite severe, especially in a combat zone. She would have been interrogated, not violated, but since surrender wasn't what she wanted, death was her only option.

Jungle warfare is a highly fluid situation, each side maneuvering for position and advantage. A firefight can erupt suddenly and just as quickly stop. A bold frontal assault is rarely used, usually when it is the best way to, maybe, come out alive.

During the day, one of the Marines was separated from his platoon and captured. His legs had been shattered. A corpsman, we called 'em Doc, stopped to help him with first aid but couldn't stay. The platoon had to keep moving and would come back later, but he was found and captured.

The NVA used him as bait to draw us in. An attempt was made to rescue him, but it was not possible without losing several more. He was tortured for hours in the night until, with one last agonized scream, he died. That corpsman carries deep regret over that to this day. What happened wasn't his fault; he had no control over that. I'm not the only one who's been haunted by those screams in the night, but I knew then and still know that it couldn't be helped. That doesn't make it better, just immensely sad.

That kind of thing didn't help the Chieu Hoi program, though. Chieu Hoi means *I surrender*, but when I heard someone say, "Chiu Hoi my ass, I'm going to kill somebody," I totally agreed.

Early the first evening on LZ Argonne, the sergeant major came to Jesse to tell him that the Red Cross had notified him that Jesse's mother had not gotten a letter from her son in quite some time, so he'd better write a letter home. He wrote one to his mother and one to his best friend, Benny. In the bush where stamps and stationary weren't available, we could use the top from a box of c-rations as a post card, no postage necessary. For some reason, Mrs. Villanueva thought her son was still working at the NCO club. He didn't want her to worry by telling her that he'd gone back into the field.

The next morning, a pallet of HE (high explosive) ammunition for our guns was brought in by helicopter on the lower LZ and we began stowing the boxes in a crater near the gun pits. While carrying a wooden box of three rounds, I noticed the battalion commanding officer, Lt. Col. George Sargent, sitting nearby, conferring with a lieutenant and brushing his teeth. Stacking the box of ammo, I stopped for a brief breather. On top of the hill was the upper LZ where a CH-46 lifted off and gave us a moment of quiet. Suddenly, I heard a whistling sound; no one had to tell me what it was. Dropping in place, I caught a glimpse of the first round as it exploded about ten feet away. Time doesn't always flow at the same rate. In that split second from the whistling to impact and explosion, everything seemed to be in slow motion. Gravity is too slow and the explosion blossomed before my eyes in such detail that I watched it grow with black smoke and red flame marbled together. There is something called the umbrella effect; if you're close enough and low enough, the explosion and accompanying shrapnel go right over you. Not so good for anyone in the immediate area though, since the kill zone is about thirty feet in radius.

They kept coming in all over the hill, 82mm mortars, with devastating effect. We had arrived with seventeen members in our mortar section. When it was over, ten had to be medevac'd along with our section leader, Cpl. Anguiano, who was hit in the neck and shot in the back of both legs. Our battalion commander, Lt. Col. Sargent, was killed instantly along with the lieutenant with him. Jesse had been right behind me when that first round came in. He was ten or fifteen feet back. Being a good ammo corporal, he worked with us to get the job done quicker. We had stacked about half a pallet of mortar ammo in the crater I was in and I didn't think that was a very good place to take cover. If a round hit where I was, there wouldn't be enough left of me to scrape up with a spoon and send home to my mother. So I jumped to a safer location in a hole a few feet away. I decided to stay where I was since I had not had time to be integrated into a gun team, and figured I'd be more in the way asking for directions. The hole I was in was about four feet deep and roughly 9x9 feet square. It didn't have a roof and was open to the sky.

While I was waiting out the barrage, another Marine jumped in with me. He was a radioman for one of our forward observers.

"I've got to do something," he said.

"You go right ahead," I told him. "I'm staying here for now."

He then jumped up and charged out. A minute or so later he fell back into the hole, holding his upper arm, saying, "I'm hit, I'm hit."

"Oh crap," I thought. I didn't have anything on me. I had taken off my utility belt with the field dressing while I worked. What was I going to do for him? I went over to where he lay in the dirt. "Let me see it," I said.

He slowly moved his hand away from the wound to reveal a little scratch on his arm. Burning hot shrapnel really stings when it hits you; it's the big ones you don't feel right away. "Shit," I thought, "I've scratched myself worse falling in the blackberries back home."

Meanwhile, Jesse looked around to see what damage had been done. In the gun pits, where most of the leadership for the section had been, there were a number of wounded. He grabbed some towels to stop the bleeding on the wounded and took one to the helicopter that was coming in. Next he went to Tom, who had caught some shrapnel in the face. Tom was blind in one eye and couldn't see out of the other. As they got to the helicopter; Jesse put the two postcards he'd written in Tom's pocket. As he moved over to let Tom on board, a sniper shot just missed him and Tom was hit again. Running to another Marine with more rounds coming in, Jesse jumped for safety, receiving a piece of shrapnel about an inch long in the back of his leg. Later when that was done, he sat down and felt something wet on his leg. Thinking that a canteen had spilled, he felt his leg and discovered blood on it. The corpsmen said he could medevac out, but he couldn't leave us leaderless.

Back home a week or so later, Benny got the mail with Jesse's postcard and noticed there was some blood splattered on it. He went to see Mrs. Villanueva and learned that she too had received a note from Jesse and it also had blood on it. You can imagine a mother's shock to learn that her son no longer had that nice cushy job in the rear. Despite what he had told her, the evidence was all over the card.

LCpl. Villanueva assumed the position of section leader, communications, and sole operation of the FDC (Fire Direction Center). He reformed the two-gun teams with three each, a gunner, a/gunner, and one ammo man. It was the minimum needed to operate a 81mm mortar in combat. In the gun pit with me were John Parch, the gunner, Ken Silka (Silky) the a/gunner and myself as the ammo man. We were all PFCs, but Marine Corps training had prepared us to interface in any position.

Our two guns faced west across a valley to the hill where the NVA were dug in with their mortars. The heaviest guns they had, but had used very effectively against us. Our FO's (forward observers) couldn't help us. They were either wounded or

139

otherwise occupied. So we engaged in direct counter mortar fire. This required the gunner to swing the bi-pods toward the enemy position and zero the gun sight, looking at the target rather than the aiming stakes. They were trying to drop a round in our pits and we were returning the favor. Just below the gun pits, in the FDC, out pops the grinning face of our fearless leader.

"Give it a turn right, one round H.E," Jesse yelled to the gunners. "Your *other* right, dummy."

Amidst all the confusion, with incoming rounds landing on our hill, we quickly fell back on our training, doing the job in front of us. Parch listening for instructions, Silky feeding rounds into the tube and I setting the increments, elongated tea bags filled with gunpowder, and lining them up against the parapet wall for him. There was no time to think about anything but what we had to do. "Hold fire, hold fire, helicopters in the air." Fast approaching our position were two jets. They came in low and fast, circling the NVA's hill and dropping bombs and napalm. When they had expended that ordinance, they began strafing runs with their 20mm cannon. Each time the jets flew over, they received ground fire from small arms. We could hear it over the roar of the jet engines. Eventually one of them caught one in a critical area and had to limp back to its base. Cost effectiveness may have been a factor in the decision to withdraw the fighter support, but all I knew was that we didn't see the jets anymore. Thanks for the help, anyway.

With our landing zone zeroed in, re-supply became a problem. The wounded had been evacuated but the dead had to wait. After a couple of days, putrefaction set in. Most people have encountered a dead animal that had been there a while, a most unpleasant smell, but it doesn't compare with that of human flesh. There were several bodies laid out on the lower LZ for almost a week. The rifle companies were heavily engaged on and about the hill, and of course there were more casualties. So the decision was made to do an emergency medevac at night. In the foxholes surrounding the LZ, heat tabs were lit, blue tablets used for cooking our canned rations, and just before the helicopter landed a strobe light was set flashing in the center. The wounded and dead were quickly loaded aboard and lifted out.

Water. How often do we take for granted that it will always be there? But when it's in short supply, it is a major concern. Either the first or second day, a water buffalo was delivered to the top of the hill. That is a water tank on wheels that could be towed by a truck but was, of course, brought in by air since there were no roads.

The more incoming we got, the more holes were punched into the tank, causing it to leak. Sticks and chunks of wood plugged the holes and an armed guard was placed on it. That sounds serious, but then we were all armed and water rationing had to be enforced. No one knew how long this would take, and for the moment re-supply was out of the question.

I found a solution to the problem. In our c-rations came fruit cocktail and canned peaches. They had plenty of water and helped to extend my ration. There is one problem with that: too much fruit juice and you get the trots.

"I need a few extra men for security to retrieve some bodies from the bottom of the hill," said a platoon sergeant.

"Oh crap," I thought. They wanted me to go down there in the dark. I wasn't quite a seasoned combat veteran yet and scared as hell. "Uh, Jesse? I've had the shits all day and I don't think I could bring myself back up the hill, much less carry a body too." This was true and a good way to skate this detail.

Night patrols are even more frightening than the day; it gets awfully dark in a tropical forest.

"Okay, Gatlin, you stay here. I'll get someone else," Jesse said.

Even though I think it was the right decision, at that moment I felt a little like a coward but also relieved that I didn't have to go. Fortunately, the retrieval patrol encountered no resistance that night and all came back unscathed. Except for the dead Marines they brought back.

Airlift re-supply, as an option, was attempted. Water would soon become critical so a C-130 flew over and unloaded a water bladder. It looked large, black and uncontrollable. As the aircraft flew over, it was pushed out and landed on the hill. A perfect air-drop except for one thing, inertia. It was a little disheartening to watch it bounce several times and impale itself on the trees to the north. Tighten your belts, Marines; it's going to be a while.

With the absence of close air support from the carrier, we were not left without any air cover. The Broncos, fixed wing twin-engine boxcar aircraft, flew over and around our position. Armed with 20mm cannon and rockets, they were used mostly for aerial observation with teeth. A pallet of mortar ammunition had been air dropped and landed on a finger of the hill outside our perimeter. We couldn't retrieve it without risking the lives of more Marines. The Broncos made several strafing runs at it and eventually blew it up. A Spooky was sent in. Everyone knew about Puff the Magic Dragon. Puff flew during the day and Spooky at night.

Shortly after dark, the drone of a fixed wing, multi-engine, prop-driven aircraft was heard. AC-130 circled over us, dropping three flares suspended on parachutes, and began to lay down an incredible amount of fire from its mini-gun on the hill across the little valley from us. As they opened up above us, the sound exhibited a Doppler effect as the steady stream of 7.62mm tracers, every fifth round, hosed down the enemy position. It sounded kind of like, AHRRRRRRROARRRRR. There is something very comforting about that much firepower looking over you. Sort of like a guardian angel. Spooky stayed on station every night for most of the next week. There were only two aerial platforms with mini-guns in Vietnam then, and to have one of them for an extended time said something about the importance of this action.

Argonne may not have been the biggest battle of the war, but it was the biggest thing going on at the time. You might have seen, *When We Were Soldiers*, about what happened in the Ia Drang valley. That will give you an idea of what it was like. Life doesn't imitate art but sometimes, rarely, art imitates life. When we got there, the hill occupied by the North Vietnamese was covered with trees. By the time Spooky was done, it was covered with wood chips and, go figure, they were still there, and maybe a little pissed off.

The night was relatively quiet, except when Spooky was around. One evening I was standing beside a lieutenant, looking across the valley at a whole section of the opposite hill. At the southern end of the hill, it was more like a ridge; hundreds of lights could be seen laid out in roughly a square.

"There they are," I said. "Why don't we just blow 'em away?"

He just smiled at me and said nothing. My ignorance was showing. I wasn't trained in tactics, only to do the job I was given. I didn't know about tactical diversions and miss-direction, but that seemed to be what they were doing. As it turned out, their positions were at the other end of the hill. The North Vietnamese were not stupid. Out-gunned, with inferior weapons and support, the NVA used anything to give them an advantage. They knew that time was on their side for the overall outcome of the war. This was their country and they weren't about to give up.

A few nights later, deep inside Laos, we saw the headlights of trucks as they came through a pass in the mountains. It was maybe five or ten miles to the west and we couldn't touch them. We had to respect international borders, but they had no such limitations. I tried to count them, but they just kept on coming. It seemed like there were hundreds of them. Intel reported that an entire regiment of NVA was moving in to re-enforce the troops opposing us. Seismic sensors had been placed inside the DMZ to detect troop movements. I guess they wanted the convoy to get through on the Ho Chi Minh trail. The next afternoon the sky flashed over like an arc light and the ground began to shake. We ran over to the north side and saw the carpet-bombing in a valley inside the DMZ. Above we could see the con trail from a B-52. It was already miles past its drop point and heading southwest. The expected regiment never showed up. Thank you, *thank you*, United States Air force.

We pumped out hundreds of mortar rounds, mostly HE (high explosive), some Willy Peter (white phosphorous) to mark a target with smoke and illumination. Willy Peter was also used as an incendiary; at night it made a beautiful explosion like a white chrysanthemum blossoming in all directions. You don't want any to get on you. Smothering it with mud can put it out, but when it's exposed to air again it re-ignites.

As dusk was approaching one evening, we started to shoot out illumination rounds. One of them broke off of its fin section and began tumbling in the air. Floop, floop, floop it went. "Short

Round!!" yelled the grunts in front of us as they scattered in all directions, fearing it was a HE round. That can happen when you use equipment from the lowest bidder.

On one afternoon, I think we were getting close to silencing their guns, but so were they. Parch, Silky and I were operating our gun, keeping our heads down below the gun pit wall as much as possible. They nearly got us with an explosive 82mm round. It landed just behind our magazine; maybe three feet outside, throwing up dirt and gravel that pelted us as we lay on our bellies. Parch and Silky got up after maybe a minute and dusted themselves off.

"Damn, *that* was close," said Silky. "Hey, Gatlin, you okay?"

I was frozen, lying on my stomach and hanging on to my helmet. If I could have said anything, it would have come out something like, "Oh shit, oh shit." But I was mute, shocked. Silky reached down and shook my shoulder. This brought me out of my shock, and standing up I dusted myself off also. "Uh, yeah, I'm okay," I said, but the shock still lingered another minute or so.

During a quiet afternoon, a Chaplin came and gave Mass for anyone who wished to attend. I hadn't been to church since I'd been twelve years old. I just didn't see the point. I had considered myself to be agnostic. If there was a God, I didn't know it, but at this time there seemed to be a very good reason to touch base with whatever was up there, so I attended the service. It was held in a crater with the Chaplin dressed in the full robes of his office. Jesse came from a large Catholic family and had always accepted his faith, but did not attend. He correctly saw that a large group in a combat situation was a potential target. I didn't care; if there was a God and I could die here, I thought it might be a good idea to pray. There are no atheists in a foxhole.

The service came from a book with sermons for appropriate occasions. The priest did not use the 23rd Psalm. The Marine Corps has its own version of that. It goes something like: "Yea though I walk through the valley of the shadow of death, I will fear no evil for I am the meanest son of a bitch in the valley." My prayer was that the fighting and dying would stop and, oh yeah, the other guys too. Unfortunately, I soon forgot that brief moment of faith and went on with the business of war.

Whenever Jesse heard the bloop sound of tubing he looked for any sign that would give away their position. Smokeless gunpowder is used by both sides, but there is a faint whiff of smoke and condensation as the round leaves the tube.

"There, I've got'm," said Jesse.

Finally, we had the position of their guns. All four mortars were put into action for what we called "Fire for Effect." Each gunner gave a turn after each round was fired. Over and down from the top corners and over and up from the bottom. This created a square that placed an explosive round every few feet within the targeted area. Their guns were silenced.

The next day, the grunts assaulted the NVA position but met with heavy resistance. They pulled back and resumed the assault the next morning, taking the hill. It was reported to us that the NVA's six-gun pits were found with craters from our mortars inside. About this time the convoy we had seen earlier was near enough to the border for the aerial observers to call in a fire mission on it. We were given the task of marking their position with smoke. It was out of sight from where we sat, but with a full load of nine increments we could reach out between 3- to 4,000 meters. The aerial observer then called in the fighter-bombers, who proceeded to destroy the convoy. Many secondary explosions resulted as the munitions they were carrying blew. It was also reported that a number of elephants were killed. This was unfortunate, but we didn't press them into service.

The mission was successful. We had eliminated the NVA's blocking force and destroyed a large re-supply convoy. All that was left to do was to pick up and leave. We used our bayonets to slice open every sandbag, dismantling the gun pits and bunkers we had used, leaving nothing the enemy could use against us in the future. The engineers produced a case of C-4, with two sticks missing; even so it was more than forty pounds of plastic explosive and would make a nice hole in the ground, which it did, maybe twelve feet wide and almost six feet deep. Inside this crater we set up our mortar and would shoot out all the remaining ammunition, but first we had a little celebration. The C.P. (command post) had left the hill, leaving behind some chow. Several #10 cans of dehydrated steaks. So a barbecue was in order. That was the best outdoor cookout I've ever had.

As the sun went down, we manned the gun and spent all night expending what we weren't going to carry out with us. In the morning, the gun was dismantled into its four pieces. Gunners hump the bi-pod; a/gunners carry the tube; leaving the inner and outer rings of the base plate to the ammo men. With three rounds strapped to our backpacks, plus all of the gear we needed, each of us were carrying over eighty pounds.

"I thought the colonel liked the gun crews to chopper out? Oh yeah, he's dead," I said.

"That's not it," said Jesse. "We had a helicopter shot down a while ago, leaving another hill, so we're going to walk out of here."

"No problem, I like walking," I said.

It took us two days to go back to Russell, but we were proud of what we had done and walked tall.

As we left, Jesse told all of us, "You're my ace beaucoup, you're my pride and joy. You're ugly but you're still my boys."

Gunny Hayes told Jesse that he would get a medal for his actions on that hill. He had saved several Marines, risking his life, receiving a wound in the process, and held together our much-depleted mortar section, and had effectively saved the whole hill by accurately directing our fire.

CHAPTER 13

SEMPER FIDELIS STEVE BYARS

Richard Everington
CPL, 0331, M-60 Squad Leader,
Delta Company, 1st Bn, 4th Marines

FIRE SUPPORT BASE ALPINE. IT WAS A FREAKISH KIND OF place where the rarest of flukes could and did happen almost daily. It was there I clearly remember seeing stars against a deep blackness with small neon creatures fluttering around, chattering in chaotic unison while I listened to a tiny voice talking to me from inside my brain. My ears were ringing and painfully throbbing. I could barely hear anything from my outside surroundings, as if I was underwater. There were some familiar noises of explosions very close. Awakening to a state of semi-consciousness, I could feel the insides of my head pulsating painfully, as if I had been punched in the face by a gorilla. Fluids flowed out of my nostrils and my mouth, there was the distinct taste of blood, my own. Combined together with the fervidly caustic smell of exploded ordnance, the sickly sweet salty flavor turned my stomach.

Peering through squinted eyelids, I could see straight ahead into the sky. In the distance were some dirty white clouds smudged against the early morning gray sky. It was a beautiful sight but at an odd angle. Low and barely audible sounds continued to emanate from all directions, including gunfire, a lot of it. There was a moment of dead silence between the explosions. It seemed like time itself had stopped. I realized I was lying flat on my back on the hard packed dirt. The continuing dull echoing sounds penetrated deep into my brain, making it almost impossible to think coherently. My grip on consciousness was tenuous and I began to succumb to the drowsiness. I started getting cold, stiffening. The voice in my mind started laughing. That was when I understood it was my enemy and I had to fight to stay awake.

What sounded like the moans of an angry thunderstorm raging miles away manifested into faint whistling resonances, at first a low shrill, then louder. I tracked the sound until I could see some black specs that continued to get bigger, ultimately screaming over me to kill some part of Alpine. Yes, you can see mortar and artillery rounds coming straight at you if you have good vision. My ingrained reflex would be to dive for cover, but I was unable to move physically. My entire body seemed to be paralyzed. I could only endure as a spectator while the heavy artillery rounds shrieked above me by some forty meters and slammed onto the top of the fire support base. The extreme earth tremor vibrations reached through the ground and into my spine. One of the explosion's pressure waves nudged me farther down the hill. Chunks of shrapnel whizzed viciously over, missing my face by inches. Dirt clods, rocks and splinters dropped down from the sky and pummeled me. Dirt dust fell onto my face, burning my eyes with gritty particles that stuck to the insides of my eyelids, causing tears to form and dry almost immediately.

At that moment, barely perceptible, came the familiar *thoop, thoop, thoop,* sound of tubing from mortars. Three tiny black dots appeared in the sky, arching gracefully downward one behind the other, whistling in with determination. I closed my eyes, which was the only thing I could do, and prayed. Recollections of my entire life flooded my mind, all of it except the part about why I was lying out on the side of the hill. People, places, good and bad stuff can blaze through your neural structure when you're at the Grim Reaper's door. Like everyone else, I religiously prayed to Jesus and Mother Mary whenever I was close to being killed. I never prayed as I was killing the enemy, not wanting Jesus to know me as a killer. That's the truth. When in combat you have to have your sense of order.

In 1st Battalion 4th Marines, our first prime directive is **God**. That name, that word is labeled on the battalion's shield, along with Duty, Country and Corps. We always assumed that **He** was on our side.

The rounds thankfully hit and exploded on some other unfortunate designated target. In the ghostly black void, I heard voices. Through partly opened slits of my eyelids, I saw two figures with sweaty faces appear over me.

Somebody shouted, "Get the ammo cans, grab his legs." They hurriedly pulled me by both boots over the dusty hard-packed hillside, the back of my head raked over bits of gravel and detritus. It seemed like a very long time for the torturous ordeal to continue. The back of my head felt like it was on fire.

I couldn't communicate or move. Someone shouted, "Mortars!" They jumped into a crater, pulling me in with them, causing my skull to bang against a rock at the bottom. Seeing shooting stars once more, along with the pain, made me want to slug and thank these guys at the same time. Again, face up I could see the black dots approaching in our direction. The objects were clear to me from my angle, approaching closer than over to explode up near the 105mm gun pits. Menacingly hot and jagged shrapnel flew slightly above us, due to the slope of the hill. More dirt clods, rocks and debris rained down on us. Those guys were hunkered down in the hole face down and didn't see the beauty of it all. I didn't have a choice.

Relieved that the body lugging stopped at least momentarily, feelings of failure and uselessness crept over me, coupled with the need to rest, to fall asleep until the torment was over. Death thinking took hold of me. If I got hit, I wanted it to be direct and immediately fatal, no pain or anguish from seeing my legs blown off. I was too cowardly for that kind of ordeal. I remembered a Marine on LZ LOON with his guts blown out. He wanted me to shoot him, but I gave him my last grenade, the one I was saving for myself. I know his name, but I can't ever remember it. I don't know what happened to him. We were being overrun and I had to run back to my gun position. I have a lot of blank spaces in my Vietnam memories, and sometimes I think Vietnam may have been just a long bad poisonous dream.

As I lay there, all kinds of bad thoughts raced through my mind, like I was probably crippled. I cried, laughed and got angry all in a single instant, used God's name in vain, then quickly begged forgiveness, asking for His mercy.

After the explosions subsided, the ordeal began again. One of the guys pulled hard on my right ankle, and because I was dead weight it felt as if my entire foot was being detached. The pain was excruciatingly intense and really pissed me off. Fear and wrath-laced adrenalin pulsed through me as I emerged from semi-consciousness. I wanted to scream out a curse and strike out at them. At the same moment, there was an opposite urge to drowse off. However, jagged stabs of agony kept me at the edge of the black well and not in it. Years later, I realized that pain prob- ably saved my life because it stopped me from going deeper into the comfortable dark space I was drifting into on that day, March 9, 1969. Inflicting pain into an almost-dead person can keep them alive. The tugging and dragging suddenly stopped and I was rolled unceremoniously into a slit trench, hitting the bottom, luckily, face up. The excruciating pain from the fall made me want to kick the guy who pushed me in.

Still in a semi-conscious state, I was aware but couldn't move or make myself talk. My eardrums were throbbing and everything visible was draped in shades of gray or black. This reality had no color to it, making it all even more surreal. I could make out some shadows of men crouching nearby, excitedly yelling to each other and glancing at me with wide crazy killer eyes, the kind you get when there's death being shared around.

I began to examine my surroundings. Alarmingly, there were shovel and pick marks on the greasy gray dirt walls surrounding me as if...I was in my grave? With that claustrophobic thought a sharp thrust of newfound adrenalin stroked through me force- fully. It freaked me out so deeply my heart started pumping wildly, and so hard I thought it might kill me. The numbness began to recede from my torso and then my limbs. The stiffness began to fade somewhat. Opening my eyes fully, I could comprehend that I was laid out on my back in a trench near a sandbagged bunker. The odor of dirt, blood, sweat and exploded ordinance caused a reflexive convulsion to race up from my bowels. I began uncontrollably coughing out copious amounts of acidic bile. Just in time, I managed to turn my face sideways for it to spill out like afterbirth onto the dirt. It lay there in a smelly putrid pool surrounding my head. It was mortifying, but I finally caught my first full breath of air and could deeply breathe again.

A voice asked, "I thought he was dead?"

A Marine appeared and hovered over me. "No, he's alive, just like I said."

I could just barely hear what they were saying, but it was Steve Byars talking to Norman Beck, both M60 gunners.

From the bottom of the trench, I watched as Steve opened the M60's top cover, locked the bolt back, then pushed the charging handle forward. He checked that the feed tray was in the down position, placed the ammo belt with the first round directly onto the feed tray, then closed the top cover with a firm tap to lock it down. All of it done in a calm, methodical manner, just like a thousand times before. Suddenly there was an explosion, someone cursed and shouted out, "They're in the wire."

Byars moved the gun's selector switch to the fire position and waited. He ordered, "Hold your fire, don't give away our position yet. Wait until they get deep inside the wire and can't go backwards." After a very long pause, Steve took in a heavy breath of air while embracing the gun, took aim, then exhaled while pulling back on the trigger. The gun came instantly alive, shivered gratefully and started to dance, belching out its opus of death. The whole side of the trench line opened up with gunfire. The M60s expended shell casings and belt links ejected out and fell carelessly onto my body and face. Mesmerized, I couldn't stop looking at the gunner's silhouette against the morning's gray sky. Hugging that vicious gun, a beautiful young slayer of men in his killer trance. He was in deep automatic combat mode, not thinking but transcendent and immersed in his own personal kill zone world of murderous death. All of it, sanctioned.

Only grunt machine gunners experience this kind of psychological killing trance state of being while doling out death in mass quantities up close, eye contact and facial recognition close. Close enough to hear bullets hitting flesh and bone. You have visions forever about how shocked and surprised they always appear to be when hit. As if it can't really be happening to them. Up close, you may get eye contact for that last instance of life as they drop straight down into odd shapeless forms. The difference from a rifleman is that a machine gunner has a long belt of ammo and doesn't need to break his hypnotic kill-zone spell when changing magazines. An M60 is a human death instrument, expressly designed to deliver industrialized murder with a touch of the trigger carried by boys, barely men. Steve had that instinctual talent that can't be taught. He was very good at killing them and had the will to do it. Like me, he found he liked it too much. The killing was the easy part, and we all knew the price of admission was getting terminated yourself. That was only fair and even expected. After a while, most machine gunners had their fill and wanted to let go of their joy of wasting other human beings designated as enemy, even those hardcore bastards who were also desperately dying to kill us.

The hot brass casings continued to stream out of the gun's ejector port, descending downward to hit my flesh with a sting, then tumble into the pool of puke. No one noticed my dilemma. One of the casings fell onto my right eyelid, searing the flesh. That hurt enough to finally wake me up all the way. I sat up abruptly, pushing my back up against the wall. Brushing the spent shells off of myself, I was feeling embarrassed, confused and panicked. *Where's my M16?* A scary thought that hit me suddenly. I managed to gather enough strength to pull myself up enough to carefully peer over the sandbags. I saw a group of NVA soldiers gathered down near the base of the hill. Some had AK-47s but most were cradling heavy canvas packs in their arms with fuses already smoking. The one in the pith helmet with the gold star inside a red dot began blowing a whistle and pushing them forward. They all began running through the breached section of concertina wire. Spreading out in a V-shaped formation they continued on with determined faces, humping awkwardly up the cleared and barren slope, straight at our position.

Byars yelled out, "Beck, click it off now!" The assistant gunner squeezed the claymore trigger together, instantly igniting an incredible explosion. The powerful blast created a blinding flash with a visible shock wave that drove ball bearings straight through the bodies of the sappers, pushing them backward and causing their own satchel charges to detonate. There were multiple secondary explosions. Most of their body parts were vaporized into a pink, disgusting mist that clung to the atmosphere in that vicinity, while some of their heads were shot into the air, looking like footballs being tossed for a hail Mary touchdown. The sight was unforgettably horrific as we watched one of the grotesque spiraling heads land right in front of our gun position with a thud. It gazed accusingly at us for a moment. Everyone froze, stunned, and stopped shooting. It might have blinked or twitched? Then, it slowly commenced rolling backward, eventually tumbling all the way back down the hill into the ravine and completely out of sight. After a few moments and a gun barrel change was managed by Beck, Steve grimly fired off another belt of ammo into the elephant grass around where it vanished. We figured he was trying to kill that head. But later said, he was just trying to eliminate any possible hidden second wave camouflaged in the bushes, waiting for orders to attack. Chalk it up to freaky fluky Alpine incident number whatever.

When the shooting eventually tapered off a bit, I started to ascertain that something wasn't right. It was odd that I didn't have my rifle. Hell, that was really bad. I reached for my 45 and it was still buttoned up and in its holster, securely strapped to my right hip. In that free fire zone territory, you always feel naked without your weapon being very close.

My hearing was compromised, but I could feel enemy mortar rounds hitting the hill somewhere nearby and close enough for the dirt kicked up to fall into our trench. The 105s began sending salvoes of rounds outbound toward the surrounding hills. Byars and Beck didn't say anything to me, but I had the impression that I needed to get the hell back to my own position. When the incoming mortars subsided, I limped and crawled back toward the other M60 position under the artillery gun pits. On the way I found my M16 and helmet about forty meters from Steve's bunker. Amongst a dozen mortar craters, my rifle was lying on the dirt, abandoned along with my helmet, which appeared to be wounded. Somehow the cloth cover was half blown off, shredded. I made it with considerable effort to my bunker as my right ankle stiffened and my head pain worsened.

I continued to feel as if I was submerged and must have smelled and/or looked bad, because the guys were acting strange, trying to keep their distance. One of the brothers asked, "You okay bro?" Another voice stated, "Shit, we thought you was'a dead mother'." Before I could lay down to pass out, Doc Overstreet appeared, knocking on the bunker doorway as he entered our squalid little hooch. His thick glasses were taped together in the middle. He dropped a tightly rolled up black rubberized fabric bundle on the floor. The corpsman began opening his kit while stating he wanted to check me out. I could barely hear his words. I motioned for him to speak up.

He said loudly, "I'm here to put a toe tag on a dead Marine. That bundle I dropped on the deck is his body bag."

I stammered, "What the hell are you saying, Doc?"

He looked very tired and then relieved. "The word is there's a body of a Marine on this side of the hill. One that laid out there for a long time, not moving."

I said, "I don't remember being hit, I do remember being out there."

Doc, in his steady manner, replied, "It was rumored that some fool grunt running between bunkers was hit and blown twenty feet into the air, did a full 360, landed on his head, stopped breathing. It was assumed you were dead, so nobody went out to retrieve you. But, apparently, and at great risk they drug your dead carcass off the side of the hill while the enemy mortar crews were using you as a sighting marker. Those two guys righteously deserve a medal. It's highly improbable that you are still living. Unless I'm talking to a dead man?"

The corpsman wiped his brow with the back of his hand and sat down on the sandbags. With a practiced method to his actions, he cleaned his military-issue glasses of dirt, then his hands with antiseptic hand lotion and a strip of white cloth. I pointed to my right ankle. He nodded, then deftly and gently untied the laces, gingerly pulled my right jungle boot off of my swollen ankle. There was one small hole where a piece of shrapnel pierced the laces and the tongue of the boot. I could see a small round bit of metal was embedded into the top of my foot. He pulled it out with tweezers and handed it to me. I took it and flicked it out the bunker door. He found two other small, jagged pieces further up on my calf. The wounds didn't hurt and were not bleeding. He splashed the holes with some red iodine liquid from a bottle marked XXX and labeled Rock Ape blood. It burned so bad it caused tears to form in the corners of my eyes. Then he reached for his needle pack. I immediately motioned that I didn't want stitches.

He laughed, then expertly covered the holes with antiseptic salve, cotton gauze and sticky white tape. After examining and wrapping my ankle, he carefully cleaned out the dried blood from my eyes, nose and ears with Q-tips and water, doing so without causing further pain. He soaked a strip of cloth torn from a military-issue green towel with soapy water and wiped the dried puke from the back of my head and neck. He worked with a practiced, skillful manner worthy of any practical nurse. It amazed me that he had so much stuff in his medical kit pack. I can vouch that he was especially good at being a corpsman, it suited him.

He pointed to my eyelid, which was red and puffy, but I waved it off as being okay. He mentioned that I was getting bald on the back of my head and told me my ear drums were more than likely blown out. Pulling out a small glass bottle of Darvon, he handed me some and said, "For the pain. It's all I can do for now, should get you medevac'd out of here but can't until the Skipper can get more guys to man the perimeter."

I really didn't want to go through the medevac deal anyway, with the hill bracketed with anti-aircraft guns. Screw that. Like everyone else, I hated being back at battalion with the lifers. He told the guys not to let me sleep for at least six hours because of my concussion. He started to leave, then backed up and picked up the bundled body bag. He looked at it, then at me, and kindly said, "It's rare that someone gets to see their own body bag." I had a slight shiver of cold reality shoot through me at the sight of it. I asked him where he was going next.

Looking very exhausted, he shrugged. "I'm going to get some Z's. It's been a busy day. I've already attended to five other wounded Marines before I came here. I saved you for last because you were supposed to be...well, thankfully not. Stay awake for a while."

After he left, I realized that I forgot to thank him. I felt bad about that, so I drank a full canteen of water while downing all the painkillers at once. Almost instantly my wounds started to bleed as I began to feel okay. Don't ever drink water after you get a few random holes blown into your carcass because you might hemorrhage to death. I was glad the holes were small.

Later that day, they went down to repair the wire and look for bodies. No one could or wanted to find enough of a body to count. The guys from Steve's gun team did not report or mention the eviscerated enemy sappers. Fuck that! We had already found out the body count was bull shit! A lot of dirty stinky soul-robbing work for nothing. Plus, you could never get the smell of the dead out of your clothes or mind. Talk about a shit detail, there were no hot or even cold showers in the bush. So at all cost we discouraged finding enemy dead as a matter of group wellbeing and personal hygiene. We killed them but couldn't find the bodies if we could get away with it. Anyone that had enemy body recovery detail once never wanted to do it again. Finding, collecting and counting dead enemy soldiers after a battle was the ultimate crap assignment.

All of it was done just so the brass could add to the score and pat themselves on the back? To heck with that! A Marine dead or wounded, we'd go to hell on earth and back to retrieve. Out in the boonies and whenever possible, from corporal on down, a dead NVA was something we didn't find or know anything about. It wasn't like after five dead enemy soldiers you'd be an Ace. Almost all of our lieutenants were in on it too, but only unofficially, very seldom noticing our dead body blindness. We didn't need the burden of being tasked with carrying the smelly stiff dead weight of corpses around. Or worse, hanging out on some unknown LZ with a pile of rotting flesh, hoping the chopper that didn't want to come finally came before dark.

Vietnam jungle dark is an unforgiving timeless space filled with a wicked blackness that pervades those unexplored mountain ridges and death-filled ravines. Somehow the darkness always creeps unexpectedly over the country before you can prepare for it. Nights in the remote mountain jungle were always chilling because that was when massive starved tigers came stalking you with a vengeance. We all have terror-filled dreams of the night radioman Frank Baldino began screaming as he was grabbed by a tiger and carried away down the hill, the bloodcurdling shrieks getting fainter until they stopped suddenly in mid-yell. The dead silence that followed was complete and the void endlessly deep. Then, they shot off hundreds of flares the rest of the night, hoping to scare off the beast. This infamous incident happened during the Argonne valley operation of November fourteenth, 1968, the first time we were in the Argonne area.

The tigers out there did not fear humans, they were too hungry for that instinct. All their normal game had been spooked away by fighting, so now we were their prey, big cat food. God only knows how many unknowns were inadvertently left behind, wounded out on the battlefield, deserted. At their final moments, the end came as they met their tiger. It was fair, it was sanctioned and had no meaning. Just some freaky fluky shit to be endured by some of us. A few weeks later we heard that some 3rd Recon team had killed a tiger near the Laotian border DMZ area. One of the Kit Carson scouts attached to the battalion exclaimed that he would not go back to that area of operation, and quit. As he was getting on the chopper, he said in a trembling voice that killing that tiger was going to be a curse on anyone going back to Argonne, including the NVA and especially us.

Finishing, the men gathered up the remaining spool of concertina wire along with the splicing tools and turned to climb the hill. The Old Man suddenly appeared about twenty meters up the slope, standing straight as a statue, his arms folded over his chest, looking stern. Everyone froze in place, stupefied. With a hint of a Southern but clear and measured tone, he projected out, "The first man that tries to salute me gets a firing squad in the morning. At ease, gawd dammit! I want the after action report in one hundred words or less by one of you that can tell it raw. Now, and if I sense one bit of bull, this entire squad goes on night patrol for the week. Am I understood?"

His face and body remained drill sergeant rigid, like a stone monument, only the lieutenant colonel's eyes shifted from one Marine to the next, searching for some misstep. The excruciatingly long pause was mercifully ended when Norman Beck, the newest guy in the company, stepped forward toward the commander. They both walked up the hill with Beck talking and gesticulating with arm motions to tell the story. That was Vietnam freaky and may or may not have happened officially, even though we all witnessed it. We should have known that we couldn't get crap past the Old Man. Evidently, he was satisfied with what Beck explained to him and we were off the hook. We heard the early morning incident was logged in as a hard probe from enemy forces. That it was scared off by extreme over-reactionary defensive fire. Luckily, there was so much sporadic gunfire interspaced with incoming and outgoing rounds at all times of night or day that it wasn't even a thing. Although, there was the telltale nauseous burnt flesh odor that emanated from that section of the perimeter. At dusk later that day, a lone F4 Phantom jet screamed over our area and released two canisters of napalm into the ravine where the head had vanished. We all had recurring nightmares of that skull on fire, glaring at us with utter contempt. No orders came down to find body parts in the ravine. The Old Man was old school and usually never tasked us with that kind of work detail while out in the bush, like the rest of the brass bigwigs often did. He was considered too Gung Ho for some of us, if that was even possible. For most, he was simply a real hardcore Marine, looking to fight and kill the enemy whenever or wherever he could find them, and he liked to do it in person. The kind of commander any general would appreciate.

I ended up staying awake that night, high as hell, watching the 105s from 3/12's G Battery working over the treacherous jungle hilltops and stream-laced valleys surrounding Fire support base-Alpine. My M60 bunker was about fifty meters below the artillery pit as a hard point of protection along the perimeter. The night was pitch black surreal, but I was close enough to hear the fire missions coming over the radio. Forward Observer Lt. Andy O'Sullivan and Radio Operator Cpl. David Ovist sent at least one hundred rounds out to designated coordinates of possible enemy activity that night. No telling how many NVA killed, if any, but there was intel on secondary explosions, so munitions were destroyed. Early the next day we were outside the wire, humping the bush, looking for the sites that were hit and of course the NVA, dead or alive. As usual, we didn't find any bodies, just blood trails. That was code for: we didn't care to find them.

About a week later I was medevac'd out while on the fog-shrouded mountain ridge line trail between Alpine and Argonne. Doc had put me on the list with the other walking wounded. My ankle was getting worse with use every day on the ragged mountain trails. I was conflicted on whether to get on that Army Slick in the ebbing light of dusk. The aircraft was waved off twice because of its shaky approach inside the mountain's rapidly expanding shadows. It was almost night when they ignited a flare, and it came in fast and hit the tiny LZ hard, bounced up and down, then settled into a hover of about a foot off the LZ. Doc Overstreet and another Marine helped guys up and into the Slick quickly as possible. Being hesitant made me the last man to board, but I gingerly put my swollen ankle and foot on the skid as shots rang out from below the ridge line. Doc gave me a hard shove as the Huey suddenly lifted, then drifted to the right and plunged downward. It stayed about two meters above the slope of the ridge, picking up speed. I assumed we were going to crash into the stream bed below as I was holding on for all I was worth to the edges of the doorway. Fortuitously, one of the crewmen had me by the flak jacket and pulled me in with a practiced hand. Face down, I kissed the floorboards of that filthy Slick as the turbine engine screamed to full power and lifted upward and we were gone.

Days later, the X-ray showed a hairline fracture, so I got an ankle cast. That only lasted for a week before I cut it off to get back in the field with the guys. When I got back out there, everything had changed. Most of the guys I knew were gone and the ones left were shells of themselves, hollowed out in spirit somehow. Soon the replacements came in and we were back out there, patrolling the strangely familiar but unknowable country, Vietnam.

Lt. Col. George Sargent, Doc Overstreet, Cpl. David Ovist, Lance Cpl. Steve Byars and Pvt. 1st Class Norman Beck, among others, were killed in action on Fire support baseArgonne. Unforgettable Marines, they were truly some of the best of us. A great loss for the battalion and impossible to replace at that time in that place.

I knew Steve Byars as one of the most aggressive M60 gunners in Vietnam. He always had the loudest and hottest gun in any firefight. Exactly what you want from a gunner going up against the bad guys. I do have regrets. I never got to say thanks to Doc Overstreet for patching me up when I was wounded and later for putting me on that chopper. None of us got to thank Beck for smoothing things out with the Old Man that day at the wire. Talk about freaky fluky, a private 1st class talking to a lieutenant colonel? I especially wanted to say thanks to Byars, a real friend who looked out for me. I remember him on patrol wearing Ray-Ban sunglasses while carrying his gun on his right shoulder and gripping the by-pod. He was a pal to most everyone and never complained about stuff like the rest of us.

I have one story that sums him up. We were out in the bush, lined up, hunkered down in an L-shaped ambush, overlooking a partially hidden enemy blood trail. Eventually, two litter teams appeared carrying wounded or dead NVA soldiers. The soldiers doing the carrying were very young women. Teenagers or younger even. I could just barely see them in the dim moonlight. I took aim and was getting ready to fire and set off the ambush when Steve touched my hand on my trigger finger to stop. He gave me direct eye contact and nodded his head no, the signal to wait. I was confused but didn't shoot. The enemy body detail passed by and into the thick undergrowth. We waited for a larger group to appear, but none did that night. I never had the inclination to ask Steve what the deal was and just chalked it up to nerves, something to mention at some later date. Some time after, I understood what happened. We were both killers, but somehow Steve had already transitioned from killing for killing's sake, to one who had mercy when warranted. Steve usually had something good to say about anybody he knew. I think HM3 David Overstreet would have been an outstanding medical doctor if he had lived. He had a likable and sincere personality that made you comfortable in his presence, a good man I once knew.

In Vietnam, with the political leadership dropping out and abandoning us without a clear goal, and as our own people turned their backs on us, we lost the will to help these people who could not fight for themselves. Not one of us volunteered for that kind of disrespect and dishonor. No one is to blame for what happened in Vietnam, but there are those who are guilty of looking the other way when we Vietnam combat veterans came home. The America we blended into was one that forgave the draft dodgers and made them into presidents. Hollywood created guys like Rambo, who made them tons of money, while we couldn't get hired by managers who were distrustful or didn't want to take a chance on a possible psycho case that would go postal at work. Gratefully, that's all in the past and if someone can figure out what the hell happened, don't bother us with your answers or conclusions. It was just freaky fluky shit and had no meaning.

To this day, I still don't recall the week right before being hit on Fire support baseAlpine, only the memory of waking up on that hill in extreme jeopardy. We veterans from those battles of the undeclared war will never forget the grinding everyday ordeal of surviving our own personal Vietnam. I don't have dreams of that body bag that was meant for me any longer, but on occasion, when I hear the choppers I recall the shadows and spirit of my brothers forever on patrol at Fire support baseArgonne.

Semper Fidelis, Steve Byars and Doc Overstreet

Rick Everington and Walter "Scotty" Scott returning from a patrol
photo credit - Rick Everington

An unknown CH-46 crew member with two NVA bullets lodged in his helmet.
photo credit - Jim Berg

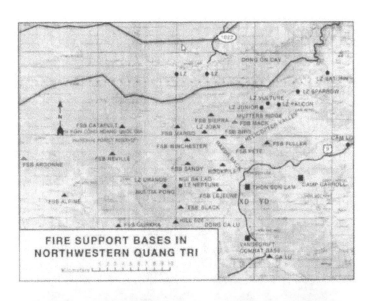

FIRE SUPPORT BASES IN
NORTHWESTERN QUANG TRI

I think we all did this one.

Dale Riley with his .50 caliber machine gun for his CH-46 of HMM-262.
photo credit - Dale Riley

View from Argonne's lower LZ looking towards upper LZ.
photo credit - Jody Caldarulo

Picture Taken about 15 min after securing the top of Argonne.
photo credit - Doc Hays

Andy O'Sullivan and David Ovist. The last picture of David alive.
photo credit - Andy O'Sullivan

Golf 3/12, 105mm howitzers on upper LZ
photo credit - Bill Black

From (L) Max Baer (KIA Argonne), Tom Bartlett (WIA Argonne),
David Ovist (KIA Argonne), Lt Caldwell (WIA Neville)
photo credit - Bill Black

Glen Compton's view of his fighting position.
- photo credit - Glenn Compton

Looking North right after a F-4 Phantom bombing run.
photo credit - Glenn Compton

View from upper LZ looking West to the lower LZ
photo credit - Glenn Compton

Recon UH-1H, #68-15340 on upper LZ
photo credit - Glenn Compton

UH-1H, #68-15340 Front view of the bullet riddled windshield.
photo credit - Glenn Compton

More bombing runs by the F-4 Phantoms.
photo credit - Glenn Compton

Perimeter view of Argonne.
photo credit - Bill Black

Corpsmen (HM) Robert Hays (L) and Bob Biebel (R) at their fighting position.
photo credit - Robert Hays

Steve Eklund (front) and unknown Marines on Argonne.
photo credit - Bill Black

Bill Black in front of the UH-1H that was rolled off upper LZ.
Photo credit - Bill Black

Unknown 1/4 Corpsman (HM) on Argonne.
Photo credit Glenn Compton

Unknown Marine at hootch
photo credit - Bill Black

Steve Eklund (L), J.P Young (R) with new Marines reading
Stars and Stripes newspapers. photo credit - Bill Black

3rd Plt, Delta Co. Marines discussing situation on Argonne.
Photo credit - Bill Black

Tim Marquart after recovering from wounds at FSB Neville.
photo credit - Tim Marquart

After Argonne, at FSB Alpine. From (L) J.P Young, Dave Nelson,
Gary Booker, John Arsenault, Bill Black. Photo credit Bill Black

Bill Black and Max Baer on patrol.
Photo credit Bill Black

From (L), Joe Michaels, Mark Abplanalp, Gary Smelcer
photo credit - Mark Abplanalp

John Arsenault in DMZ, after leaving FSB Argonne.
photo credit - John Arsenault

Jim Berg before a flight at Phu Bai.
Photo credit - Jim Berg

Jim Berg's CH-46 ready for a flight at Phu Bai.
Photo credit - Jim Berg

Larry Deason and unknown Golf 3/12 Marine at Khe Sanh.
Photo credit Larry Deason

LZ Stud - AKA Vandegrift Combat Base (VCB)
Photo credit - Kinser

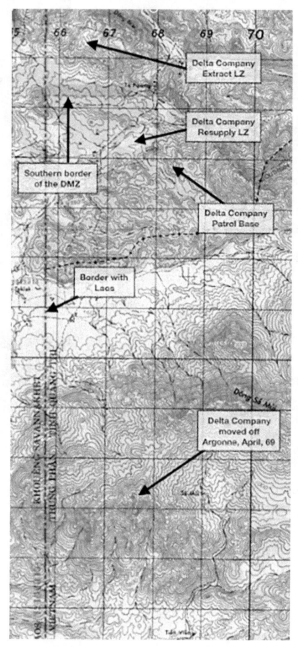

Delta Company's movement north after leaving FSB Argonne

178

Hill 1308 in 2019, where FSB Argonne was located.
Photo credit - Thomas Gourneau

CHAPTER 14

SHORT TIMER

Marcelino Anguiano
Cpl, 0341, Mortar Section Leader
H&S Company, 1st Bn, 4th Marines

ABOUT 200-250 MARINES AND I ARRIVED AT THE DA NANG AIR

Base, Da Nang, Vietnam, on the first week of April 1968. Supposedly, we had arrived just as the Tet Offensive (Vietnamese New Year celebration) had ended on the last week of March. Right away they separated us into groups by MOS and we were assigned to different barracks. Of course, all the 0311s, 0331s and 0341s were kept in barracks separated from everyone else.

We were not issued any weapons or armor gear of any kind the first day we arrived. I myself thought, "We must be in a secure area and we don't need weapons to defend ourselves." Well, was I wrong? Later on that night, we were awakened as "rockets" were hitting the air base strip and we found ourselves scrambling to find bunkers to hide in. That's when I realized, "What the hell did I get myself into? And where can I find a weapon of some kind in case we get overrun?" I am not ashamed to tell you that I was one scared puppy. Now I know why dogs are afraid of thunder. I and the rest of the Marines there with me were scared shitless. I did not move from inside that bunker until the following morning, when they called us out to be loaded onto 5-ton trucks to take us to our new homes.

Well, after they fed us some C-rations, a formation was held and names were called out and we were assigned to different groups. About fifty Marines, including myself, were assigned to a truck convoy that was going south of Da Nang to join the unit we were assigned to. Again, to my surprise, we were not issued any weapons or armor gear to wear while we were trucked down to our unit. One of the Marines on our truck got wind that we were going to the 27th Marine Regiment Compound, about twenty to twenty-five miles south of Da Nang. Well, here we were, about fifteen Marines per truck, just taking a Sunday drive down to this compound where the 27th Marines were at, with no weapons. The only security we had was a 50 caliber machine gun on a turret atop the truck, with the gunner scanning the area as we're driving down the road.

Everyone was crouching down into the bed of the truck as far as they could. I was thinking, "If I hear a round go over my head, I'm jumping out of this bad bear and into a ditch and take my chances." It seemed like forever before we arrived at the 27th Marines location. Upon arriving, we were met by the Admin Section of the 27th Marines and we were called out by name and asked what MOS we had. All of the 0311s were separated into a group, along with the 0331s. As a 0341, I thought, "I'm going to be assigned to H&S Co, 81 mm Platoon." **Wrong**. I was assigned to Bravo Co, 60mm Mortar Section, Man, was I disappointed. It was like going from shooting a 16 gauge shotgun to firing a 22 cal. rifle. At the time I figured, "What the hell, I can handle this little peashooter."

It was there at the battalion area we were issued our weapons and armor gear. I thought we were going to be issued the M-14 rifle, but instead we were given the new M-16. I took a look at it and I couldn't tell "shit from shinola." The day after, we were taken to a small target range to zero in with the weapon and get our battle sights. The rest of our battle gear (helmet, cartridge belt, magazines, canteens and backpacks) was a gimme. That afternoon we were trucked out to the position of the Bravo Company, who at the time were conducting patrols in the vicinity. The 60mm Section was with the company headquarters. When I arrived there, I was taken to the mortar site on a "mule" (M274 Mechanical Mule ATV). This was where I met my mentor, Cpl. Clifton L. Broyer. He was a Marine's Marine. He taught me a lot about survival and how to take the good with the bad. He was like me, he wanted to be something else besides a mortar man, and he wanted to be a M60 machine gunner so he could be where the action was. He had joined the 27th Marines when they arrived here from Kaneohe Bay, Hawaii, a couple of months before I arrived. They were on a six-month deployment and were due to return to Hawaii in August of 1968.

He, along with the rest of us newbies, was transferred up north to the 4th Marine Regiment in Dong Ha. When we all arrived there, we were separated... he went to one of the line companies, I believe Charlie Company, 1st Battalion, 4th Marines. I myself was assigned to Headquarters and Service Company (H&S), 81mm Mortar Platoon, 1st Battalion, 4th Marines. All of us were dispersed to our assigned companies as they flew us to LZ Stud (later in 1968 renamed to LZ Vandegrift).

It was there I met my longtime friend, LCpl. Jesse Villanueva from Yakima, Washington. Jesse and I hit it off as if we had been friends forever. I was assigned as a gunner in his section, and within a couple of months I was promoted to corporal and assumed the duties as section leader for the 4th Section of the 81's Platoon. He became the ammo sergeant of our section.

During our stay at LZ Stud, seldom did we have enough personnel to complete a full section. Although we had to provide fire support for the companies, or when different forward observers called in fire missions, we had to man the mortars with the gunner/a-gunner and maybe two or three ammo carriers per gun. That was pretty much our situation when we had to man a fire support base that we were assigned to. When the sections were back at LZ Stud, we were given the opportunity to clean the mortars, clean personal weapons and maybe take showers. It was also the time for the company gunny to use our personnel for working parties, such as "burning the shitters." Mostly, we would run mock fire missions to keep our gunners/a/gunnersmore proficient on setting up the mortar as quickly as possible and train the ammo carriers on the mortars so they too could be proficient at manning the mortars.

During the months of September through November, our 81mm section was assigned to different fire support bases all along the southern region of the DMZ (Demilitarized Zone). These fire support bases included LZ Mike, LZ Alpine, LZ Sheppard and LZ Russell and last but not least, LZ Argonne. Our mission was to provide fire support for the infantry companies in our area. We also provided fire missions for any forward observer (sometimes artillery FO's) that would call in for fire support on enemy targets as well. Sometimes we would occupy these fire support bases for two to three weeks at a time.

The following is a recollection of events that took place from the month of November 1968 till March 21, 1969, for the 4th Section, 81mm Mortar Platoon, 1st Battalion, 4th Marines leading up to the "Battle of LZ Argonne."

Fire support base(LZ) Argonne (also known as Hill 1308) was a U.S. Marine fire support base located northwest of Khe Sanh, Quang Tri Province in South Vietnam, approximately two kilometers east of the Laotian border. You could say that it was right on the corner of Laos and the DMZ. It provided good observation of the North Vietnamese Army transporting weapons and other supplies by using the roads in Laos to infiltrate into South Vietnam. The Marines of 2nd Battalion, 4th Marines built the fire support base from 4-11 November 1968. Because of U.S. policy, the Marines could not call fire missions into Laos to try to destroy the convoys carrying all those supplies. Eventually, the fire support base was abandoned. Before it was abandoned, the 1st Battalion, 4th Marines relieved the 2nd Battalion on the second week of November and occupied the fire support base until the 18th of December 1968.

After leaving LZ Argonne, our section was flown into LZ Russell to provide fire support for the infantry companies occupying the firebase. We stayed there for a period of about two weeks. Not that I didn't mind, but it seemed to me that we were just jumping from fire support base to fire support base with hardly any action. As we were getting comfortable with our new fortified bunkers and FDC, we got the news that we would again be moving to another firebase, "So get your shit ready." It was kind of ironic because the battalion we relieved at LZ Argonne was the same that was relieving us at LZ Russell.

The battalion commander informed us that we would be sharing the fire support base with the Army. The firebase, none other than the infamous "Rockpile," was going to be our next hotel for no telling how long. I used to hear stories about that place, and I wondered, "Why is our battalion commander punishing us?" Come to find out that it was one of the safest places to be. The fire support base was literally an inaccessible location, it could only be reached by helicopter, but it made a very important and essential observation post, both for the Army and Marine Corps. The best thing that could have happened to us was that the Army had a mess hall there, so we got to eat hot chow and "mid-rats." We certainly took advantage of the situation, believe me. Once again, we packed up our gear after a couple of weeks and we headed to LZ Mike and then back to LZ Stud.

At LZ Stud, we started to receive new personnel, little by little. Our platoon and sections started to get back to almost full strength. We started to train our new people on the guns to get them ready in case we were to be flown to another firebase. I wanted to make sure they were familiar with the mortar from top to bottom. I knew there was something in the air, I could just feel it. I was beginning to be a "short timer," and I was hoping that the administrative section of the battalion had not forgotten about me. Well, needless to say, they did. I kept looking at the calendar and counting the days, and I had calculated that I only had about fifteen to twenty days left in-country. Well, low and behold, we got orders to pack our gear and get ready to fly out to a place where we would be given a so-called in-country R&R. I knew it; something was coming down the pike. When we arrived at Cua Viet, a secure area, the battalion had prepared a "going away dinner" for us. We were resupplied with ammo, new jungle fatigues, and water. We were given a "hot meal" and some even attended a small USO show that was in the area.

All the company commanders, platoon commanders and section leaders were assembled with the battalion commander to receive the orders of the retaking of LZ Argonne. Right at that moment, I realized that "something was in the air" was about to come true. After we were dismissed, I gathered my ammo NCO, L/Cpl. Villanueva and told him the news. We gathered the rest of the section and gave them the word about the retaking of LZ Argonne. I took Jesse aside and told him, "Look, I got a bad feeling that I may not make it this time, and if something happens to me, make sure you take care of the section, because they are going to depend on you to lead them."

On March 20, 1969, my section of 81mm mortars boarded the CH-46 that was to fly us into LZ Argonne. As we sat in the chopper, shoulder-to-shoulder, we looked at each other with blank stares. We didn't have any idea as to what awaited us at the LZ. All we knew was that when we disembarked the helicopter, we were hitting the deck running and setting up the mortars to provide fire support to whoever we could. Fortunately, I had kept the old maps of the firebase, so I knew more or less the area we had to concentrate on when we had to provide a barrage of rounds for counter-battery fire. We didn't know if we would have ammo waiting for us on the LZ, so we each had to carry at least two rounds of HE (high explosive) on our backs, so when we landed, we had some ammo to fire. This was apart from the mortars the gunners/a/ gunnershad to carry. I believe that some of our line company personnel also carried some rounds for us too.

As we approached the LZ, we kept circling around and around and we could see from the portholes on the helicopter all the smoke coming from atop the LZ. I asked the crew chief why we were not landing, and he looked at me with those big eyes and said, "We can't land because it's a hot LZ, and they are receiving incoming artillery and mortar fire from the NVA." We were waiting for the "air support" to fly over the LZ to take out their positions. It seemed like we were up there forever.

Finally, the chopper started to descend and I knew it was the moment of truth. Previously, we had occupied the lower LZ at Argonne when we had relieved 2d Battalion, 4th Marines in

November of 1968. The LZ was facing west toward the Laotian border. The crew chief of the helicopter had said that all the artillery and mortar fire was coming from that direction. As the CH-46 landed, we ran out and immediately started to set up the mortars. I was kind of skeptical to set the mortars in the same mortar pits as before. Because the LZ had been abandoned, it was easy for the NVA to have access to the fire support baseand boobytrap all the bunkers and gun pits. That was exactly what they did. The battalion sergeant major met me and I told him that I was setting the mortars away from the old pits. Well, little did I know that the battalion commander and the sergeant major occupied the old FDC bunker that I had previously.

As we went around checking the LZ, we were stumbling over dead and burnt bodies of NVA soldiers that had been recently killed and ones that were burnt the day before by napalm. If you have ever smelled a burned body, you know that it is a horrible smell. We continued policing up the immediate area and trying to reinforce our positions for the gun pits. After the fire support basehad been bombarded for two days, it seemed as though a tornado had swept through the area. Nothing was intact anymore. We tried to scrounge up some sandbags that were not completely destroyed so we could reinforce our gun pits and also dig some fighting holes for us to take cover, in case of incoming fire.

During the night, we could hear sporadic fire going on outside the perimeter. On the morning of the 21st of March, "the day after," at around 7:00 AM, we got the first barrage of mortar fire from across the Laotian border. We had just gotten up to police the area and try to make the LZ a little cleaner and to work on fortifying our positions. I remember hearing a whistling sound in the air. In a split second, the round exploded about ten to fifteen yards where I was standing. Hearing the whistle sound, my first reaction was to hit the deck, facing down and trying to cover my head at the same time. And then another round and another hit the LZ. At first, I didn't feel any pain, and immediately I yelled to my section, asking if anyone was hit. I heard no response because I couldn't hear anything. My ears were humming from the blast that the round had made when it exploded.

As I started to look around, I felt a burning pain on my neck, and saw the blood all over my flak jacket. My left hand started to burn and I could see a piece of shrapnel sticking out of my wrist that had penetrated through my watch. It was protruding about an inch out of my wrist and on my left thumb was another piece of shrapnel that had gone completely through on both sides. It was then that I started feeling the burning pain of all the shrapnel in my body. I looked toward the FDC bunker, where the first incoming round hit, and I saw the battalion commander and the sergeant major lying on the ground with their bodies unrecognizable. One of our gun pits was no more than ten yards away from the FDC bunker, so I knew that some of my people from the mortar section had been wounded or killed. I felt so helpless at that moment because I couldn't move to do anything to try to help anyone, because I myself was lying there bleeding. I knew something had to be done, so I started to get up and run to the nearest gun pit and set it up to return fire, because I knew where it was coming from. As I got up and started to run, I felt like someone had hit me on the back of my legs with a two-by-four. I didn't find out what it was until I arrived at Dong Ha, at the medical hospital. Apart from the shrapnel wounds, I also got shot on the back of both legs by enemy fire just outside the perimeter.

When I woke up, I was in the FDC bunker, all bandaged up. Along with me were some of my section personnel who had been wounded when the barrage hit the LZ. L/Cpl. Villanueva came into the FDC bunker to check on how I was doing and asked me what I wanted him to do.

I looked at him and told him, "It's your section now, and do what we trained together to do." The barrage of artillery and mortar fire kept pounding the LZ throughout the morning as the medevac helicopters were trying to land on the LZ to take out the wounded. They were hovering around the LZ for a few hours until air support from the jet fighters of the Marines and Navy were able to knock out the NVA artillery and mortar sites. Finally, after the mortar fire was suppressed, the medevac helicopters flew in and started to take the wounded out of the LZ. As I recall, the first helicopter landed, it came in with guns blazing, firing into the direction of the incoming mortar fire. I could not believe how good the CH-46, twin .50 cal machine guns sounded, tearing up the jungle. They were awesome in spraying the area while the wounded were being loaded. L/Cpl. Villanueva and Mark Abplanalp carried me into the helicopter.

As I flew away from LZ Argonne, I look down and I felt that I had abandoned my section of mortars. The only consolation I had was that I had left the section in good hands. My best friend and comrade L/Cpl. Jesse Villanueva was in command and all would be well in hand.

CHAPTER 15

CORPSMAN UP

Robert E. Hays
HM2, USNR, Corpsman
1st Bn, 4th Marines Command Group

ON MARCH 20,1969, WE WERE DIRECTED TO GO TO FIRE SUP-
port base Argonne, the northwestern-most fire support basein
South Vietnam. The battalion commander, Lt. Col. Sargent sent a
UH-1H Huey up to look things over before we were to go in. The
Huey got shot down. The colonel decided to go anyway and the
assault was on.

We had six CH-46s to launch our operation with; each CH-46
would only hold about twelve or thirteen men. We sent two at a
time, so we didn't exactly overwhelm the NVA holding the hill
with a massive show of immediate force.

I was on the third round of helicopters in. In other words,
by the time I got there, we had landed about fifty men and had
been engaged for maybe ten minutes at the most. As the helicopter I was in began its descent, we could hear small arms fire
everywhere. Our machine guns were going, stuff was happening
everywhere. Looking out the window as we approached the LZ
(Landing Zone), we could see a pitched battle in progress. The
ground was exploding everywhere on the hill as rounds of small

arms, mortars, RPGs (Rocket Propelled Grenades) and other munitions landed all over it.

As we hurled toward the LZ, they told us to roll off and exit in a hurry when the helicopter reached around six feet off the ground. We were either going to get off while it was going down or going up, for it wasn't going to stay there waiting on us to move off. Marines started jumping off it when it was still five feet or so above the ground. By the time it touched down, it was empty of passengers and ready to get out of there fast. It just sort of bounced, as I recall.

On the ground, with small arms fire everywhere, mortar rounds going off, and utter chaos everywhere, there is but one thing that runs through your mind: get to the top and kill all the people you can identify as being on the other side before they get you. There is a drive that takes hold of a person and makes him do something he would not usually do: go through bullets to stop the bullets and hope there's not one there destined for him. To stop and try to hide would be suicide. It's the fastest who survive in this action — or at least, who have the best chance at it.

So we shot our way to the top and held the hill. It was ours, but we had a tiger by the tail. Smoke was oppressive from burning trees, set off I suppose from all the explosions. We were still taking small arms fire and mortar rounds from neighboring hills. Dr. Sheppler and a couple of corpsmen, Rick McGaffick and Bob Biebel, and I found a depression in the hillside and began to construct a hooch over it before the NVA got mad and tried to take it back.

After it was over, as I remember, there were thirteen dead Marines laid out on the LZ to be taken away. One of them was a fellow named Stephen M. Frye from Citrus Heights, California. Just a few days earlier, he had asked me to cut all his hair off because of the heat, since I also served as a company barber, and I had refused. I told him that if he got killed, I didn't want his mother mad at me when he got home with no hair. He went home with a good haircut.

One particular incident that I remember occurred when a lieutenant asked for a group of men to go to the base of the hill and wipe out a machine gun nest that had been giving us a hard time. They took M-79 grenade launchers and went down the hill. The plan was apparently to take the nest and emerge as heroes. As the small group of four or five slipped out of the lines for the nest, they made two mistakes. First of all, they sneaked too close to the nest before they began firing into it. If memory serves, an M-79 grenade had to twist something like thirteen times before it would be armed. That way, it wouldn't go off too close to the one firing it if it hit a tree or something. These guys were so close to the nest that the grenades wouldn't arm before they got there. I heard someone say later that after the action was all over, they found a pile of grenades on the floor of the nest.

The second mistake they made was leaving the perimeter without telling anyone. That mistake proved particularly costly, because while they were down there shooting unarmed grenades into the hole, someone on top decided to call in some shelling of some sort on the nest, also. And since these guys were so close to it, they got all shot up, also. Suffice it to say that the lieutenant was in hot water.

As we sat on the hill trying to establish some order to be able to take care of the Marines, an officer and senior enlisted Marine came up for treatment of their "wounds." One of them had a strawberry scrape, as I remember, and the other must have had something equally heinous. I looked down at the LZ and saw the dead Marines waiting to be taken out, while these so-called leaders were whining up to the Doc so they could get another medal – a Purple Heart.

I don't remember everything I said to these two "casualties," but I do remember some others telling me I needed to be a lot more careful in what I said to whom. All these two were interested in, it appeared to me, was furthering their own careers by collecting medals, and the dead Marines on the LZ apparently didn't mean squat to them. I remember saying something about how I ought to put myself in for a Heart for a scratch I incurred on my finger coming up the hill.

The next morning, Dr. Sheppler, McGaffick, Biebel, and I were trying to dig a hole in which to jump in case of mortar attack.

The going was slow; the mountain was like solid rock. We were between the position where Lt. Col. Sargent and Lt. Carl Wilson were standing and the location of the big guns. The two officers and the guns were about twenty-five feet either side of us, respectively. All of a sudden, an explosion occurred right at the feet of the two officers. The lieutenant colonel and the lieutenant were killed instantly, with no apparent mark that I can remember. The four of us digging the hole decided it was time to try it out, so we jumped in it. That was when the reality of how shallow it was set in. It could not have been more than eight or so inches deep by then. We flattened out as much as possible to await whatever was ahead. Then another mortar round landed and went off. This one was between where the two men had been and our "hole." The NVA were trying to get their mortars zeroed on our gun pits, and we were between where their rounds were impacting and where they wanted them to. They had to go through or over the four of us in the hole! The next round landed inches from the lip of the hole on the right side, and I was the right side man. It could not have landed more than a foot away, and all the dirt and shrapnel went somewhere else. God had kept me safe thus far. I wondered, where would the next round land? It landed on the left side of the hole! They had skipped right over us! Then they put a few among the guns and called off the attack for a while. We decided to quit trying to dig a hole in rock, and go back to trying to reinforce the hooch over the depression we had acquired when we first got there.

The afternoon we took Argonne, one of the officers got medevac'd out. He left his pack. Later, some guys were going through it, and found a bottle of Christian Brothers brandy. There were six or so of us in the hooch; we all wanted to share with each other, of course, so we devised a way to stretch the brandy, so we invented a new drink: the Argonne 82. The reason we called it that was because the NVA had 82 mm mortars, we were on Fire support base Argonne. The recipe was the officer's brandy and anything else. Canned peach juice would do. Kool Aid. Whatever someone had would be fine, as long as the brandy was in it. It wasn't very good, but we had a good time joking around about it.

Argonne was a high stress situation. We were mortared several times a day from an adjacent hill. Someone sitting on his hooch would hear the *whoosh whoosh whoosh* of several shells leaving their tubes, and he would yell, "Incoming!" and everyone would jump in a hole for a few minutes. We had lots of rounds land on top of our hooch, but none ever got through. We just got dirty, but who could tell, or who even cared, after a while? We called in air strikes day after day against the adjoining hill where the NVA were tunneled in. The jets would roar past, drop bombs, and as they were flying off, we could hear an NVA machine gun firing after them. Their tunnels were something else in that hill. Five hundred-pound bombs didn't faze them. We tried to spot them, and couldn't. They were better at that stuff than we were.

Our patrols got ambushed every day. We would send one out and the NVA would let them alone until about dusk. Then they would ambush it. It would be around 10:00 PM or so before they would get back to the lines with the wounded and dead. My job and that of the other corpsmen would then be to start IVs on the LZ with red-lensed flashlights (as though the NVA didn't already have the LZ zeroed in), and arrange stretcher teams to get the wounded on board. Then we'd call in the medevac helicopters, and when they would swoop down to pick up their loads, the teams would get the wounded on as quickly as they could and head for holes because the mortars were going to start landing immediately.

This went on night after night. Mortared all day, harassed all night. I had at least five mortar rounds land within five feet of me, and no telling how many landed on top of our hooch. This went on until the 4th of April, seventeen days of non-stop stress. By then it had been some twenty-five days without a bath. Sleeping, eating, living in dirt. We had dirt in our beards and in our hair, in the skin under them. It wasn't until days after we got to the rear before we would be able to get all the dirt washed out of us.

When we left Argonne, I wrote home that I left the hill with no regrets except that there were still some live NVA there. I had changed in my attitude toward them completely. The doctor put Rick McGaffick, Bob Biebel, and me in for a Bronze Star for our part in the action on Argonne, but there had been no heroism on our part; we had simply done our jobs. It was downgraded to a Navy Commendation Medal with Combat V (for valor under fire) device.

When I got to the rear later, I discovered someone had indeed put me in for a Purple Heart and it had been approved. About all that can be said for it was it was legal. I received it; however, in 1998, I wrote my US Senator, Trent Lott, and asked him to begin whatever process was necessary for me to return it and have its award expunged from my service record. God had protected me all the way through the Vietnam experience, and my taking that award was almost, to me, a slap in His face. In addition, I felt that in no way did I deserve that for a scratch when so many others gave so much more. The word I got back was that an award could not be legally expunged. After several more attempts, I gave up the effort

As it turned out, Rick McGaffick and I did get our Navy Commendation medals (with V device for valor) for this action and for others — mainly just for doing our jobs well. Biebel never got one. I always thought that was an egregious oversight that should have been rectified.

CHAPTER 16

SIXTY-EIGHT DAYS

Jody Caldarulo
PVT, 0311, 2531, Field Radio Operator
Delta Company, 1st Bn, 4th marines

ON MARCH 20TH, WE WERE ON THE OUTSKIRTS OF FIRE SUP-
port base Alpine, where the CH-46 helicopters were coming in to
pick us up to take me and the rest of 1st Platoon to Argonne, which
was the last platoon to go to.

Prior to the Marines landing, the first helicopter in was an
Army UH-1E Huey on the upper landing zone, and as it touched
down, the NVA ran up to it and fired, the pilot was killed and the
NVA that were in the defensive positions on that hill.

The first platoon that was inserted was the 3rd Platoon, followed by 1st Platoon and lastly 2nd Platoon. A couple of days
before that, I had become 1st Platoon radio operator. So I was
attached in everything I did to the platoon commander. I got to
hear all the things that were going on whenever he heard it. In
any case, several properties, you know, the first two platoons had
gone. 3rd Platoon had hit Argonne and were under fire because it
was not a cold LZ. 1st Platoon finally got aboard a helicopter, and
it was a rather eventless flight into Argonne.

As we came into the lower LZ, 1st Platoon was assigned security for the artillery, so we were on the west side of our guard up

the lower LZ with positions all around where the headquarters was, on the edge of the upper landing zone about fifty yards in from the wire that surrounded Argonne.

By the time 1st Platoon got there, the fire support base had been secured. We were still taking fire, both mortars and small arms from outside the wire from the west throughout the first day and completely that night. We were worried of being overrun by the NVA, We had support from Puff the Magic Dragon (C-47), which was flying around. The next night, Puff wasn't there, but Basketball was. Basketball was a C-130 built just like the C-47 Puff the Magic Dragon. Only difference was the C-130 had tons of flares to drop. They literally turned the night into daylight continuously and also fired their guns outside the wire on suspected positions. This was my very first assault in my career and I felt that it went very successfully as we secured Argonne.

One of the occurrences on the second day (March 21st) was from mortar fire that involved battalion Lt. Col. Sargent. He was hit, and eventually word made it down to my foxhole that they needed help getting the lieutenant colonel down to the lower LZ. I volunteered for it and went up the hill to his position, which was not that far from my position. As I arrived to render assistance, I noticed the lieutenant colonel was not wounded. He was deceased. He had been hit in the head with mortar round shrapnel as he was outside of his bunker. We put the lieutenant colonel inside a poncho and carried him down to the lower LZ, where we designated a location near my foxhole to store the dead bodies of our comrades. The helicopters couldn't come in because of the mortar fire that the NVA would fire at us every time the sound of a helicopter came to support us. The NVA had the landing zones zeroed in with their mortar rounds. They couldn't miss that LZ. So the wounded and the dead had to wait.

The next couple of days we took mortar fire, hit or miss mortar rounds they fired on us when helicopters would come in. Or if they happened to see people hanging out on the LZ, they would fire at them too and one of those times I was wounded with shrapnel from a mortar round that landed in front of my position. It was superficial, very minor, just in the left hand and arm. HM3 David

Overstreet treated me and he cleaned me up so I wouldn't have to worry about jungle rot, and I carried on. I was lucky that I didn't have to be evacuated, but it was just another occasion where HM3 Overstreet and I got to be close buddies. He was 1st Platoon corpsman, so he was in 1st Platoon headquarters just like I was. We both entered Vietnam roughly about same time.

As we received incoming motor rounds throughout the day(s), a mortar round landed and I had seen where it landed. So I went out on LZ. I left my position and went out on the LZ with my compass and I did a back azimuth on the crater hole to pass the word on as to where the back azimuth was. I returned to my position, and the platoon sergeant chewed me out for exposing myself to the fire. The platoon sergeant voiced his displeasure about that move. Well, I still passed the word on to the mortar teams as to what the back azimuth was.

On March 23rd, 1st Platoon was sent on a patrol. This was a platoon patrol of our sector of the Argonne perimeter. We numbered twenty to twenty-five men. The platoon sergeant led us since the platoon commander was wounded when he rolled over the booby-trapped (grenade) body of the 3rd Platoon commander, Lt. McCormick, who was killed the same day as the initial assault. The grenade didn't kill Lt. Gates, but when we next saw him in the rear, some six months later, he was a changed man to say the least. I was the RTO for 1st Platoon and was in the hip pocket of the platoon sergeant for the duration of the patrol.

The patrol route did not take us very far outside the perimeter, maybe 200 to 300 meters at most, but was through thickly wooded jungle on the hillside below the fire support base and visibility was extremely limited. The first half of the patrol went quietly, with the only interruption coming when we stumbled upon some fresh graves. There we found several recently (two to three days) dead NVA in shallow graves. After quickly checking the bodies for intelligence, we re-buried them and continued the patrol. We were soon on the back leg of the route home to the fire support base, when our point Pfc. Norman Beck walked upon a bunker and was shot dead where he stood. He died right on top of that bunker. The next three to four guys behind him were wounded also. A fellow squad member we called the "professor" was running back toward the platoon HQ, hurdled a waist-high fallen tree, crashed on landing, rolled onto his back and scurried on his hands and legs another couple of feet away from the enemy fire that had gut-shot him. His first words when he stopped scuttling away were, "They got me!"

In an instant, it seemed, we had reacted to the fire and were returning same. The platoon sergeant was barking at me radio in what the situation was, while directing the fire and disposition of the platoon. L/Cpl. Steven Byars set his M60 machine gun up where the platoon sergeant told him to, and returned fire for a few minutes into the firefight, before he too was hit. The call went out for "Corpsman!" and HM3 David Overstreet responded quickly and was there in seconds. While HM3 Overstreet lay on his left side to avoid the withering fire coming from the bunkers (yes, by now we had seen fire coming from a couple more bunkers), I could clearly see him (five to ten meters) in front of me, struggling to turn Byars over to access his wound.

Overstreet's next move was one that showed total disregard for his own safety and shall for the rest of my days on this earth live etched in my memory. He bounced up into a flat-footed squat and began to flip Byars over to render assistance. It was the last thing he ever did, for he fell over like a statue, never coming out of the squat, even in death. It was just an awful tense time for me because I was desiring to kill the NVA. But with me being the platoon radio operator, they had to keep me secure so I could keep communications with battalion headquarters. I have lived with this event all my life.

Twelve days later, we abandoned Argonne on foot and headed north into the DMZ. It took a couple of days to get up there. During one of those days, we had left our positions, but then we were going up a ridge. We noticed an NVA soldier going through our position we had the prior night before and the company commander had about six guys fire on him until he went down. He then sent a patrol down to check on the situation. At that time they found he had no intelligence on him.

SIXTY-EIGHT DAYS

Once we arrived at our base camp, it was about sixty-eight days we had spent on patrol.

CHAPTER 17

LIGHT THE MATCH

Tim Marquart
L/CPL, 0351, Assault Man
H&S Company, 1st Bn, 4th Marines

MY EXPERIENCES IN OPERATION PURPLE MARTIN ON FIRE support base Argonne, also known as Hill 1308. I arrived in Vietnam January 1969, flew into Da Nang Air Base, and was assigned to the 3rd Marine Division. I was an 0351 anti-tank specialist and my weapons included one on six recoilless rifles, LAWs rocket launcher, 3.5-inch rocket launcher, flamethrower and light demolitions. It was my expertise with flamethrowers that would eventually land me on Argonne.

We flew up to Dang Ha and then to Quang Tri, where I was assigned to the 1st Battalion, 4th Marine Regiment. Because I was an 0351, I was in fact assigned to H & S company a 106 mm anti-tank platoon. Because you have an MOS of 0351 doesn't mean that you'll be assigned to an entire unit, they put you wherever they need you, but it just so happens I was assigned H & S. It was March 20th that we were sent up to Argonne.

I'll never forget that day. We were summoned to our platoon sergeant, Staff Sgt. Ryerson. I can still remember the solemn look on his face and it actually concerned me. He just stared at us for a moment or two and started to speak.

"We've been tagged for a mission that is potentially very dangerous on Hill 1308, otherwise known as Argonne. There's a lot of trouble up there. The 4th Marines are taking this hill and we're sending a 106 up there but there is a problem with some NVA occupying a cave; they can't be hit by airstrikes. They have failed to get them out other ways; they failed to get them out other ways possible. We are going to burn them out with flamethrowers."

This would be the beginning of my participation in Operation Purple Martin.

Sgt. Ryerson said, "I'm not going to blow smoke up your skirts, there's a good chance you may not come back." Well, that sent a chill up my spine. But I wasn't trained on a flamethrower to start campfires. Sgt. Ryerson told us, "Go to the ammo bunker to get the flamethrower ready for the mission." We had to go quickly, mix a batch of fuel. We mixed napalm powder into a fuel oil mix in a fifty-five-gallon drum, and we had to mix that thoroughly. We had a homemade sifter. We shifted the napalm into that drum and had to stir it and stir and stir it. We had to make sure there were no jelly balls. These balls could plug the holes in the nozzle of the gun and cause a backup or an explosion.

When we finished filling flamethrower tanks, we reported back to Sgt. Ryerson. He told us "saddle up and report to the LZ for transport to Argonne." I'll never forget the look on his face. It was a very solemn look, a look of goodbye. We moved down the hill to LZ Stud, also known as a Vandegrift, field headquarters of the 3rd Marine Division for the northwest I Corps. We had to walk down a winding hill from 4th Marines to the LZ, and shortly after Marine Corps CH-46 helicopters arrived for a ride up to Argonne.

I had the flamethrower on my back, as I was the designated gunner for this mission. We were told by the crew chief on the chopper, "This is an extremely hot LZ," which translated that it was under heavy fire from 82 mm mortars and sniper fire.

Mike Dean, who was my partner and a good friend of mine, was with me on the helicopter for our ride to Argonne. The 106 mm recoilless rifle was on a helicopter ahead of us, so it was set up when we flew in. There were two landing zones on Argonne, an upper and a lower. A UH-1H Huey helicopter that had been shot down blocked the upper LZ and the pilot was killed. It was sitting on the upper LZ. So we came into the lower landing zone with 82 mm mortar rounds raining in on us, machine gun and sniper fire also being fired at us. The crew chief yelling, "We're not landing," and we were instructed to jump out of the helicopter.

We're about ten feet off the ground. When you jump out of a hovering helicopter with a flamethrower on your back, you can't roll very well when you hit the ground. I tried to log roll, but was stopped with a thud at that point. Mortar rounds were coming in. I noticed that little indentation in the ground, somewhat of a ditch. It was covered with ponchos. I slid into it, never realizing what I was about to encounter. I slid into this shallow cut out that contained about four or five dead Marines. They had been covered, so I didn't realize it until I slid right into the middle of them very suddenly, then very suddenly it dawned on me what the situation was. I'll never get rid of the absolute feeling of horror I felt in my body as I shuddered violently. But I had to stay where I was as we were still being shelled by the NVA 82 mm mortars. Chopper after the chopper flew off, and shortly after then the tubing stopped. And I can tell you, quite frankly, this may have been the absolute worst day of my life or the worst moment of my life.

There was still a machine gun nest at the top of the hill that was believed to have shot down the UH-1H Huey helicopter. I went to set up the 106 mm recoilless rifle with Otto Tunips, also known as Chief, a full-blood Comanche Indian They loaded a heat round into the chamber. Heat round is a high explosive anti-tank round, 106 millimeter round. They fired it at the machine gun nest. It was a direct hit and killed every NVA in that position. Since this all happened very quickly and it was completely chaotic, I'm relating these events as best as I can remember them.

With the machine gun nest taken out, as I stood up, another Marine joined me in covering the Marines in the ditch back up. The LZ was so hot they could not remove the bodies at that time.

I remember looking up the hill to the upper LZ. It looked like the surface of the moon because all the shelling that had been going on caused a lot of craters up there. I also remember that feeling of impending doom as I walked up the hill toward the upper LZ. I can actually remember saying, "I'm in a world of shit," going up the hill. I can remember the images of my family, mother, aunts, uncles, siblings, cousins, friends; their images just seemed to flow through my head. I thought, "I don't think I'm ever going to see any of them again."

When we got to the top, there were bodies and body parts scattered around. Fortunately, they were all dead NVA soldiers. When we secured the perimeter, we were instructed to throw the bodies over the hill into the brush.

An additional event took place with our commanding officer, Lt. Col. Sargent. I was not present or did not know and did not see this action. I heard they charged with Delta Company with grenades and took out a machine gun nest. However, I did not witness this. A time later, an 82 mm mortar round killed Lt. Col. Sargent. He was awarded the Navy Cross posthumously. He was an extremely brave man. It was a tragedy that he was killed up there.

When the perimeter was secured, we were instructed to dig holes and operate and create some shelter. My fellow squad member, Mike Dean and I started digging as deep as we could to make a secure foxhole. When we finished digging, we found some tree logs to put over the top of the hole and covered them with filled sandbags. Then we made a little opening on the side, which allowed us to slip in and out quickly. Our foxhole was right next to the upper LZ, just maybe about thirty or forty feet from the UH-1H Huey that was shot down

It's important to remember that Hill 1308 was very close to the Laotian border and to the DMZ. So we were up in the upper corner of this South Vietnam inquiry province. Now, we were surrounded by NVA troops who were extremely accurate with their 82 mm mortars.

After Col.Sargent was killed, we got a new battalion commander, Lt. Col. Claire Wilcox. I remember seeing him on the upper LZ giving instructions as to what we needed to do. You see, the problem was, we were basically trapped up there. Any time a helicopter got near the hill, the NVA would start mortaring us, with a barrage of mortars. The only advantage in a mortar attack is that we could hear the tubing as the rounds were being fired. It sort of made a sound like a "doop doop doop." When we heard this, we knew the rounds were about to fall right on top of us, so everyone yelled "incoming," and we jumped into our hole, which was one of the reasons we never strayed too far from home.

There were times at Argonne when it was silent and nothing was happening. We were on top, they were on the bottom of the hill. Some of us managed to get into a few hands of back alley, the popular card game in Vietnam. After a time being up there, the days just blended into each other. We got the word that the flame-thrower raid on the caves was scrubbed. We were never really given a definitive reason as to why. But I found out years later that the attack actually took place, but it was by another unit. My unit did not go ahead with the mission of burning out the caves, but we didn't let the fuel go to waste. The upper LZ was still use-less as the UH-1H was still blocking it from any use. Col. Wilcox ordered that we had to get that thing off the LZ. Not only was the helicopter blocking the LZ, but also the bodies, the dead NVA sol-diers that we threw in the brush started to stink really bad.

We gathered up some old small logs that were blown off the trees and put them in front of the landing struts of the helicopter, and we lifted. We lifted the helicopter up onto the struts. A squad of Marines is more than capable of lifting a Huey up.

We started to push the helicopter at and rolled it on along pretty good. We repeated the process until we were able to push the heli-copter over the hill onto its side. It was now off the landing zone, however, we never left anything the enemy could use against us. There might be parts or machinery or metal or something else they could find a use for. They were very resourceful that way. We still had the flamethrower full of fuel. So we embarked on a two-fold event. I was instructed to light up the helicopter with the flamethrower. The bodies of the dead NVA were still lying in the brush next to where we pushed the helicopter. And again, as those bodies were lying there for days, it was a horrifying stink to a level that was sickening. The stench of those dead bodies had to be addressed. I was instructed to burn the UH-1H Huey helicopter and the bodies all at once.

The effective way to use a flamethrower is to saturate the area with fuel, then light up. A flamethrower has two triggers that are independent from each other. One contains the fuel flow. The other is called the match. The match works like a revolver. Every time you press the trigger to ignite a match, when you release it, it rotates to the next match. If you just pull a fuel trigger, only fuel will come out of the hose. The fuel is stored in the tanks strapped to your back. The hose comes around your body so the match trigger is in your left hand and the fuel trigger is in your right hand. You stand about fifty or sixty feet back from your target, because when the fuel and napalm mixture ignites, it gets seriously hot. I took up a position and aimed the hose, pulled the fuel trigger, and saturated the helicopter and the bodies. You don't use too much fuel because you need plenty of it for the flame. The next step, you let go of the fuel trigger, you light the match trigger, then hit the fuel trigger again. It sends out an awesome flame, igniting all the fuel that was previously sprayed out, and will keep a steady flame for about ten or twenty seconds. The helicopter was completely consumed and the bodies were incinerated.

Charlie must have been getting an eyeful from their position, because just as I was finishing up the tubing started. "Incoming" was the shout. I don't think I ever took a flamethrower off my back that quickly. Mike then helped me pull it off and we dove into our holes. They were landing the mortar rounds relatively close to the ground. So the ground shook violently but we got through that attack unscathed.

I believe it was the following day we saw some enemy movement down below. Since we still had the 106 mm recoilless rifle with the H.E rounds, we thought we'd take some target practice at the NVA. From what we could see, we hit them pretty good. Of course, they retaliated with and without massive mortar attack. It was biblical.

So now it was getting to the point as to what do we do about the situation? That night we were treated to an awesome light show, Puff the Magic Dragon, a.k.a. Spooky, a World War II, C-47 cargo aircraft, refitted with Gatling guns. These weapons put out more firepower than can be conceived, barrels rotating by machine.

Every fifth round was a trace around and it looked like a laser beam. Well, and there was a whirring sound, so we couldn't even distinguish between the individual rounds, coming out of there so fast.

Well, that night, the gunship was ordered to attack the enemy positions. We sat in our bunkers and watched this show. It wasn't likely there would be any mortar attacks that night with the amount of ordnance raining down on their positions. The mortars were silent for the rest of the night.

The following day after the light show is a bit hazy in my mind. The next thing I remember, we were told to muster up by the LZ. I can still remember, as I was in a position about ten feet from Col. Wilcox. He was on the radio with the pilot of the CH-46, who was a major, and Col. Wilcox was blasting him really good. I remember this like it was yesterday. Apparently, this major didn't want to bring the chopper in because he was concerned about a mortar attack. Col. Wilcox told him, "You get this fucking chopper down right now, and the situation may not get any better. And I've got people down here who are wounded and injured, land now or face a court martial. And I mean, fucking now, that's a direct order." Well, the pilot did come in to the LZ and landed when the ramp came down. As the helicopter was nearing the hill, the tubing started and the incoming could be heard loudly all around the LZ.

As I ran for cover, I must have stepped in some sort of hole or something that caused me to twist my ankle and I went down. The mortar rounds started to hit close to where I was lying. At the moment, it suddenly felt like somebody hit me in the stomach with a sledgehammer, because I had the wind knocked out of me severely. The concussion of the round just really shocked me. I was totally out of wind. I remember my mouth was full of dirt and excruciating pain in my ankle. I couldn't move. Two guys from 81 mm mortars came out of their holes and dragged me to safety. Seconds later, the attack ended as the helicopter flew away without attempting to land. As it turned out, my ankle was sprained. It was swelling up and started to turn purple. I couldn't walk without help; a Navy corpsman wrapped it tight and gave me something for pain. I remember thinking that if we got attacked, I couldn't move very well. The next thing I remember is that we were told to muster at TLC that comes.

The pilot came in on the LZ and landed when the ramp came down. I hopped as quick as I could to get into the helicopter. The wounded got on and some of the bodies were loaded. The helicopter was not on the LZ for more than about thirty seconds. I'm not sure what happened or whether there was a mortar attack, because we as we took off, I was just concentrating on getting out of there. We were off so quick. I'll never forget that feeling of anxiety surging through my body as we lifted off.

When we came off the landing zone, the helicopter kind of dipped into a valley, slightly going downward. The door gunners on both sides were at the ready in case of sniper fire, but it never came. The helicopter surged upward and we were out of there. I remember feeling relief as we put distance between Argonne and us. When we flew back to LZ Vandegrift and landed at the outset, Mules (a very early version of a utility ATV, small flat deck that could carry a few Marines) were waiting to drive us up the hill to the battalion aid station. When we got there, a corpsman unwrapped my leg, which was quite swollen, and put an ice pack on it, which was not available up on Argonne.

He noticed some blood trickling down the sleeve of my utility blouse. He said, "You're bleeding; I'm surprised you never felt anything." We took off the blouse. There was a flesh wound just above the forearm by the bicep. It was slight. He asked me what happened. I said that I really didn't know, as this was the first time I realized that I was bleeding, between the pain in my ankle and the gut wrenching pain in my stomach. I never felt anything else. I guess I was in a mortar attack earlier, when it must have happened.

Then he said, "I can't write you up for a Purple Heart as it was not witnessed."

I replied, "I don't know where else it could have happened."

The corpsman said, "I just put a bandage on it, a little antiseptic and a bandage."

Technically, the corpsman was correct. It had to be witnessed to receive a citation. It's certainly not the first time or the last time that this has occurred. I was just thankful I was alive and in one piece after the ordeal on Argonne, thus ending my part in Operation Purple Martin.

CHAPTER 18

THE LZ

Andy O'Sullivan
1st Lt, 0801, Artillery Forward Observer
Golf 3/12, Assigned to Delta Company, 1st Bn, 4th Marines

THE TIME: 1962. THE PLACE: BROOKLYN, NEW YORK. THE SIT-
uation was a young man planning to be the first member of the
family to attend and graduate college. But in 1965 the US made
moves to become more involved in a place called Vietnam. There
were classmates of mine who were getting drafted out of school
and I became very aware of what could happen to my education.
I also felt a need to serve in my country's call and do the "right
thing," but I wanted to finish what I started with my education and
be "properly prepared" for my future. My solution was to sign into
the Marines. They would either let me finish college and go into
the OCS program, or if I dropped out I would go to Camp Lejeune.
PS–I got a draft notice in September 1965 and declined the offer.

After graduating in June 1967, OCS in September 1967, The
Basic School 1968, married in June 1968, Artillery School in July
1968 and off to Vietnam in September 1968, I thought I was prepared for any situation that my country would throw at me. After
the initial "welcome to Vietnam," I was off with my team as a forward observer in an infantry company. The first thing that was very
evident to me was my training did not prepare me for all situations.

208

I also realized that I needed "the old salts" who walked with me to draw from their experiences and to stay alive.

Now fast forward to March 1969, and the command group decided to occupy a place called LZ Argonne. Other Marines were there earlier in the year, but when they left it the NVA just walked back in. As the forward observer assigned to "D" Company, it was my job to prep the landing zone and surrounding area for the safest possible insertion to follow the next morning. The prep operation required extensive coordination with fixed wing (F-4) and Huey gunships. During that night and early morning artillery batteries in the supporting area expended 2604 rounds – 105mm, 428 rounds – 155mm and 800 rounds – 175mm. I thought, as many others who preceded me, nothing could live through this. The morning of March 20th would prove just the opposite! The morning of March 20, 1969, we piled on to the CH-46s and started the assault. The first indication of a problem was when I saw a UH-1H helicopter shot down on the LZ we were going into. Being a college graduate, I also realized that the pelting on the outside skin of our CH-46 was bullets trying to enter my space and kill me along with my fellow Marines. This increased my pucker factor, and when we set down all my Marines got off quickly and started returning fire. It was amazing how much you can squeeze into a helmet and flak jacket when necessary. The NVA was well prepared and had locations on the hill zeroed in with a constant barrage of 82mm mortars, and small arms fire seemed to be coming from all directions. With all this activity, I realized that the eighteen- to early twenty-year-old Marines were the best qualified and trained to deal with these stressful and dangerous situations because they knew what to do and did it.

I was blessed to be with young men who had the commitment to do whatever was required to protect the Marines next to them. That dedication included the sacrifice of their lives if necessary. Some of these men included Mark Abplanalp and David Ovist. They were just two of my RTO's, and in many cases the ones who kept me alive. Mark was well trained and knew the tricks to communicate when it was deemed impossible. He could remember our fire missions and tracked them either in his head or on a piece of paper, a trait essential for safety and coordination. David was the person you wanted around you when the shit hit the fan. He had a calming personality and knew his job. If you would look in the dictionary and find the term, "calm under fire," you would see his picture. He gave the ultimate sacrifice on March 22, 1969.

We stayed on LZ Argonne for about three weeks and got pounded every day and night. There was a time the command group thought we were going to get over-run and we got Puff on station, which was a World War II C-47 plane with rapid fire automatic weapons out every window. All we saw was a steady stream of red/orange tracers hitting the ground all around the hill. To light up the area at night there were flare ships on station, coordinating with fixed wing attack jets and gunships. These weapons gave all of us on the hill a false sense of security, but it was amazing to watch. At the end of our occupation, we lost eighteen Marines (KIA) and had thirty-eight injured (WIA). The NVA responded during our occupation with 159 - 82mm rounds and countless RPGs and small arms. When I look back, my question is *Why*? At my command level I did not see the big picture, but I did see Marines do unbelievable actions of courage. Some of which were recognized with awards, but most went unnoticed except for the people around them.

These are the people who came back to the world (United States) after their service without a parade or a thank you, but did get the scorn of many and the blame for a war they did not start. In some cases, it has never left them. I see eighteen and twenty-year-olds today who get upset when a speaker says something they disagree with and they require counseling to repair their mental stability. I lived with young Marines who would do almost anything to get the job done – and that included sacrificing their lives. God bless them **all**!

As for the title of this note, the LZ was a lost cause from the start and seemed to be just another stopover in an endless war, but Panel 28 West is the place on the Vietnam Memorial in Washington, D.C., where you can find the names of those who paid the ultimate price for this action.

CHAPTER 19

OPERATION PURPLE MARTIN

Bill Jones
L/CPL, 0844/46, Field Artillery Control Man
Golf, 3/12, Assigned to Delta Company, 1st Bn, 4th Marines

MARCH OF 1969, OPERATION PURPLE MARTIN. WHO THINKS of these names? It sounds like a bird-watching excursion. We should have known something was up. Back at the battalion headquarters there are clean clothes, showers, beer and steak at the mess hall. The scuttlebutt is we are going to a place called LZ Argonne, just east of the border with Laos and a little south of the DMZ.

The NCO's make sure we have plenty of personal ammunition. This is a bit unusual and we suspect they know something the rest of us don't know. I put together fourteen loaded magazines and stuff a bandolier with seven fragmentation grenades. We are encouraged to take as much as we think we can carry. This latest move seems curiously different, for reasons difficult to pinpoint. An air of foreboding surrounds the men of the battery, akin perhaps to someone facing major surgery. There is a sense of dread coupled with stoic resolve. The men are unusually quiet as we board several CH-46 helicopters and head west to the Laotian border.

We begin our descent onto a smoke-filled hill and the door gunners begin firing in long bursts from each side of the helicopter. (I am thinking that coming into any LZ is a strange place for them to be test firing their weapons. The capacity of a human being at self-deception, I later conclude, is limitless). Out of a side window I note that one helicopter has landed at the top of the hill, but the rotors are not turning, Strange, I think, for it to just sit there exposed.

We land at the bottom of the hill and run off the back ramp. Along with my FDC buddy Risk. We are carrying a wooden ammunition box full of charts, maps and other gear. Our assignment is to establish a fire direction center (FDC) at the top of the hill. An incoming mortar round lands a few feet behind the helicopter, which is already lifting off. Risk looks okay and I surprisingly don't see any blood coming from me. The round is close and least one of us should have been hit. A grunt at the edge of the little LZ (this would be known as the lower LZ) is firing furiously into the nearby jungle. I don't see anything, but then again you almost never do. Grunts spend a great deal of their time firing at trees in the jungle and these particular trees are shooting back at them.

We start up the hill and more mortars fall, but not nearly as close as the first one. In addition, supersonic bumblebees are whizzing around amidst this unbelievable noisy and confused chaos. Somebody in those trees, I think somewhat incredulously, is shooting at Risk and me. Risk apparently reaches that same conclusion at the same time and we collapse in a hole a few feet away. A young Marine already occupies the hole. By his clothes and new boots, he is obviously a new guy and could not possibly have been in-country more than a couple of weeks. He is also newly dead, having caught a round directly between his eyes, most probably one intended for us.

"Don't look at him," Risk says. "Don't look at him and don't think about it. We need to get going." Risk is a lot braver than me. I would have been content to spend the rest of war in the relative safety of that hole. Soon, we are at the top of the hill next to the disabled Army UH-1H Huey full of holes and blood that we saw on the way in. The dead and wounded Marines have already been removed. The two machine guns on either side are also missing. Someone says the NVA waited for the helicopter to land and then raked it with automatic weapons fire. A discarded, shattered and gore-filled flight helmet indicates that at least one of the pilots was killed. I don't know who got the machine guns, but I hope it's not the NVA.

Most people live out their lives, in the words of the poet, in "quiet desperation," without really being afraid. Not just anxious, nervous, concerned, upset or a little worried, but flat out convinced your life is about to be over soon. A fear that is palpable, consuming, debilitating, drying your mouth, constricting your throat, and immobilizing your limbs. Thanks to Risk, the fear does not overwhelm and leave me frozen to the extent I cannot function. But there is definitely some beginning frostbite and it is spreading rapidly. The fear does not win this time. But it comes close. Entirely too close.

We make it up to the top of the hill and begin to organize our maps and charts in an abandoned bunker. From the time we leave the hole with the dead Marine till we reach the crest of the hill is a total blank slate. I have no memory how we got there. None.

The battalion commander Lt. Col. George T. Sargent, along with Lt. Wilson, were killed on the first or maybe the second day. The Lt. Col. led Marines from the front, which is the very reason we seldom if ever see any high-ranking officers in positions of great danger. But at least Lt. Col Sargent is down among his men and not flying safely overhead barking orders at semi-panicked lieutenants and captains. Although he is killed about forty yards from me, I do not see it happen or ever hear about it until later. Such is the pervasive element of confusion and lack of information in combat environments. Apparently an old-style World War II type gung-ho Marine officer, his death causes me to reconsider my cynical attitude toward those Marines in higher-ranking leadership positions. This officer has balls and is with his Marines. As he should be. Unfortunately, he is the exception, rather than the rule.

A couple of NVA soldiers are dead in a hole next to the downed UH1H helicopter and a few feet from the bunker Risk and I have just occupied. One of them (NVA bodies) has a folded picture from a *Playboy* magazine in his pocket and the discovery infuriates me. This close to Laos and the DMZ, there is no way he could have obtained that picture except by going through the gear and/ or pocket of a dead Marine. There are also a couple of letters in Vietnamese, which I take and keep for several years. At the time, the grim irony of this situation escapes me.

Doc, since the death of our other corpsman and another friend, pulls the NVA bodies (now beginning to stink) down the hill a little ways and sets them on fire. Their fight hole, about the size of a six-foot-long grave, I quickly claim as my new home. It's a little messy, but one can't be choosy. Inside I find a couple of NVA-issued freeze dried rations that look just as good as anything the Marines have, but I throw them away because they are "gook food." The two bodies along with some others burn and smolder until the day we finally leave, almost two weeks later.

Our dead and wounded are having difficult time being evacuated because the helicopters are taking too much incoming fire into the LZ at the bottom of the hill. For our dead this obviously does not matter, but the poncho-wrapped bodies lined up at the bottom of the hill are a somewhat troubling moral issue, at least for me. I try not to look down there. Our three cannons are in position now and we begin to initiate fire missions. Soon we are nearly out of ammo and water. The resupply helicopters have stopped coming. The LZ is much too hot.

To solve the ammo problem, large pallets of 105 howitzer shells and mortar rounds are parachuted onto the hill. This does not go well. The chutes miss the hill and drift leisurely off into the jungle. The NVA mortars are 82 millimeter in size, whereas our motors are 81 millimeters. The NVA can use our ammo in their mortar tubes but their rounds will not fit in ours. For the next several days we are mortared with what is more (probably our own ammo), which we conveniently supply. Air strikes are called in to try to blow up the ammo pallets before the NVA get them, but this is only partially successful. Sending out patrols to retrieve the ammo is simply out of the question; there are too many NVA out there in all directions. They surround us.

We can hear the NVA drop mortar rounds in their tubes. It makes a distinctive sound that sends everyone scrambling frantically for cover. Since this is a previously abandoned firebase, they don't have to fire any "adjustment" rounds. The first round is always on target and they are more than a little proficient. A good mortar crew (and admittedly these NVA crews are extremely good) can get a number of rounds in the air before the first one ever hits. I resolve that at my first opportunity, I am going to make my new home mortar proof. Under the circumstances, the former NVA hole is starting to resemble a grave a little too much for my liking.

After a couple of days, it suddenly occurs to me that unless things start to change pretty quickly, we may not make it off this godforsaken hill. Later, I think it somewhat curious that this thought contains the noun " we" not "I."

LZ Argonne had been occupied previously in November of 1968, so there is still junk around that will be beneficial in fortifying my new residence. I find a piece of steel airplane matting and drag it over the top of my hole/grave and place a couple of sandbags over the metal sheet for good measure. A couple of sniper rounds buzz nearby but not that close. I am surmised that as long as I keep moving, the chances of being hit are fairly minimal. It is the incoming mortar rounds that are the biggest, most lethal danger and the source of my gut-wrenching fear. Unless a lucky incoming mortar round happens to fall in my two-foot hole entrance, I will be reasonably safe. That is, if not caught out in the open like Lt. Col. Sargent.

The skipper is in the FDC bunker a few feet away. He eyes my new fortification. "Nice hole you have there, Jones," he says in a friendly manner. Real nice."

"Thank you, sir," I reply. " I have been working pretty hard on it." I do not volunteer the reason for my ball-busting industry is that I am scared shitless! These NVA incoming mortar rounds are eventually going to kill us all, I think.

"You know," the skipper continues, "that hole being close to the FDC and all would make a nice home base for your battery commander." So I think, there is a reason for this little social chit-chat. I should have known!

"Well, sir," I counter, "this is my hole. I guess you will have to find your own."

The skipper then laughs like the whole conversation was a joke, but we both know it is not a joke. I quickly resolve that I will not give up the hole without doing something. What, I don't know, but apparently the skipper has second thoughts about confiscating my fortified grave and drops the issue.

Later I think about how intimidated I was not that long ago when I watched a troop handler sergeant beat a friend with a tree limb in infantry school. Now I more or less told a captain (respectfully) to go fuck himself. Amazing what a few months in Vietnam can do, especially when survival becomes part of the equation. I often wonder what I would have done if the skipper had in fact ordered me out of my little fortress. In reality, probably nothing.

The incoming mortar rounds keep falling again, kawumping outside our flimsy bunker as we take cover inside. Trying to make myself as small as possible inside my flak jacket and helmet, I look across at the Marine squatting across from me. He has a leather shoulder holster with a .45 caliber pistol. The holster is unusual. I have never seen one up to now. When I look at his face, I realize it's the supply sergeant from back at battalion. This explains the holster. The supply guys get all the good stuff before anyone does.

"Sarge," I say between the incoming motor rounds, "what are you doing here?"

"Well, I heard you guys were in the shit, so I hitched a ride with a medevac and came on up."

Wow! Apparently, he does this on his own. It is not something I would have done. I mentally forgive him for scarfing the holster, even if he is in a rear area. The dude is very brave or else a fool. Anyway, my estimation of the guy immediately spikes hundreds of points. This Marine Corps mentally is hard to explain.

That afternoon, some NVA are spotted running around the hill a few hundred yards west of us just inside the border with Laos. The FDC gunnery sergeant, my immediate supervisor who seldom if ever leaves the safety of the bunker, happens to be outside and quickly takes charge of a gun crew, ordering the crew to swing the 105mm howitzer around and lower the tube for direct fire. He shouts words of encouragement, makes elevation adjustments and pours high explosive rounds into the position. "Willie Peter!" he yells. "Burn them!" (Willie Peter is the term for white phosphorous shells that are banned to use in this fashion by the Geneva Convention.) The gunny has apparently not heard of this rule, or if he did he does not care. Neither do I, nor any of the rest of us fighting for our lives on this isolated, very small hill. Watching gunny take command and work his expertise, I swell with a somewhat surprising sense of pride. This is my gunny and he is a killing machine.

Ron "Hutch" Hutchinson comes walking up from the other side of the hill. We are surprised to see him; he didn't come with us. Apparently he hitched a ride with one of the first arriving platoons. Smiling broadly, he is in great spirits despite the obvious and dire predicament we now find ourselves in. He's a man in his element. Confident and self-assured and still crazy.

"We killed some NVA on the other side of the hill, do you want to go see them?"

I shake my head no. I have already seen enough dead NVA.

"One of them is a woman." A NVA nurse or something. "Maybe," he adds a wink, "is still warm."

Ron laughs at his little joke and seems slightly amused at my reaction. Up to this point I considered myself to be kind of shockproof. Ron, I conclude, has been here too long. The war has damaged him possibly beyond any hope of redemption. Later, actually many years later, I realize that war damages everyone in one way or another. Even those who don't go. The extent of damage is a matter of degrees.

For the first few days on LZ Argonne the airstrikes are continuous during daylight hours. The fight jets, in radio parlance called "fast movers," put on quite an impressive show all around our position. Roaring in from different directions they carefully drop high explosives and silver tumbling canisters of napalm. I am especially fond of the napalm, because being overrun in a ground attack is a real possibility and the more NVA who are fried, the more it increases our odds for survival and lowers the enemy's chances. Thank God for Dow Chemical.

One day an F-4 Phantom drops all its ordinance in several passes and comes screaming low level over the top of our hill, and in a final run doing at least 400 knots or more before climbing straight up while doing a victory roll. Apparently he knows we have our collective asses in a sling and this last gesture is a tribute of sorts? I like to think this is probably a Marine fighter pilot, but really don't know. Nevertheless, it is a goose bump-producing and unforgettable moment.

After about three days, airstrikes have suppressed incoming mortar fire enough to allow resupply helicopters to bring in ammo, water, supplies and evacuation of the dead and wounded. The water situation is approaching situation critical and many of us suffer from dehydration. The water arrives none too soon. The incoming mortar rounds begin falling a few moments later. These NVA mortars are good, too good, and most probably are targeting a stack of artillery shells. A few moments later a mortar round hits exactly where I was standing with another Marine. It misses us by less than thirty feet.

The bunker is in some sort of frenzied commotion a few yards away near the FCD bunker. From the sound and tone of the voices, I know something tragic has happened. Something really bad. I hear someone yelling. The voice sounds like Ron "Hutch" Hutchinson. Running back to the FDC bunker, I see Hutch, distraught and weeping, running around in a small circle. "The Big O is dead!" (David E. Ovist) he is saying over and over. "The Big O is dead!" David is prone at his feet, not moving, with a hole in the back of his flak jacket the size of a dinner plate. A mortar round has fallen directly into his foxhole a few feet from mine, killing him instantly. There is nothing anyone can do.

I didn't know David, a radio operator who just returned for a second tour. Ron Hutchinson and David apparently had a history. (This is another Marine I think who should never have come back. You can only dodge a bullet so many times.) Ron quickly composes himself and calls for a poncho to carry David down to the lower LZ. There are no ponchos, for we have used them all up. Ron becomes cold, menacing and quite clear.

"I want a poncho," he says evenly, "and I want one now!" Ponchos start appearing from all directions.

The skipper comes running up with a poncho in an outstretched hand saying, "Here, Hutch, Take my poncho."

I grab one corner of the poncho and we start carrying David down to where his body can be evacuated out. It is uneven ground with a heavy shifting load. One Marine, a new guy drops his corner, and so picks up and starts again toward the lower LZ. A few more steps and he, no doubt having difficulty with this grim scenario, drops his end again!

Ron looks at him steadily and says, "You drop him one more time and I will kill you."

I believe him and so does the new guy, because we stumble shakily down the hill without any more incidents.

At dusk, standing in the entrance of my hole, an incoming 122 mm rocket hisses a few feet overhead and slams into the bottom of hill where the dead NVA soldiers are burning. It is a huge explosion and it is close. There is no way any of our bunkers, inclining my steel-roofed tomb, could have taken a direct hit from one of those.

There is a dead, putrid smell in my hole. I find a piece of scalp still with some black hair on it. It was from one of the dead NVA soldiers we set on fire. (I wished it was from the one who had the playboy fold out in his pocket.)

After ten days, LZ Argonne is abandoned for the second time in less than a year. There is an article in *Stars And Stripes* newspaper, saying the operation was a huge success, with light casualties, but it failed to distinguish which side. The NVA or us. We boarded the helicopter to join the other half of our battery. We are unshaven, stink, and giddy with relief — glad to be alive! I sit next to a gunner. One of the FDC Marines elbows me. "Show him your scalp!" I hold up the scalp by a string and the gunner gives me thumbs up.

CHAPTER 20

ADVANCE PARTY

Arthur L. Sandle
PFC, 0811, Field Artillery Cannoneer
Golf, 3/12, assigned to Delta Company, 1st Bn, 4th Marines

MY NAME IS ARTHUR L. SANDLE. TO MY FRIENDS, I'M BO, AND to others PFC Sandle. PFC was the nice name, anyway. We newbies all got the tag NFG, or the "New Fuckin' Guy". You earned that particular nickname solely on your new arrival to the unit and in the section to which you were assigned. You'd only lose the NFG tag when another, newer NFG, your replacement as NFG, arrived and was assigned to your section.

I arrived at the 12th Marine Regiment in late September 1968. Twelve of us from the same artillery class shipped over to Vietnam on the same flight. The 12th Regiment then assigned us to our individual battalions; some to 1st Battalion, some to 2nd, some to 3rd, and some to 4th Battalion and their self-propelled 155mm Howitzers. Four others and I were assigned to 3rd Battalion, Quang Tri, in Quang Tri Province. When we arrived at the Battalion Headquarters, three were assigned to a 155mm Howitzer battery, one assigned to Battery India, and I was assigned to Battery Golf.

Once I received my gear, I was transported to Fire support baseCa Lu, (LZ Stud) where I was ushered before the battery's gunnery sergeant, a tower of a man with no-nonsense expectations, who immediately put the fear of God in me, and told me exactly who the people were that he did not want me associating with, before introducing me to the commanding officer (Skipper) and the executive officer (XO). He then gave me an escort to my gun section's chief, and the members of my assigned piece, Gun 5. After several weeks at Ca Lu, the battery displaced to Fire support baseCarroll. It was here that I experienced my first enemy mortar attack.

In November 1968, we displaced to Fire support base Alpine. This is the LZ on which I was introduced to the Marine artilleryman's morbid sense of humor. Periodically, we would get a mortar attack in the early evening around sunset. These attacks would always be from the west, as the sunset would make it difficult for us to see the muzzle flash from the NVA's mortar tubes, preventing us from effectively making counterattacks with our 105mm Howitzers.

One day, to break the boredom, someone decided to organize a game of touch football on the LZ. So, we made a ball from the tape that sealed the 105mm ammunition canisters, and began to play. Just as the game was getting interesting, we began to receive incoming fire from the enemy. Not to be deterred, we kept on playing every time we were bored, usually around sunset. After repeating this event on several occasions and getting incoming fire each time, somebody came up with the brilliant idea to start the game earlier and see if they would attack us earlier, letting us see their muzzle flash.

So, we posted a man on watch, and lo and behold, they fell for our trap. The man on watch was able to see the muzzle flashes and provide information to direct a counter-mortar attack on their position. My gun section (our mortar tube's name was Beatrice) was in the best position to deploy direct fire on the enemy's position, and was successful in destroying the enemy and his position. After they were dead, we went back and finished the game!

During my time at LZ Alpine, I recall a few other memorable events. One was the LZ's 155mm Howitzer battery had an in-tube explosion of a live round that killed two Marines and wounded seven others. The second occurrence was when a tiger ate a Marine assigned to a Recon Team while on patrol.*

After this event, we were often on 100 percent alert when we received word that grunts had tiger movement near the parameter lines. This meant that every Marine was to man our predestinated defensive positions. A short time after this tiger event, a Vietnamese tiger hunter was flown to the LZ with a little dog and set out to kill the tiger. After a few days, he left without succeeding in killing the tiger. Maybe the tiger didn't have much taste after having had American. Another morbid joke.

Another thing I remember happened when we were socked-in by fog. Helicopters couldn't bring us a resupply of fresh water, and a ragtag group of us artillerymen humped down the hill with five-gallon water cans to bring back water to our battery. We were just lolly-gagging down the hill, banging the water cans and making all sorts of noise. We had no clue we were sitting ducks for the enemy. As the saying goes, "God takes care of babies and fools," and I am glad He does. We found a stream, failed to put someone on watch, and began to play in the water as though we were in a pool on a base back stateside. All of a sudden, we got interrupted by a pissed-off rock ape. I guess we disturbed his noonday nap.

While on our way back with filled cans of water, one Marine found a small red pouch on the ground. Picking it up to inspect it, it blew up in his hand. Although it didn't do much more damage than what you'd expect from a firecracker, it did get all of our attention when we realized what might have been. Turns out, these small pouches were dropped by aircraft to serve as an H&I introduction to the enemy.

In early December, we displaced to Fire support base Neville. This was an adventure. We were located on a ridge of a rock hill with a steep cliff on one side of our gun position. We threw our trash and spent brass from our 105mm guns off this cliff. Our greatest enemy upon arriving was the huge rats. They were **big**. They were brave. They were aggressive.

Often, they would even be so bold as to drag away your open C-Ration cans with you looking right at them, no shame in their game. We tried, without success, to get rid of them any way we could, stabbing, beating, poisoning, and so on.

Unfortunately, I became a little too acquainted with one in early February, and it bit me. I had to be medevac'd back to the rear to receive thirty painful rabies shots in the gut. During my time in the rear, my duties consisted of a few shit-burning details, guard duty, and working on trucks in the motor pool.

It was during this time at LZ Neville that our unit was attacked in the early morning of February 25, 1969. During this attack, we lost Cpl. Jeffrey Barron. the section chief on Gun Number Six, Doc, our senior corpsman, and a member of our FDC section. Ironically, Cpl. Jeffrey Barron, and L/Cpl David Ovist had just signed on for another tour and were both recently returned to Vietnam from leave in the States. Both men would die within a month of each other, Cpl. Jeffrey Barron on 2/25/1969 at LZ Neville, and L/Cpl Ovist on the 22nd of March at LZ Argonne.

In early March, the battery relocated to Fire support base Vandegrift to recover and await reassignment for the next operation, Purple Martin. On March 20, 1969, we displaced as a split-battery operation. Three guns remained at Vandegrift and three were to displace to Fire support baseArgonne. I was a member of the Advance Party for my gun bound for Argonne. Our responsibility on the advance party was to arrive on the LZ prior to the guns so we could make ready the gun positions and inform the LZ team where to direct the CH-53 helicopters that delivered the guns to the designated positions.

The start of our helicopter lift seemed normal. I thought it would be business as usual. It was usually a CH-46 helicopter ride to the next firebase. It wasn't my first advance party, so I wasn't too worried. The artillery advance parties normally arrived at the position well after the LZ had been secured by preparation fire days before and after the Infantry units swept the position to remove enemy combatants before our arrival. This time, however, we had to make a pit stop at LZ Alpine on the way to give the Infantry time to secure the hill. As we sat there at Alpine, we all gathered around the radio operator to listen to the fighting on the radio. From the sound of the radio operators in position in and around Argonne, the fighting was fierce. Meanwhile, our guns at Fire support base Vandegrift were already picked up and en route to Argonne.

This was the beginning of an entirely new experience as an artilleryman. We watched the guns approach in the distance, slung under the CH-53s, en route to Argonne. As we watched, a CH-46 helicopter landed and called for the arty advance party. We all ran to the helicopter, and a very unusual thing happened. The pilot shut down the engines, and the crew chief told us to gather around. He began to inform us of the situation.

"We are going into a hot LZ," he told us. "There is likely to be incoming small arms fire. We will come in hot, which means the wheels will only be on the ground a few seconds. When I give you word to disembark the bird, you must be ready to un-ass the bird. If you are hit and wounded, stay on the bird and we will get you back to medical. Does everybody understand? Again, if you get hit, **stay with the bird**, otherwise you be turning and burning assholes and elbows getting off the bird. Understood?"

Silently, we all climbed aboard and took our positions on the red jump seats with our rifles pointed toward the floor, as per policy. I began to feel my ammo bags to check how much extra ammo I had. My mind was in a whirlwind, working out how I would respond to the different situations now playing in my mind. Although I had been shot at several times before, I had never been in this situation. To add to the drama, as the chopper circled the LZ, the gunner pointed out a CH-46 on the side of the hill that had been shot down, as well as a downed Huey at the top of the hill that had met the same fate. This really got the old pucker factor going.

At this time, my mind began to say, "Someone could get hurt here." I think we often thought in terms of someone else getting hurt to relieve the pressure of thinking it could be us. Without a warning, the helicopter made a sudden hard turn, tilted at about a 45-degree angle, and swooped towards the ground at a high rate of speed. Before I could gather my thoughts, or myself, the previously mild-mannered instructor-type crew chief was howling and pushing and shoving me like a raving madman.

The helicopter wheels never touched the ground. I fell face-first in a thud from his boot square in my ass. My helmet went one way, my rifle another. When I was able to raise my head, I looked around. Before I could figure out what had just happened, I heard the bullets hitting all around us. Although I couldn't appreciate it in the moment, I was later grateful that those guys were piss-poor shots.

Just as I was trying to locate my helmet and rifle, the Skipper started to give instructions. "Okay, men, on three, we are going to make a run toward the top, and when I say hit the deck, you hit the deck." We did our first quick run, and hit the deck. I looked toward the top of the hill, and there was a Black Marine beckoning for us to come on, aiming and shooting at the wooded area from which the enemy was shooting at us. We did a second quick run, and hit the deck again. I looked again, and he was waving his arms faster now. I took it personally that he needed help. I set my mind that I was going to get all the way to him on the next run, even if it meant getting shot in the process.

So, when we started the next short run, as the Skipper gave the order to hit the deck, I kept running and dove through the 60mm parapet like a baseball runner stealing home. For a moment, I felt safe. Then the panic hit me. I had no helmet and no rifle. Bullets were flying and incoming mortars fell like rain.

Using the Skipper's tactics, we finally made it to the gun positions. The LZ Team met us, and we showed them where each gun was to be placed. Usually, the helicopter lowered the gun into its position very softly. This, however, was to be another new experience.

As the helicopter began to lower the gun, it started taking enemy fire. We were watching the little black dots appear along its fuselage. The crew released the gun some twenty to thirty feet above the ground. We all had to scamper out of the way to keep from being smashed by a 105mm Howitzer. Nevertheless, nobody was hurt, and the gun was still in good working order. This happened again for the delivery of the three remaining guns.

In the midst of preparing the gun for action, we did not realize that we were under attack from snipers, small arms, and mortars at the same time. Again, this was the first time that I had occupied a gun position without the fire support base being secured by the infantry prior to the arrival of the artillery. We were in the fight for sure. When my gun pit received two direct mortar hits, flattening a tire on our 105, I thought again, "Someone could get hurt here!"

Just outside the gun pit, a Marine was in a shooting exchange with a sniper. After about what seemed like an eternity, the Marine was killed. Since I had lost my rifle during that unexpected ejection from the helicopter, I retrieved his rifle. The rest of the day and through the night, fierce fighting continued. As night fell, Puff the Magic Dragon (C-47 Sky train) came on-station and dropped flares, giving us a sense of comfort as it poured continuous red streams of fire from its Gatling guns.

The next morning, March 21, we were just beginning to get ready for another fun-filled day. As the choppers approached Argonne with reinforcements, supplies, and our batteries, all hell again broke loose. Mortars, snipers, and small arms fire started up again. Upon hearing incoming, I jumped out of the hole that Ray, my good friend and gun mate, and I had slept in that night. Ray was trying to throw the sleeping bag out of the hole when a mortar round landed a few feet in front of him. He caught shrapnel in the arm, chest, and face, just missing his eye. Fortunately, his injuries were not fatal.

During this attack, the infantry commanding officer, Lt. Col. Sargent, Lt. Wilson and some of his staff, were killed. Ray and the other wounded and dead were sent to the lower LZ to await a medevac helicopter. Each time a helicopter approached Argonne, we were hit by an incoming mortar attack. These attacks were extremely scary because the rounds were falling into people's holes. It seemed that these holes weren't the safest place to hide. I never again took cover in the hole Ray and I shared when we got incoming. I was pissed after it was over, as I found our gun had suffered another flat tire, the same one I'd replaced the day before with the tire from a Water Buffalo (Water storage tank on wheels).

The sergeant then arrived, and we began to get our position ready for fire missions. We fired all that day in support of the operation throughout our area of support to both infantry and artillery units. There were enemy dead on Argonne. There was a call for a detail to come to help drag them to the trash berm and burn their bodies. There is something about burning flesh that never leaves you.

Because of my position on the gun, I did not draw that detail. As I understand it, some of the people from our fire direction center (FDC), lucked out for that.

The next morning, March 22nd, it began all over again. A helicopter would come to bring supplies, drop off Marines, and medevac the wounded and dead, and the mortars would rain down on our position. After this attack was over, there was a lot of commotion near our gun pit, over by the FDC group. We later learned that David Ovist had suffered a direct hit in the back while in his hole. I got that feeling again, "Someone could get hurt here!!"

The sergeant decided to increase his odds of surviving future attacks by reinforcing his hole. This would prove to be a wise decision. On about the fourth or fifth day, we got mortared and took several 122mm rocket rounds on our position. One round hit directly on top of Sgt. M's hole. Were it not for the roof he had put on his hole, he would have met with the same fate as David a few days earlier! Sure enough, my 105 had another flat. By now, we didn't want choppers anywhere near the hill, but we needed resupply of ammo, food, water, and the like.

The higher headquarters decided to attempt nighttime resupply operations by parachute-dropping the resupplies. This did not work well at all. Twice they missed the hill entirely, and the last time they dropped it directly on the home of a PFC, who was shaken up and dirty, but unhurt.

So this is the story of my stay on what Bill Jones designated as LZ Sitting Duck. We spent the rest of the days fighting intermittently, and fearing the barrage sure to come on the next chopper approach, waiting for the one coming to lift us from this hellhole of a place.

Unfortunately, we lost some great young Marines there.

CHAPTER 21

I NEVER KNEW

Dale Riley
SGT, 6173, Helicopter Crew Chief
HMM-262, 3rd Marine Division

I NEVER KNEW FOR SURE IF I MADE A DIFFERENCE IN VIETNAM

for my fellow Marines or their families. I did know that we helicopter crews as a whole had an important mission and that the only reason we existed was to support the grunts as they fought through the most miserable conditions on earth to accomplish theirs.

On my journey in the last five years to make sense of my memories, to have them somewhere other than bad dreams and cold sweats, I have tried to put some of them on paper. I was actually looking for some paperwork on an Army Commendation Medal that the three star CG of the 101st Airborne Division pinned on me one day at LZ Stud/VCB Combat Base, when I received my file from the National Personnel Records Center in St. Louis and discovered some letters of recommendation written by pilots. Now my fellow crew chiefs out there can understand my surprise. I never knew, and all these years I thought the only thing pilots could write were yellow sheet gripes to keep me working all night till the mess hall was closed and the showers shut down and it was time for the next day's mission. In the statements there were references to call signs of the units from this day of too much medevac and I felt I needed to find out just what ground units were "Heritage 81" and "Jawbreaker E3" at that zone we were into so many times that day, where the desperate look on those Marines needing our help has been burned into my brain.

This is what I remember and have found out to be factual for the day I spent with what turned out to be a perfect crew for the Chatterbox Medevac Package of March 25, 1969, Marine Medium Helicopter Squadron 262 out of Quang Tri.

In the cockpit were Lt. James C. O'Connor Jr. and his co-pilot Lt. Wagner. In the cabin, myself, Dale Riley – crew chief with Mike Griffith and Bill Wassinger as my gunners, and, of course, HMI "Doc" John Hillhouse.

Some facts from the After Action Report: We left Quang Tri at 0845 and returned 1850 (ten hours and five minutes) with a total flight time of 7.7 hours. Touching down in zones ten times, expending 1,000 .50 caliber and 600 M-16 5.56 mm rounds, conducting twenty sorties on ten tasks and, our reason for being there, twelve emergency – six priority – eight routine or KIA brought on board that day. Along with delivering one ton of ammo and water on one of our return trips into a zone I will describe shortly. But those are just the numbers. Let me tell you what those men did that long, hot, dry hellish day.

We started off with a call of several emergency medevac's from "Heritage 81" (which I believe to be E/2/3) in heavy contact with the enemy and supported by two UH-1E (Huey) gunships from VMO-6. One of the gunships sustained several hits and had to return to Quang Tri. As the one remaining covered our approach, it quickly became apparent that the LZ was too small for our CH-46 Sea Knight helicopter (BuNo 154021). The only way I saw was to back in up a gully and get the aft gear down. Lt. O'Connor did not hesitate and spun us around and followed my directions precisely as I checked out the clearance on both sides of the aircraft as quickly as I could with help from my gunners and with very smooth and steady handling by the pilot. We got the wounded on board and slowly pulled out of the zone as all hell broke loose and my gunners and the gunship opened up on the enemy muzzle flashes. I emptied out several M-16 magazines myself, as it seemed to take forever to climb enough to swing away over the ridge and gain speed. Doc Hillhouse never looked up as he got to work on some very badly wounded Marines, and once we hit altitude he directed me and the gunners as what to do to help stop the bleeding and help the men as the pilots squeezed every knot of speed out of the aircraft. This was just the beginning.

On a personal note, I cannot put into words what a horrible experience flying medevac can be. Stretched out or crumpled up before you were these young, strong, straight U.S. Marines. Bloody, torn, butchered flesh, with extremities missing or dangling, attached but not. The deck of the helicopter was coated with a non-skid material to protect you from slipping on the ever-present oil and grease, but it did not work against blood. There never seemed to be enough water to wash it away and I found bringing in a sandbag or two back at base to use as a sweeping agent worked best, as disgusting as it was.

We were then tasked into a zone on Dong Ha Mountain where "Jawbreaker E3" (Echo Co/2nd Bn/9th Marine Regiment) just received a mortar attack as they reached the top after setting out from Khe Gia Bridge the night before. They climbed the mountain under the cover of darkness. The company commander, Lt. James Glenn Upchurch, was killed in that attack and five Marines were wounded. It would be the start of a battle that had us into their zone at least four times.

As a crew chief my job was to check clearances around the aircraft, and I was constantly hanging half out the port or starboard hatches. A lot of days you really felt for the grunts that you saw down in the swirling dust or sticky mud. This day, instead of lowering their heads to avoid our rotor wash or flashing the usual V sign, they were shaking their canteens and making a drinking motion as we came in. I grabbed what canteens I could and tossed them to the ground. I always had probably eight or ten canteens scattered throughout the cabin. I closely guarded the metal ones for making c-rat coffee in the engine compartments, but these guys needed them badly and I only wished that I had more.

Our port gunner, Mike Griffith, was answering the fire from the tree line to the north as I got the wounded Marines and their

KIA lieutenant onboard. Till we lifted out, Mike had gone through close to 200 rounds. It was apparent how the brutal heat of that zone with no cover at all was taking its toll. Lt. O'Connor could see it also from the cockpit and he radioed LZ Stud to get a load of water and ammo together for us after we dropped the casualties at Charlie Med. This was very unusual for a medevac mission, but he knew we were going back in for more. After unloading at the med pad, we hit the fuel dump. I sent one gunner out for more .50 caliber ammunition and the other for loaded canteens as I fueled the aircraft. We then air taxied over to the supply pad and I hooked up to a cargo sling loaded with five-gallon cans of water and ammo.

We proceeded back to Dong Ha Mountain and into the zone. I remember it as a small grass-covered, narrow ridge with the men of Echo, 2nd Bn, 9th Marines on both sides as the top was a killing zone. As my attention was down through the hellhole talking the pilot in, I heard our .50 caliber machine guns going off in bursts. I settled the load down, released the cargo hook and keyed my mike with "hook clear." As I was getting up, I thought we were hit and on fire, as I was blinded by big flashes of flame; it was the port .50 with a burned out barrel. Lt. O'Connor had to execute a go round after we dropped the sling load as the fire was intense and there wasn't room until the grunts cleared the cargo.

I cleared us to the starboard and then as I was getting up from closing the hellhole hatch, I panicked as I realized Mike Griffith was pulling his burnt .50 caliber machine gun from the mounts and I said, "No, we are going back in." But he and Bill Wassinger were a real team and just switched out the starboard gun to the port mount, and we never missed a beat.

The forward air control and the Marine who took command on the ground were on the radio urging more .50-caliber fire as it was spot-on and the enemy fire was ceased from that tree line. The acting company commander, 1st Lt. Jay Standish, was standing up exposed outside the port gun directing our fire as we touched down and loaded more wounded and guys prostrate and in real trouble with heat stroke. The day continued and the After Action Report tells the story with the zones listed and casualties counted, etc., for my crew of ET-14.

Our wingmen that day in ET-15, crewed by pilots David and Trigalet with crew Nelson, Matlock and Boersma, flew also with a corpsman, Doc Westervelt. Unusual, but this was the day for unusual. They worked in perfect sync with us and carried out twenty sorties on fourteen tasks carrying seventeen casualties and fourteen replacements to those magnificent Marines of "Hell in a Helmet" E/2/9 on Dong Ha Hell.

I never knew the outfits back then. It's just as well, as E/2/9 was my brother's unit and finding this out now is very emotional for me. He was often on my mind over there, especially on medevac's, as I tried my best to help some other family avoid that damn telegram that devastated mine on 13Sep66, with the news that their son, PFC Neil E Riley was killed in Vietnam.

Having the opportunity today to contact several of those Marines on the ground that day and hear that they remember it as intensely as I still do, I now know that we did make a difference for those Marines on the ground. I also know too well the price, not only my own friends with HMM-262, but all the helicopter crews paid to make that difference as the memories of them are with me today and will be to the day I die.

This day of March 25, 1969, that I remember, just kept going and turned into night medevac package with Lt. Barton, Lt. Mix, Doc Cavanagh, my gun team of Griffith and Wassinger. Twenty-nine more wounded to load onboard from missions to Jawbreaker F and a nerve-wracking one to LZ Argonne, as an AC-47 Spooky gunship prevented an overrun with the most impressive firepower I have ever seen on my darkest, scariest night. I can't say it was the first time I was scared in Vietnam, but unlike the other times that just happened and you were in the moment; here we were watching this scene from hell, knowing that we would soon descend into the inferno ourselves.

CHAPTER 22

BACK HOME

Susan Sargent Jones

THAT WEEKEND IN MARCH HAD BEEN LACED WITH A TENSION
my mother could not define. She had been ill at ease for no apparent
reason the whole weekend. By Sunday evening, March 23, 1969,
we three Sargent girls were getting prepared for school the next
day when the doorbell rang. The next thing I heard was my older
sister screaming, "Not my Daddy! Not my Daddy!" Unfortunately,
it was our Daddy and he would not be coming home alive. My
mother, sisters, and I decided that I would call my brother's girlfriend's house to get him to come home because I did not sound
as upset as the others. Bull! He picked up on it right away and
made it home in record time.

Within minutes it seemed that all of Daddy's Marine buddies
from Parris Island (we had moved to a house in Beaufort, South
Caroline, before Daddy left for Vietnam) had descended on the
house to swap stories and remember. I mostly remember some of
the older guys telling my brother what it was like to get hit by a
mortar. My sister and I kicked them out of the house after telling
them that type of information was not what any of us needed at
that time.

I realized several things, looking back from the perspective
of fifty years. First of all, we were not the only family getting that

news that weekend. Lt. Carl Wilson died from the same mortar impact that killed my Daddy. Reading the accounts from the Marines who landed at LZ Argonne, there were at least eighteen families who got the same news we did. From personal experience, that's eighteen mothers and fathers, untold siblings, children, and extended families whose worlds were shattered by that one battle. My heart weeps for those family members.

Secondly, we were lucky in a way. When Daddy left for Vietnam, his children were thirteen, fifteen, sixteen, and seventeen years of age. We had an opportunity to get to know him and have memories of him. So many of the Marines on Argonne at that time were only slightly older than I was (fifteen) at that time. Had they had the chance to marry or have children? How many babies born in that era never got to meet these brave, young men who were their fathers?

Thirdly, and it took me a long, long time to come to this realization, the Marines who survived the inferno of Vietnam and came home and I have another common bond. We were not able to share our experience with anyone. Instead of the crowds cheering and welcoming our returning warriors, these young men were almost universally despised and castigated. I felt isolated as well. I could not talk to others about how good a man my Daddy was. He fought in an unpopular war, so it was better not to talk about it.

Finally, I would like to say how proud I am that my Daddy was able to serve with fine, young men like all of you. I know he held you to a high standard and your stories tell me that you reached that standard. I thank you for the vignettes you have given me of him "over there." I thank you for taking the time to write your recollections down for posterity; for yourselves, for you families, and for future generations. I thank you from the bottom of my heart.

Susan Sargent Jones

NAVY CROSS CITATIONS

Navy-cross

GEORGE THOMAS SARGENT

NAVY CROSS

GENERAL ORDERS:
Authority: Navy Department Board of Decorations and Medals

CITATION:

THE PRESIDENT OF THE UNITED STATES OF AMERICA TAKES
pride in presenting the Navy Cross (Posthumously) to Lieutenant Colonel George Thomas Sargent, Jr. (MCSN: 0-51686), United States Marine Corps, for extraordinary heroism while serving as Commanding Officer of the First Battalion, Fourth Marines, THIRD Marine Division (Reinforced), Fleet Marine Force, in connection with operations against the enemy in the Republic of Vietnam. On 20 March 1969, Lieutenant Colonel Sargent was in command of a heliborne attack against enemy positions in Quang Nam Province during Operation PURPLE MARTIN when the lead helicopter came under a heavy volume of North Vietnamese Army fire, causing it to crash in the landing zone. Directing the debarkation of the battalion at a smaller zone on the slope of a hill below the designated area, Lieutenant Colonel Sargent took command of the lead company, and after starting up the hill, the Marines encountered a hostile force occupying a well-fortified position. As he led his men in an aggressive assault against the enemy emplacements, Lieutenant Colonel Sargent observed a machine gun which was pinning down a portion of his unit.

Fearlessly moving across the fire-swept terrain toward the North Vietnamese emplacement, he boldly hurled several hand grenades, which killed two hostile soldiers and destroyed the enemy weapon. Skillfully maneuvering his men, he secured the slope of the hill, and early the following morning, despite a fragmentation wound sustained during the previous day's engagement, commenced the final assault against the enemy soldiers. During the ensuing fire fight, the Marines were subjected to intense North Vietnamese mortar and small-arms fire and rocket propelled grenades. Ignoring the hostile rounds impacting near him, Lieutenant Colonel Sargent remained with the forward units, effectively controlling the actions of his men and exploiting every enemy contact to the maximum extent until he was mortally wounded. His timely actions and aggressive leadership inspired all who observed him and were instrumental in the accomplishment of his unit's mission. By his courage, intrepid fighting spirit, and unwavering devotion to duty, Lieutenant Colonel Sargent upheld the highest traditions of the Marine Corps and the United States Naval Service. He gallantly gave his life for his country.

HERBERT E. PIERPAN

NAVY CROSS

GENERAL ORDERS:
Authority: Navy Department Board of Decorations and Medals

CITATION:

THE PRESIDENT OF THE UNITED STATES OF AMERICA TAKES pleasure in presenting the Navy Cross to Major Herbert E. Pierpan (MCSN: 0-82433), United States Marine Corps, for extraordinary heroism in action while serving as Operations Officer of the First Battalion, Fourth Marines, THIRD Marine Division (Reinforced), Fleet Marine Force, in connection with combat operations against the enemy in the Republic of Vietnam from 20 to 22 March 1969. On 20 March 1969, Company D and elements of the First Battalion's command group were heli-lifted into Fire Support Base Argonne, located northwest of the Vandegrift Combat Base, to commence a sustained operation against North Vietnamese Army forces in the area. As the Marines landed they came under a heavy volume of mortar, small-arms, and automatic weapons fire, and their lead elements were pinned down by hostile soldiers occupying well-fortified bunkers overlooking the landing zone. Unhesitatingly maneuvering across the fire-swept area to a forward position, Major Pierpan shouted words of encouragement to his men, restoring their confidence and enabling them to provide a base of fire as he and a companion advanced toward the enemy strongholds. When his comrade was seriously wounded, Major Pierpan seized the man's weapon and boldly assaulted a bunker, killing two North Vietnamese soldiers. As he led continuing attacks against other enemy positions, he tossed a hand grenade through the aperture of a hostile emplacement and was wounded when a North Vietnamese soldier returned the grenade. Ignoring his painful injury, he resolutely continued his determined efforts until the bunker was destroyed. When his commanding officer was mortally wounded on the following morning, Major Pierpan unhesitatingly assumed command and, maneuvering his men with skill and daring, continued to lead the battalion against the enemy until he was relieved by a new commanding officer on 22 March. By his courage, dynamic leadership, and unwavering devotion to duty in the face of grave personal danger, Major Pierpan contributed significantly to the accomplishment of the battalion's mission and upheld the highest traditions of the Marine Corps and the United States Naval Service.

MICHAEL P. MCCORMICK

NAVY CROSS

GENERAL ORDERS:
Authority: Navy Department Board of Decorations and Medals

CITATION:

THE PRESIDENT OF THE UNITED STATES OF AMERICA TAKES pride in presenting the Navy Cross (Posthumously) to Second Lieutenant Michael P. McCormick (MCSN: 0-107462), United States Marine Corps Reserve, for extraordinary heroism while serving as a Platoon Commander with Company D, First Battalion, Fourth Marines, THIRD Marine Division (Reinforced), Fleet Marine Force, in the Republic of Vietnam on 20 March 1969. Second Lieutenant McCormick and a fire team from his platoon were heli-lifted into an area north of Khe Sanh as the assault element in an operation to secure Fire Support Base Argonne. Immediately upon disembarking from the aircraft, the entire team was pinned down by a heavy volume of fire from hostile soldiers occupying fortified bunkers overlooking the landing zone. Reacting fearlessly, Second Lieutenant McCormick moved across the fire-swept terrain from one man to another and, shouting words of encouragement, restored their confidence. Under cover of machine gun fire, he then initiated an aggressive assault upon the bunkers, and charging up the slope, he and his three-man team stormed and systematically destroyed three of the fortifications with hand grenades and close-range rifle fire, thereby providing security for the remaining Marines landing in the zone. Later that day, Second Lieutenant McCormick led one of his squads during a search and destroy operation in the surrounding area and encountered intense automatic weapons fire from a well-concealed emplacement. Repeated attempts by the Marines to recover their injured point man were thwarted by machine gun fire from concealed enemy soldiers. Unwilling to risk further Marine casualties, second Lieutenant McCormick directed his squad to provide protective fire and, with complete disregard for his own safety, maneuvered toward the casualty. He had almost attained his objective when he was mortally wounded by hostile fire. By his heroic actions, aggressive fighting spirit and unwavering devotion to duty, Second Lieutenant McCormick upheld the highest traditions of the Marine Corps and the United States Naval Service. He gallantly gave his life for his country.

EPILOGUE

FOR MANY OF US WHO WENT THROUGH THIS BATTLE ON THIS
remote mountain in Vietnam, walking off the Argonne in April
was more painful and sad than fearful. We had lived on that mountain and shared time with the most heroic Marines we had ever
known. These Marines performed acts of bravery and sacrifice
that were beyond our ability to even imagine, until we witnessed
these events ourselves. Moving off the mountain felt like we were
leaving those heroes behind as ghosts, because we knew in our
hearts that no one would ever return to this place and honor the
sacrifices so many of them made there. So, when we walked off
Argonne we carried their spirit with us. Those Marines who gave
so much for the "Corps" and country have never gone away. We
carried them in our hearts off of that mountain. And even now,
over fifty years later, all of us still carry those Marines with us
every day and everywhere.

Semper Fidelis

GLOSSARY

Word	Definition
.45 cal	The M1911, also known as the Colt 1911, semi-automatic, magazine-fed, recoil-operated pistol chambered for the .45 ACP cartridge. It served as the standard-issue sidearm for the United States Armed Forces from 1911 to 1985. It was widely used in World War I, World War II, the Korean War, and the Vietnam War.
"46"	CH-46 Marine Corps medium lift helicopter
"Huey"	UH-1 light helicopter used for Recon Team insert/extract, also gunships
"Puff the Magic Dragon"	Converted WWII C-47 cargo aircraft that became a gunship. Much appreciated by Grunt Marines, because of "Puff's" ability to deliver massive machine-gun fire from the air.
"the six"	Battery six is the CO usually a Captain
105mm	105 mm M101A1 howitzer has a 105 mm breach dimension, has a max range of 11 Kilometers, but is most effect if directed fire is in the 1-7 kilometer range. Developed in WWII.

Word	Definition
106mm	The M40 recoilless rifle is a lightweight, portable, crew-served 106 mm recoilless rifle made in the United States. Intended primarily as an anti-tank weapon, it could also be employed in an antipersonnel role with the use of an antipersonnel-tracer flechette round.
155mm	The M114, 155 mm howitzer is a towed howitzer developed and used by the United States Army and Marine Corps in the Vietnam War. It was capable of firing a 90 pound HE round approximately 15 Kilometers.
1st Lt	1st Lieutenant
2nd Lt	2nd Lieutenant
AO	Area of Operations
ARVN	Army of the Republic of Vietnam
BAS	Battalion Aid Station–medical facility at LZ Stud (VCB)
Bn	Battalion
C-Rats	Canned meals that field units ate. Packaged for a complete meal with several canned serving in one box. Two of these meals was considered a daily ration. This seldom was the rule due to the difficulty of resupply in the triple canopy jungle of I Corps.
Ca Lu	Village on route 9 just south of Vandegrift Combat Base.
Capt	Captain–O3
CAR	Combat Action Ribbon
CAR -16	Early version of a more compact M-16
Chieu Hoi	Vietnamese for "give up," name of a program to entice NVA soldiers to surrender

Word	Definition
Claymore	The M18A1 Claymore, is a directional anti-personnel mine developed for the United States Armed Forces.
CMC	Commandant of the Marine Corps
Cmdr	Commander
CO	Commanding Officer of a Marine infantry unit.
Co	Company
Col	Colonel–O-6
Con Thien	Marine Combat Base in the eastern I Corps, just south of DMZ
CP	Command Post
Cpl	Corporal–E-4, the first rank as a Non-Commission Officer
Div	Division
Flag Officer	Reference to General grade officers, 0-7 to 0-10, who have a flag flown at their CP
Flamethrower	US M9A1-7. This is the most common model used in Vietnam and is much lighter and easier to use. Tanks were commonly found, but most wands were destroyed by the military.
FNG	A derogatory term for a new Marine in country. "Fucking New Guy"
FO	Forward Observer. A Marine attached to an infantry unit, whose job was to call in supporting fire from artillery batteries.
FSB	Fire Support Base
FT	Fire Team, 4 Marines. 3 FT+ Squad Leader = one Squad

Word	Definition
Fuse VT	Artillery round with a "Variable Time Fuse" The artillery round can be timed to explode in the air, just over the target.
Gunny	Marine E-7, Gunnery Sergeant
Guns	M-60 Machine Guns
HE	Abbreviation for High Explosive
Hil number -	Hill number–example hill 414, is a hill 414 meters above sea level
HLZ	Helicopter Landing Zone
H&S	Headquarters and Service Company–
Khe Sanh	US Marine Corps forward base on Route 9, just east of Laos
KIA	Killed In Action
L/Cpl	Lance Corporal–E-3
LAW	Light Anti-Tank Weapon
LP	Listening Post
LtCol	Lieutenant Colonel, O-5
LZ	Helicopter Landing Zone
LZ Stud	Forward resupply base on Route 9, renamed Vandegrift Combat Base in late 1968–most Marines continued to refer to LZ Stud
M-14	7.62mm (.308) best damn gas operated, magazine fed infantry rifle the USA ever made.
MACV	Military Assistance Command Vietnam
MAF	Marine Amphibious Force
MarDiv	Marine Division. 1/4 was assigned to 3rd MarDiv, 3rd MAF
Medevac	Helicopter medical evacuation from the field
Medevac	Medical Evacuation from combat
Navy Cross	Award for valor in combat, 2nd to the Medal of Honor.

Word	Definition
NCO	Non-Commissioned Officer
NVA	North Vietnam Army
OIC	Officer In Charge
Ontos	Light tracked, anti- tank vehicle with 6X 106mm recoilless rifles–used by the Marines in Vietnam.
OP	Observation Post.
PFC	Private First Class–E-2
Rockpile	Marine/Army artillery base on Route 9 north-east of Vandegrift Combat Base, AKA, LZ Stud.
RPG	Rocket Propelled Grenade–very effective weapon of the NVA.
Rubber Bitch	Inflatable air mattress for sleeping in the field, they never stayed inflated, so few Marines carried them in the field.
S-1	Battalion Administration Office
S-2	Battalion Intelligence Office
S-3	Battalion Operations Office
S-4	Battalion Supply Office
Sgt	Sergeant–E-5, Non-Commissioned Officer
Skipper	Commanding Officer of a Marine infantry company.
SNCO	Staff Non-Commissioned Officer
Spooky	Another version of "Puff The Magic Dragon" used at night time.
SqLdr	Squad Leader
SSgt	Staff Sergeant–E-6, Staff Non-Commissioned Officer
Standing Lines	Mission for "Grunt" Marines when we came in from the "bush." Standing Lines was being the front line and our day off.

Word	Definition
TAOR	Tactical Area of Responsibility
Tube'g	Marine slang for the NVA 82mm mortar attacks–the mortar round makes a THUMP sound when leaving the mortar "tube"
USNA	United States Naval Academy
VCB	Vandegrift Combat Base, primary resupply base for Marins in I Corps, on route 9, was stood up after the abandonment of Khe Sanh Combat Base.
VC	Viet Cong, Communist insurgents
Walking Point	Marine at the very front of a patrol column. This was considered the most dangerous job in a Marine infantry company.
WIA	Wounded In Action
XO	Executive Officer of an infantry company and other Marine organizations. The 2nd in command.

CPSIA information can be obtained
at www.ICGtesting.com
Printed in the USA
BVHW091400290621
610728BV00003B/825

9 781662 813139